DATE DUE

THE HOSPITAL ALWAYS WINS

A MEMOIR

ISSA IBRAHIM

CHICAGO
REVIEW
PRESS

Copyright © 2016 by Issa Ibrahim
First edition
Published by Chicago Review Press Incorporated
814 North Franklin Street
Chicago, Illinois 60610
ISBN 978-1-61373-512-1

Library of Congress Cataloging-in-Publication Data
Is available from the Library of Congress.

Interior design: Jonathan Hahn

Printed in the United States of America
5 4 3 2 1

For Mom,
who nurtured and protected my creativity,
and mental patients everywhere.

The story you are about to read is all true. Names have been changed to protect anonymity and deter the litigious.

1

"OH, MA, WHAT AM I GONNA DO?"

I'm working on my latest painting, a large unstretched canvas tacked to the main wall of my place. Mom enters dancing and keeps in step with the ska, one of many retro musical touchstones that I embraced as a black teenage new waver and now, forty years later, am reluctant to let go of. Mom identifies with it too, being of Jamaican/English roots. She calls out, "Keep working, son, you'll get it," beaming with pride while gingerly pinching a joint. Guiding me through this artistic roadblock and recurring waves of memory and regret, Mom skips and shimmies, pleased at my persistence. I smile too, my mood lifted.

Less a haunting than a benevolent visitation, Mom is just as I remember her. Small but matronly, mercurial and frisky, moving like an amalgam of bohemian and dervish, seven-veiled Scheherazade and Salome, lost in the rhythm, possessed by melody, body swaying and arms waving. Never missing a beat or dropping an ash, she prowls as her reefer smoke swirls around her like the brimstone of a magician on the verge of a daring feat of prestidigitation.

When I was growing up, Mom, like my older sisters, was quite the mystic, proficient in tarot reading and astrology, treating me as an unknowing subject for pot-inspired soothsaying and prognostications. I was earmarked for greatness, or so the cards kept coming up and my chart seemed to indicate, yet I was oblivious to the doting, the preparations, and the expectations. But being born Issa—Arabic for Jesus—I had a lot to live up to.

The music is crosscut and drowned out, augmented and bastardized, by the constant bass and drum thuds that emanate from more than one loud sound system in my apartment building. The sounds continue farther down the block and into Richmond Hill, Queens, New York, a Trinidadian/Guyanese/Indian neighborhood. The music is busy, drunk, designed to get you to shake your ass and get some ass by the end of the night. The cacophony created by two or three of these deranged DJs, battling it out for bragging rights, is a true jungle of call-and-response beats, booms, and blares punctuated by unintelligible shouts, rambling and incongruous sound effects, and the occasional wail of females beckoning for a big stiff dick. As I'm not from that part of the world and am a wee bit older now, and as I was weaned on the genteel pop of the Beatles, Burt Bacharach, and the Beach Boys, I bristle at the musical mélange's descent into outright noise. Yet when it does quiet down, in the post midnight hours, I can play my own songs, bluesy, insular freak-pop creations about my hard-knock life and how I've survived it, and make my own kind of din. And when I do Mom says, "I like the sound of that," listening close, head cocked and eyes narrowed to parse the details. "You may be on to something, son."

When not writing or recording, I'm immersed in painting. The magic happens after 10 PM. I am usually up till dawn and have grown used to painting quickly and not sleeping until I am finished. It's a habit I developed out of necessity, when for twenty years I had to work on my craft from the last evening head count till the morning wake-up call, at which point thirty other mental patients and I had to exit our bedrooms for breakfast and a full day of programming.

2

I T'S A LOVELY, CRISP SPRING MORNING. I arrive at Kew Gardens Court a bit early, at 8:30 AM, so Miss Debra, my escort and a very pleasant, matronly, and supportive treatment aide I've known for years, suggests we go to the deli across the fearsome Queens Boulevard. There, where we sit for a moment with coffee and breakfast sandwiches, we encounter Judge Freed. He is cordial and upbeat, valise in one hand, morning *Times* in the other, topcoat slung over his arm, wearing a dark wool suit and sporting a colorful tie, which has become his trademark over the course of the trial. Large in stature but not intimidating, he drops his head and peers at me above his bifocals, then smiles.

I believe Judge Freed has heard my case and I hope he has gone over the testimony very carefully, ready today to render a fair and just decision. He impressed me from the very beginning as a wise, rabbinical fact-finder and I hope my instincts are correct. My mind races as he orders his morning meal. Should I hit him up for information on where his axe will fall? Opting to play it cool, I sit and drink my coffee and say nothing more than "Good morning, Your Honor."

In the courtroom, the spindly attorney general walks in at about 9:50. He informs me, through my escort, that "Judge Freed has called the Mental Hygiene Legal Service office at Creedmoor. Mr. Ibrahim's lawyer should be here closer to noon." This means a long wait but as I've waited almost twenty years for this, another two hours won't hurt.

At 11 AM, my stand-in MHLS attorney Leslie Boobala enters. We have never formally met but I recognize her face from her trips into Building 40 visiting other patients. She shares a suburban ordinariness with all the MHLS attorneys, saving her firebrand liberal warrior stance for the courtroom and the cases she believes are worth it.

I don't know if I will need her for any negotiations, and she asks, "Are there any stipulations that you want me to argue if it comes to that?" I hand her the list of "demands" that my now-retired MHLS attorney Barry and I cooked up that I could live with for Level 4, unescorted off-grounds privileges, if that is where Judge Freed would lean. Leslie reads the printout but says nothing.

"I still would like to hear Judge Freed's decision, though," I say, aware that only discharge or retention are on the table. I have hope that I made my case.

"OK, I hear you."

We sit in silence for about an hour, watching Judge Freed dole out justice in two quick cases. He then says, "I see Mr. Ibrahim is here, and his attorney is here, and the attorney general is present. All we need now is Mr. Mullin, the district attorney, and we can proceed. It is a very lengthy verdict and I need to put it all together, so if we can get in touch with the DA, and you can give me another, say, fifteen minutes, we can proceed."

"A lengthy verdict; that could be good or bad," Leslie whispers.

I excuse myself and go to the men's room. Here, as I deposit the residue of the coffee, I pray one final time, hoping it will count. Eyes raised to the ceiling, I whisper hoarsely to whoever will listen, "Come on, come on, let's do it. Let's do it! Justice! Let's get justice!"

Then I pause for a moment, do away with the fist-pumping and sotto voce soccer-thug hysterics, and say quietly, "Please, Mom, let me come home. I wanna come home."

Back in the courtroom, the DA saunters in, and in a short time Judge Freed steps out of his chambers. He has a stack of papers stapled and collated, fifty pages each. He asks for the three attorneys to step up to the sidebar. Handing out the papers, Judge Freed says, "Here is a copy for Mr. Ibrahim. I believe he would want one."

The three attorneys all walk back into the seating area, leafing through the great tome, all looking to the last page, where the verdict will be. Leslie, after reading the last page, gives me the thumbs-up with a broad smile. Walking back from the bench, beaming while sitting down next to me, she hands me my copy and says, "Read the last page."

"Conditional release." I read again. "Conditional release." There is a great deal of verbiage surrounding this phrase but it really doesn't matter. I got my conditional release.

Stunned, I am asked to approach the bench. Judge Freed doesn't look directly into my eyes but imparts a powerful bit of wisdom and caution. "Mr. Ibrahim, you are being given a tremendous opportunity. If you succeed that is good. However, if you fail not only do you fail on your own but you fail and let down all others, some you know, some you will never know, who will use your verdict, your footnote in the history books, to perhaps gain their freedom. So don't take this lightly. Use this as an opportunity to live your life as an example, and do so for the greater good. So go, Mr. Ibrahim. Have a good life and try to be mindful of your responsibility."

Judge Freed's caution brings to mind the final words said to me by a former fellow insanity plea patient, before we drifted apart, largely because of my humiliation and shame at still being inside. David told me, over ten years ago, "You're gonna change how people look at us. Your case is gonna be a landmark case. It may take a while but I know your case is gonna make a difference." It did take a while, and it was painful at times, but David was right.

Gathering my coat, my copy of the verdict, my mind as it reels about my head like a whirligig, I stand in the back of the courtroom, disbelieving. As the lawyers all move on to other cases the AG is trembling while stuffing the thick judgment in his valise, as if he were thinking, "Oh crap! My bosses are going to be pissed. I fucked it up!"

From the bench, as all parties pack up, Judge Freed remarks, pleased and relieved that he made it through the laborious, seven-months-long hearing, "In my forty plus years, this is the longest judgment I have ever written." He also has an extra copy for Barry, my attorney in absentia, which he gives to Leslie. "Here, give this to Mr. Newfeld. It's a tree, I know, but he will appreciate it."

The DA, a barrel-chested, hardscrabble, tough Irish cop-type, peers at me through steely, spiteful blue eyes. I am still wavering at the back of the courtroom, unsure if it is real, taking it all in, my victory. DA Mullin motions to me, telling Leslie, "His case is over. Tell him to scram, wouldja?" Leslie steps over and says nicely, "You can go if you want." She doesn't have to tell me twice.

Miss Debra and the transfer agent escort me back to Creedmoor Psychiatric Center, my home for the past seventeen years. Exiting off the Grand Central Parkway, as I did as a child on Sunday drives with Mom some forty years ago, and then as an arriving patient twenty years later, I look at that big beige building differently: no longer my towering prison, it is now just temporary housing. I'll go back before Judge Freed in a month to finalize and officiate my order of conditions and then we'll see what comes next. Albany might appeal. Creedmoor forensic director Dr. Anne Maggoty might craft and attach very tight restrictions on the order for me, just out of spite, even though Judge Freed suggested no enmity or animosity should creep into the process. Either way, if all goes well, I can add my name to the list of "short-timers."

All those years inside and soon to be a free man, healthy, painting, creating, being the artist she encouraged, even ordained me to be, I think about Mom.

3

I AM THE YOUNGEST OF FIVE CHILDREN, and definitely Mom's favorite. She never says this, as it is bad form, but my siblings, I, and even my dad feel it and know the truth. As a result my sisters and brothers often find opportunities when alone with me to toss taunts and epithets like "spoiled brat" and "mama's boy" in between bouts of typical sibling abuse. Upon finding out, Mom admonishes them, then soothes my unease.

Dad gigs on New Jersey bandstands every weekend, sleeping through the days of the week, while I am by Mom's side as she does housework and shopping. Many a day's grocery run finds me staring up at her from the metal shopping cart baby bin, where I sit way past age-appropriateness, chomping on an uncooked frankfurter that she slips from the as-yet-unbought package and into my mouth. She does this to keep me preoccupied and oblivious to the Saturday morning animation-inspired Froot Loops and Sugar Smacks.

When Mom has free time she works on a number of unfinished canvases placed about our small home. She usually uses acrylic paint but is also proficient in watercolor, and employs mixed media, quilting, interior decorating, and garden landscaping to express herself and offset the household expenses when Dad's Friday through Sunday bandstand gigs don't measure up.

Mom sets me down at her feet with a starter set-up of paper, colored pencils, crayons, and water-based paints. We sit for hours in the downstairs living room, decked out in jungle decor complete with palm plants, African masks, and a huge mural of the veldt featuring a noble but friendly elephant beside a giraffe and native huts in the background.

In this ideal artistic setting we listen to plenty of jazz, Derek and the
Dominos' *Layla*, and Traffic's *John Barleycorn Must Die* (her favorites
among many), and I request anything by the Beatles while I trace and
paint my approximations of the wondrous feast for my young eyes that
is the *Sergeant Pepper's Lonely Hearts Club Band* album cover. I take in
a great deal of Mom's influence and it is apparent from early on that I
have a gift for rendering. Mom's approval encourages me.

"That is so beautiful, Iss," she whispers. "Looks just like Paul. Wonderful. You are a great artist, son."

I bounce about the family home in a red towel that Mom pins onto
my Superman T-shirt. With dungarees stuffed into a shiny pair of red,
knee-high rain boots, up and down the stairs I fly, sometimes taking a
nasty spill. I run to Mom, not to attend to my bump, bruise, or scrape,
but just to make sure my cape is still on. When tired of superheroics I
retreat to my bedroom, my Fortress of Solitude, where my art table calls
me. There, with the proper pop coordinates fixed, I start doodles, that
beget sketches, which grow to patient drawing. Needing an explosion
of color, out come the crayons, then the colored pencils, then, boldly,
Magic Markers. Finally, needing to expand, I experiment with watercolor techniques, gouache, acrylics, and inevitably oils. When the paper
and canvas seem too small I start a mural on my bedroom wall, usually
of my latest pop-singing fascination.

I'm the type of kid who leaves the house late. What's there to see
out there in the world when I can draw or paint something infinitely
more compelling and entertaining? Although I have friends, I'm more
comfortable with my record albums and comic books—and my paintings, which often look like a merger of the two.

Mom and Dad always light up a reefer preceding an artistic
endeavor. They, like other drug-inspired artists, believe it helps the
juices flow. Mom nurses a healthy joint while painting her gigantic
monochromatic portraits of charismatic and controversial figures like
Purple Mao, Yellow Che, and Red Fidel, with me at her feet breathing
it all in. When four-foot canvases present limitations the paint eventually
falls upon the walls. Every room in the house, except for my grandfather

Arthur's austere residence, has a mural or painting on the wall, started by Mom or Dad and later completed by committee. My oldest sister, Lauren, is a good portrait painter but she will often use collage, which is easier for my less talented second sister, Carol, to participate in and feel included. First brother Smiley resorts to graffiti. His preoccupation with this art form reaches a point where he reeks of chemicals constantly as his propensity for vandalism blossoms. I feel most sorry for Kal: it's bad enough being the middle child of the three boys, but he also seems to be bereft of any discernible talent. He loves listening to music and appreciates art but cannot produce anything of his own.

I feel blessed that I come from this home. Dad is always into something musical and artistic, creating original cartoon characters of a multicultural bent, all set to music, which is unheard of in the 1970s. He also crafts African awareness presentations, highlighting his gifts for storytelling and creating imaginative sound effects. He encourages us all to take up musical instruments and is a collector of them, so we have an upright piano in our living room, numerous guitars and basses, plenty of percussion, several brass instruments, and a drum set in the basement. Though I was slated to be Ringo in the family, I lose interest and the drums go to Smiley, who becomes quite good. He bangs out a lot of his frustrations and issues, which, having to deal with me eclipsing him in the family's esteem, must be plenty.

Of the family staples that I enjoy, the salons/house parties my parents mount are certainly electric, but the jam sessions are transcendent. From near and far various musicians gather at our house and pick up those abused, neglected instruments and breathe fire into them. These jams of New York City's best and largely ignored jazz musicians are the stuff of legend. They play for hours, banging tune after tune out of these things that I run around the house with and use as toys. On these special occasions they are the Tools of the Gods.

Of course, they are all high. The partygoers, the hangers-on, and the children who arrive with these jazz giants are catching the same contact high that I am. But my real high is the music.

As a result of the counterculture that my parents traveled in during the 1950s and found themselves immersed in during the '60s, now as breadwinner and housewife of the super modern '70s they are really ahead of the curve. My teenage half-sisters are having a ball being the offspring of artsy/jazzy/pot-smoking parents, whom they show off to their boyfriends and schoolmates. Everyone wants to be invited to our house, where New York's musicians, artists, writers, and hip people congregate. You've arrived if you're rolling up and sharing a toke with Mom while Dad regales the company with animated tales, complete with dialects and sound effects.

Many summer nights see the lights turned low in the house, party lights strung in the backyard, and in every corner a collection of people getting high. Not the crack house or shooting gallery kind of getting high, but the harmless, black bohemian, suburban house party kind. Where the trees in the backyard are a leaning place for dreamy college kids sharing a joint in the colored half light and a guy just back from a tour in 'Nam strums a guitar and sings Jose Feliciano's arrangement of "Light My Fire," all while a lanky blonde in fringe and little else tries catching fireflies in a jar.

Excited by all the company and the attention I hope to get, I run through the narrow gangway at the side of the house into the side door that leads to the basement. Down there in the fluorescent purple darkness, sweating amidst the black light posters of astrological sexual positions and psychedelic icons, are more postadolescent kids of all races, dancing and humping and tripping to music from Motown and Philadelphia and San Francisco. The record player plays slow jams, romantic freak-outs, and the occasional novelty for levity and a much-needed breather from the grinding and to replenish whatever was helping their high.

Feeling out of place down in the basement I run back up the stairs, past the side door entrance, to the first floor kitchen. Here the adults sit around the white oblong pressed-wood dining table, sifting through a mound of grass resting on the cover of one of the LPs Mom and I were listening to earlier, separating the seeds and stems. Dad is in full bloom, standing on tiptoe with outstretched arms in his animated telling of the tree of life. The parents of the kids downstairs, in the backyard, and in various huddled corners of the house, are all former '50s and '60s entertainers. Now that jazz has gone fusion and burlesque has gone hardcore these talented musicians are settling in to a life of lowered expectations and polyester. The drummers will end up marrying the strippers and going into construction. The piano players will always find work so long as there's a bar with a jar and a keyboard in tune. Dad opts to sing Top 40 at weddings—while the bills get paid, it's a creative death.

Not wanting to endure the embarrassment of my raconteur father, now becoming a tree, nor be present while the gathering indulges in more weed, I bound into room after room, floor to floor, inside, outside, all around the home. I wind up under a tree in the yard, ogling the fireflies with the blissed-out blonde, calling out requests to the guitar player: "Up, Up and Away!" "Come and Get It!" "It's Not Unusual!" Nothing too abrasive, just things that are pleasing to my young ears. The major chords and la-la choruses quell for a while my disappointment at being ignored. By my family, which by now is nothing new, and by the house full of people; all of them interesting and fun, and all too high to give a damn about me.

4

"MAHATA." I SAY IT TO MYSELF with the intonation of a noble savage, like Tonto, or Frankenstein's monster. I mutter it at the oddest moments, absentmindedly, while painting in my bedroom or rising from a fitful slumber. The feeling it engenders is neither friend nor foe, but cresting a middle ground, between benign and insidious.

The word was strange to me when I first heard it, as if from another land. But Creedmoor Psychiatric Center is just that, a land of the lost, and the Mahata is one of many denizens in this lunatic's landscape.

I'VE SURVIVED EIGHT MONTHS IN JAIL and fifteen in a prison-hospital for the criminally insane hidden in the boondocks upstate, and now I am escorted down state to Creedmoor in the center of the suburban serenity of Queens Village, New York. It is unsettling and ironic: I remember taking drives with Mom when I was very young and her pointing to the huge building from the Grand Central Parkway, stating, "Do you see that big building over there? That's where they keep all the crazy people!" She said this with such dread that I knew this was someplace I didn't want to be. And yet here I am cruising down the off-ramp, being driven past the Gothic surrounding gates, onto the grounds, to that building . . . to *reside* . . . hopefully for just a short while.

I can tell already, from the New York State van as we idle outside the police outpost of the hospital, where I assume they will be informed of my arrival and my offense, that this place is looser than Mid-Hudson Psychiatric Center, a facility for the criminally insane where I was committed for a little over a year. People who look like mental patients are walking the grounds. And what sprawling grounds they are. The green seems to go on forever, in all directions. How could such a beautiful-looking place have such a bad reputation? But a further tour of the grounds, after we get lost on several unmarked streets and winding pathways, reveals long-abandoned buildings constructed in an era when aesthetics was not the main concern. They look like what I imagined buildings in an asylum would look like, with heavy doors and barred windows, only worse for the overgrown vines and obvious neglect. The architecture suggests these structures were built in the 1920s, but clearly they have been abandoned for decades. In fact, with the dilapidated, institutional buildings and the shambling, glassy-eyed patients in ill-fitting clothes roaming the premises, these grounds, though lush with summer greenery, resemble a haunted cemetery.

I enter the main building, a great, beige, seventeen-story behemoth called "40." Erected in 1959, according to the cornerstone just outside the front door, I assume it's the fortieth structure built on the grounds since the land was dedicated as a state hospital site and insane asylum at the turn of the twentieth century. The shutting and then locking of doors behind me is a depressing procedure that I am already becoming accustomed to. After a brief routine physical I am shuttled up the elevators with all my see-through plastic bags of personal belongings to the sixth floor admissions unit, 6-A. This unit is all male.

The building, shaped like the letter H lying flat on its back, is separated by an elevator bank, which would be the center stroke of the H. There is an A-side, right, and B-side, left. Entering the ward, through the half stroke of the great H, there are several double bedrooms running down the long main hallway. The professional staff's offices and the visitor's room make up the doors located at the top of this hall, nearest the main door, the only door through which you enter and exit the ward. Rounding the corners leading to one H post there is a formidable dayroom down one hall and down the other a large dorm room, where I will be lodged.

In a small, windowless conference room the chief psychiatrist, Dr.

Kara, a small, muscular, mannish Filipina, conducts my intake. Never making eye contact, she asks, "Any family?"

"Yes, but they're not talking to me."

"Any outside contacts besides family?"

"Well, there's a girl I used to know who visits me once in a while, but otherwise, no."

Leafing through my chart for relevant information, she finally closes the book of my life with the declaration, "You're pathetic." As insulted as I am, I also believe it to be true. Either way, this is my initiation as one of Creedmoor's multitude.

ONE GOOD STAFF MEMBER is my new treating psychiatrist, Dr. Singh, a kind but detached Indian woman who lowers my dosage after her evaluation. Now I'm on only 15 milligrams of Stelazine and I have no side effects. I guess I could get used to taking medication if it remains this simple. I feel fine and believe I don't need it.

Walking the long, dark, enclosed hall and emerging into the large, windowed, sunlit dayroom gives me hope that it's a new and better day and maybe my mood, my spirit, will be lifted. However, I am met by yellow nicotine-stained walls, the hardened, noncommittal gaze of the Mahatas, which I discover is an acronym for Mental Health Treatment Aide, intrinsic to Creedmoor, and the distracted and dismal faces of the other patients. My peers are all broken-down malnourished or obese vacant-eyed zombies, doped up on medication, staring emptily, as if hypnotized, watching the television mounted to a corner ceiling. The TV is running simultaneously with a static-filled radio, in-between stations, blasting some bad rap music. The staff's interests win out when choosing television and radio stations. The Mahatas are less disciplined here than the aides in Kings County or Mid-Hudson, my previous short-term hospital stays. They play cards or table games among themselves and only include a patient if they are proven to be coherent and subsequently "cool" in their circle. The main card game is spades and it is played with a passion. The patients are counted on the half hour but otherwise pretty much ignored. There's a lot of walking of the marble floors and stone-walled halls and I can be found in those halls when cigarette break arrives because I am literally smoked out of the room. The huge day hall fills to the brim three times a day with a thick cloud of cigarette smoke, where only disheveled legs and broken shoes can be seen, milling, mingling, shuffling. It's as if they're amidst dry ice in a discotheque of disease, slow-dancing to the thump of distorted bass and drum.

A psychologist runs therapeutic community meetings where groups make meandering and mundane observances about the weather, sports, or last night's TV lineup. Then there's his reading of yesterday's newspaper when today's goes missing, with not-so-current events winding up in the horoscopes and then the funny papers. The meetings end with him doling out soggy, unappetizing peanut butter and jelly sandwiches. I catch him checking his watch often. Dr. Singh seems grateful to have an office door that she can lock behind her, for she does this with alarming frequency. In fact all of the professionals do. They arrive in the morning, convene in the treatment room, come out to see a few patients, maybe conduct a group, run to their office, then break for lunch. They go back to their office, make a brief appearance in the afternoon, into their office for one last stretch, then off to their homes, one day closer to retirement. You literally have to position yourself at the door of the day hall and sprint down the long hallway to catch them entering or exiting their office before they lock that damned door. And knock all you wish—they will not answer you.

Though the food is tasteless and ill-prepared I am always hungry and grateful to eat when I can. One patient sitting across from me in the cramped dining hall mixes in multiple packets of salt and pepper, ketchup, mustard, *and* mayonnaise that he saves and pulls out of his dingy grey socks in an attempt to make his food more palatable. He then scarfs it down, belches loudly, and launches into a profanity-laden complaint about that evening's meal.

The only other recurring dining disturbance comes whenever they serve mashed potatoes, which is often, and the very distinct medicinal aftertaste they have. I would normally chalk it up to poor preparation if not for the steady decline of my sexual drive and infrequent ejaculation when I do become erect. Surely I'm paranoid but that doesn't stop my suspicion of the kitchen staff responding to unwritten orders to put saltpeter in the food. I ask the other guys if they notice the taste of the potatoes but they shrug it off, grateful to have a meal. When I broach the subject of erectile dysfunction they look at me as a queer kook, so I let it drop and make a mental note to avoid the mashed potatoes.

I notice I am sleeping too much. I feel lazy about always laying up somewhere like the rest of the patients, but sometimes I sleep alongside them in the uncomfortable cheap wood and cold hard vinyl chairs, made, it seems, to keep you awake and miserable. This appears less like a place of help and treatment than like a bus station. The dirty, bloated, and broken bodies that line the corners would remind anyone of dead mice in a glue trap.

My dreaming is thick and lugubrious, and always of Mom, when I'm not dreaming of bizarre institutional scenes. I often wake up moaning, which sounds like piercing, fearful screams until I come up from under that final blanket of sleep. In real time I am a sick dog releasing short bursts of groaned code. I always look over to see if my dorm mates can hear. I realize that what is deafening to me goes unnoticed by the other patients. All I can hear when awake at lights out is the stereophonic psychosis riding in and out of various corners of the huge dorm room, the constant low hum of thirty sick men murmuring their own tormented monologues, giggling manically, cursing their internal demons, and shouting out incongruous tangential gibberish, waking the few like me who aren't on a medication cocktail so potent that we could sleep through a car bomb. I also learn to sleep light and keep a close eye on my shoes, socks, and underwear, some of which gets stolen in the middle of the night by light-fingered fiends. I often smell the sulfur of matches and then cigarettes and even reefer smoke waft through the room. Sleepers rise around me like the dead from chemical coffins to shuffle toward the smoke, begging and even bullying to get a hit, as a chorus of "Bust me down! Bust me down!"—institution slang for "save me a drag"—repeats deep into the evening.

With the introduction to my system of a prescribed appetite-increasing neuroleptic and no consistent exercise, I gain fifteen pounds within my first two weeks on this locked ward. My introduction to the hospital privilege system and off-ward activity comes with doctor's orders not to go to the basement gymnasium but to spend a half hour down at the building's lobby snack machines. Many patients use this time to score cigarettes and lighters to take back to the ward bathrooms to smoke. Others squeeze behind pillars and into blind spots to feel up the female patients, themselves agreeing to the grope for a cup of coffee or bag of chips. Many turn their backs from staff and stuff their snacks under their armpits, in their socks, or down their trousers, supplementing the poor ward fare in favor of Pepsi for breakfast, a Honey Bun for lunch, and Doritos for dinner. I resist the blatant offenders of the snack machine but still sheepishly secure a couple of packages of Reese's Peanut Butter Cups. It doesn't help that a psychiatric inpatient leads a sedentary life, where even your supposed role models the Mahatas sit around all day, barking orders from a comfy chair behind the nurse's station. To combat the bloat I start a regimen of dorm room push-ups and sit-ups, and after a couple of weeks I get myself in pretty good shape. The Mahatas start to notice, the men intimidated by a patient who may overpower them during a takedown, and the women treating me like eye candy.

I don't feel I have much in common with the Mahatas. The staff is predominately black yet they tend to abuse and victimize the white patients as well as the chronically ill minorities. The Mahatas watch the patients during "prime time," when the professionals are on duty, and pretty much allow them to work out their various issues in the safety of this asylum. That is, until the weekend. All the patients are conditioned to dread Saturday morning because this is when the Mahatas rule with impunity. They come in, put their feet up, eat their sausage, egg, and cheese sandwiches with light and sweet coffee delivered from the local deli, and begin exacting punishments for long forgotten misdeeds during the week.

I sit in the dayroom, astonished and scared, while the young black male Mahatas, decked out in oversize designer T-shirts, gold rope chains, immaculate sneakers, and baggy jeans, call out names, days of the week, and the petty offenses.

"Greenberg! Remember on Tuesday morning when you wouldn't put your cigarette out after I told you smoking time was over? How many times did I tell you? How many times? Into the bathroom!"

"Klein! Snack time on Wednesday you took *two* puddings! *Two!* I saw you, Klein! Into the bathroom!"

Then the offending parties are taunted in their walk of shame by the female staff: "Ooop! I told ya, Klein, didn't I? I guess you won't be so greedy next time, huh?"

And the doomed beg and plead for absolution, only to be mocked by the other, luckier, trained patients in a maddening play of pathos. Screams echo screams, cries for mercy meet overriding manic laughter. All while the radio blasts Bobby Brown and Mariah Carey, and the TV broadcasts cartoon violence that dulls the senses and acts as a precursor and colorful visual to the bathroom beatdown given to the Greenbergs and the Kleins and a smattering of others who didn't put their cigarettes out. Or wanted more pudding. Or changed the channel without asking. Or did anything to run afoul of these employees who create a pecking order of snitches, gofers, sycophants, and enforcers, while I sit in the audience and wonder what my role is, desperately trying to blend into the wall.

I often wonder what I will do if I am targeted, humiliated, or even assaulted for some ridiculous infraction. I thank my shaky belief in God that I am not so far gone as to do the sometimes mindless and annoying things that mentally ill people do to incur the wrath of these sisters and brothers. They are supposed to be role models, not just guards but guides, leading us back from insanity to a life of cleanliness and functionality, but they only end up making me feel embarrassed, ashamed, and disgusted by my own people.

I just hope I can survive the threat of a beatdown and the boredom of the wait until I get my privileges to get off this locked ward and taste a little freedom. There is nothing worthwhile to do here. I watch the wall-mounted clock creep slowly to the next minute, hour, and day, while the same songs play on the radio. The same shows are watched on TV. The same patients line up for meds, and meals, and smokes. And the same Mahatas sit in their favorite chairs, and chatter about hospital gossip, boast of sexual prowess, what they bought and for how much, and periodically look up from their bull sessions to yell at a patient and count the census. I don't want to play the board games, all of which have missing pieces, and I am not good at table tennis or competitive enough for the loud spades games that go on. I just find a quiet corner, put on my Walkman, and draw most of the day.

Some of the other patients engage me in a pantomime while I wear my headphones, as if they are interpreters for the hearing impaired. Not wanting to be rude I slip the phones halfway off my head, only for them to ask to borrow my music. After being generous on Rikers Island, where several radios were "lost" by the inmate borrowers, I learned never to lend out your recreation. Unsuccessful in acquiring my radio, a lot of the guys resort to disturbing my flow. Some drag chairs across the day hall floor to sit next to me, others kick the table, some interrupt to engage in mundane and inane conversations, usually centering about themselves, still others pick out subtle flaws in my unfinished artwork.

"What's that supposed to be? It looks like a Dalmatian taking a dump. Doesn't it?" they'd call out, inspiring a small critiquing session. Fortunately most of the patients have come to enjoy my artwork, and the fact that I mind my business and don't bother anybody allows me a little bit of respect and some peace.

After a while I become ward artist. I get a lot of requests from the guys for drawings of sexy superheroes, S&M Wonder Woman being a popular fave. They use them to decorate their "walls," which are the dividers in the huge dorm room, and to send home to mama or their girls. I don't charge at first, just thinking of it as practice, something to pass the time. Willie, one of the seedier patients, looks at me disbelievingly through his one good eye. He suggests I start charging the guys. "Do it for cigarettes! Food! Anything! This is your *hustle*, man. You're lucky to have one. Most guys either have to stick you up or get dicked down for anything in here." I don't like his smile behind that bit of information.

The Mahatas are my best audience as an artist. They notice my detailed pen and ink with light washes of watercolor treatments that I paint while in the dayroom and ask, "You do tattoos?" My reintroduction to real currency comes from plenty of requests for Celtic tribals surrounding dragons devouring babies quoting Chinese, and a myriad of hypersexual and ultraviolent imagery. While I'm not a fan of this self-indulgent art form now slowly growing in popularity, I comply with their requests. Not so much because I need the money but because I'm bored and need the practice.

The process starts with the Mahata sitting down next to me and going into a detailed reverie on his or her life as if selling me the treatment to a Hollywood film. His troubled childhood, her first sexual experience, legal issues, personal philosophy, astrological sign, and intimate zingers that they expect me to wrap up neatly and distill into a kick-ass drawing to adorn their forearm, shoulder, or back.

I start at an affordable $10 a sketch, then, when Mahata demand increases, graduate to $30, then $50 for full color illustrations, $50 being like $150 in Creedmoor's underground economy. All of this commerce is against hospital policy and kept on the q.t. It feels good to make money from my artwork. Like it's worth something. Like I'm worth something. And as the weeks and then months of being on a locked ward progress, and the word gets around the hospital that I do "really fly artwork," I feel a sense of validation and pride.

I use my newfound "institutional wealth" to barter and buy more books, paper, pens, pencils, and paint, sketching almost constantly. And though I start to flourish, becoming the ward's "favorite boy," deep inside I am sad. I'm so ashamed of my work and talent—it feels more like a curse. I get so much praise for my talents that I believe I don't deserve. Not now. It is so much of an influence and outgrowth of Mom.

After what I've done I don't feel worthy to have even the most remote connection to her.

AFTER GETTING MOVED FROM THE DORM to a two-person bedroom, the Mahatas have a habit of checking my room, not to harass but rather watch my artistic development. I share my room with Billy, who has absolutely no belongings and doesn't mind that I encroach on his space or keep the lights on all night. "So long as you don't mind my psoriasis," he says, which is severe, causing scaling as large as wilted corn flakes (which he sometimes eats), requiring constant sweeping of the floor and which often wind up on my bed and under my covers. The walls of our nine-by-twelve-foot bedroom begin to fill with two-by-three-foot canvases I complete over numerous nights while Billy's bald flaking head sleeps under his sheets. I also paint in the laundry room under the auspices of catching up on a load or two. The blank canvases are bought for me by staff sometimes in lieu of payment for various pieces, and I cover them in oil paints that I smuggle in with an old girlfriend's help and hide successfully from the staff. Oil paints, toxic and considered harmful contraband, would never pass muster on the ward so I stick to harmless nontoxic watercolors when I paint in the dayroom.

Coming into the system an insanity plea patient, mentally ill with a criminal component and drug history, I see myself as the worst of the worst—unwanted by society, abandoned by my family, and unloved by myself. After many long looks at what I have become, I render a self-portrait of the artist on a gurney, surgical instruments by my head. A man who, similar to Camus's stranger, is empty, literally, eviscerated only to reveal a bloodless void where my heart should be, a hollow man with nothing (good) inside. Looking deeper, I am victim and perpetrator, exemplified by my signature on the scalpel. This is my *Autopsy of the Damned*.

Another painting, with four iconic leaders of men walking across the Beatles' *Abbey Road*, represents a metaphorical self-portrait of the artist. One who can love as strong as Jesus, hate as hard as Hitler, is as fearless as Malcolm X, but who has a healthy dollop of the rock and roll pageantry that was Elvis in his later years, all with an underpinning of British Invasion rock. In addition to the personal Passion play, I thought to myself, "What four historical figures would provoke the most fascinating conversation if you got them all in one room?"

My *Wizard of Oz* parody, featuring four more archetypes, provokes the most laughter and Mahata daps for its sexual imagery. It began as a lecherous joke. What they may have done to pass the time on that long trip to Oz, Dorothy seductive with her skirt hitched up to her panties, the Scarecrow displaying a turgid ear of corn, the Tin Man a greasy gasoline pump. I enjoy how viewers slowly discover that something wicked is afoot on the yellow brick road.

The final and best painting in this whirlwind series completed within two weeks is my depiction of a worn-out Superman, slumped in a recliner before the TV in his small, dark, single room apartment. His cape hung up on a door, gorging on beer and Doritos, with what could be a burning joint in his mouth, glassy eyed and weary, he is not so super. Someone with tremendous potential letting it go to waste.

"Yo man, this shit is dope," the Mahatas say in praise of my artistic efforts. My fellow patients don't say much but give me a wide berth out of deference and respect. When alerted by staff of my work, the Department of Rehabilitation's response is "that's nice," reinforcing the overall vibe of grade school or, even worse, special ed. When my social worker discovers a state-funded artist-in-residence program that would garner me an income, more freedom, and improve my morale, the director of rehab refuses to sponsor me, stating, "All funds go to patient programming." This is reminiscent of Mr. Spock's epitaph in *The Wrath Of Khan*, "The needs of the many outweigh the needs of the few, or the one." While I understand their rationale I feel slighted. It leaves me with few options as I grow from just another patient who paints to an artist with ambition.

I hope my art, the only thing that I have, that I feel connected to, will get me out of here, but movement is slow. We all just sit around and watch game shows, of which *The Price Is Right* is the highlight; soap operas, where Erica Kane is the bitch/goddess of the ward; and *Jerry Springer*, whose violence and depravity are quite a hit here. I pass the time by working on various paintings, while trying not to arouse too much interest or suspicion. I have several clandestine spots—under my bed, the dirty clothes bin in my closet, and tucked under my groin—for hiding cash, as it's forbidden for patients to have more than the eight dollars a week allowance given by the state.

While I believe everyone aware of my transgression, including my family, would rather I rot forever in this mental hospital, I am actually thriving. With the tattoos and portraits of Mahatas' kids, dogs, girl-friends, and grandmothers, custom greeting cards, and other artistic ephemera, I have a successful art business going from the inside, saving every penny. I do it to feel like a man, like a human being, and to hire better representation. I may need to. There are other insanity plea patients on my ward, some who've been in this hospital for fifteen, twenty, thirty years.

5

THE MOST ENDURING OLFACTORY MEMORY I have is of marijuana. I can identify this fragrance quicker than that of a rose. The smell of pot is the smell of my home. It filled my senses as I nursed at Mom's bosom and never left. The mix of mother's milk, weed smoke, and my hungry saliva created a smoothie of unusual potency that I taste still. It is a memory that seduces and repels me, causing instant symbiosis with my mom and a simultaneous forty-yard distance. I watch her beam vacantly, far away in her head, totally out of contact with me, as I wander in my own fog of nostalgia.

Mom was born Audrey Louise Phipps, which always sounded quaint and somewhat refined, as if she were friends with Grace Kelly and Jackie Bouvier, or that she came from a long line of English butlers. Yes, there is English blood in the family, "but probably introduced by the masters in the slave shacks on the plantations of the West Indies," Mom would always say, usually while smoking a joint.

As I always saw a burning stick of reefer perched on Mom's lips, I assumed this was the norm. I often wondered which of my other boyhood friends and schoolyard chums' mothers were pot smokers, but I never broached the subject. There was a quiet understanding in my home, and I assumed in other smoking mothers' homes, that though they loved getting high, it was best kept secret because, as Mom said, "the fuzz is always on the lookout to bust people like us for having too good a time."

As a young child I began to feel disconnected from her. I noticed her getting high and occasionally scrunching up her face in mid-laughter while looking at me, as if I were a leprechaun or a Lollipop Guildsman, enchanted and strange. When I saw her addled and dizzy like this a part of me felt I had to be the parent to my mother, but I didn't mind it too much. In fact I relished Mom's animated monologues, laughing with me for hours after she smoked, walking off her high through the back roads of Jamaica, Queens. I learned to take what I could get from her, appreciating whatever attentions she could muster. Off the main roads, Mom would smoke openly, with me as her sounding board and confidant, her voice soft and warm, or laughing gently between drags, though for years I didn't get the jokes.

MOM HOLDS MY HAND as we walk the neighborhood. During these times alone with me she tells me about her life and her dreams. I listen quietly, as if walking with a sage. And I feel her rage as her hand periodically tightens while griping about Dad and his women, peppering her diatribe with the impassioned whisper, "Don't be like your father, son. For God's sake."

We wander well past dusk. She smiles pleasantly, handing me her slippers while walking barefoot on freshly cut, dew drenched summer lawns and then tossing me into massive mounds of autumn leaves, apologizing to the homeowner who raked them into the neat pile we just demolished, giggling with me as we walk away.

"My mother never did this with me, son. I don't ever want you to feel that shame. You know, when I was your age finishing shopping errands with her, your Granny would tell me before rounding the corner to our block in Brooklyn, 'Walk ahead of me. Go on run. Run into the house.' Then it was, 'You know what to do.' Eventually it became ingrained, me running far ahead of my own mother into the three-family brownstone. This so the German and Irish neighbors wouldn't know that I was her daughter. You know, Granny was Jamaican, but with her fair skin and wavy red hair, she wasn't above trying to pass. They may have called her 'Pinky,' and me a tragic mulatto, or quadroon, or octoroon.

"This is how we of mixed race were classified in the pseudoscientific language of the white power structure," Mom recounts, and I can tell it hurts her deeply, even now, wincing as she laughs the odd names off, trying not to harsh her mellow. I watch Mom inhale deeply and take long thoughtful pauses as we walk, the pot jogging her memory and loosening her lips.

"I was a petite model, art student, and gay divorcee with two small daughters in the mid '50s when I was first turned on to marijuana, son," she says. "It was very much a part of the artsy, downtown New York crowd that I ran with." I'm aware of these types through my constant television intake, mostly from *Dobie Gillis* reruns and film noir.

Bereted, goateed, chain smoking, deathly pale artists and models dressed in tight black schmattas, snapping their applause for the explicit homosexual wanderlust rants of bespectacled, wayward, drop-out poets above the discordant squall of soul-patched, dope fiend Negro jazz musicians wearing sunglasses indoors, in squalid smoke-filled basements with sweating walls and cheap castaway furniture. Lost and found run-aways from "anywhere but here" congregate and cohabitate with the jaded native New Yawka, sharing paper plates of a slice with pepperoni, a bagel with a shmear, chicken and greens, regular coffee, and passing a thickly rolled joint of wacky tobacky. Mom frequented all of the hip Greenwich Village nightspots. "I loved Café Feenjon for the Mediterranean music and Turkish coffee, and Gerde's Folk City for the beat poetry and great pot."

At four feet eleven with just-out-of-high-school baby fat still clinging to her cheeks, she caught many a wary eye from doormen and bouncers, "but my good looks usually got me in." With soulful eyes, dimpled cheeks, and a winning, girlish smile that she retained all her life, at her best she looked like Elizabeth Taylor with a mean tan.

In between modeling gigs and art school classes, Mom and her best friend and fellow model Joan, a sultry, raven-haired, Jewish beauty, ran what she calls a "salt and pepper operation, selling loose joints." I know Joan as a middle-aged mom whose best days are behind her but is still outgoing and sexy, and I harbor a boyhood crush, delighted when she visits our house parties, where she approaches me with wide-open arms, pinching the cheeks on my face and my bottom, begging, "Give me some sugar!"

"Soon everyone in the Village looking for a good high knew Audi and Jo," Mom says proudly. "We were welcome in every after-hours drinking establishment, turning on the discreet in the gay bars on Christopher Street, the blacklisted Communists on Bleecker, and even the junkies in Alphabet City. We courted the drifters, the loners, the misfits, and the dreamers who clung to the underbelly of lower Manhattan, because we were beloved and valued for our cool, our chic, and our top shelf smoke."

With street competition fierce, the girls were approached and protected by Deon. "He was a part-time jazzman and reefer dealer," Mom remembers. "Deon enlisted us to gain access for his product in places that he could never go. He gave us an ounce or two out of which we would still sell loose joints to cats between sets, but focus on nickel and dime bags to the rich and privileged from Jersey and the outer boroughs too scared to score from the brothers."

One of the major benefits in Mom's partnership with Deon the dealer was her introduction to any- and everyone who played, sang, wrote, or produced the cool jazz music of the time. While her freelance job in *Jet* magazine's model stable brought Mom face to face with the "safe" black idols of the day such as Johnny Mathis, "for whom I acted as a beard whenever he was in New York," she confides, in the evening she would share a joint and julep with the jazz cognoscenti. It is in this elite circle that she met a brown-eyed handsome man recently transplanted from Tampa, jazz bassist Jamil Ibrahim.

"When I first met him he often talked about not knowing his father, the shame he had of being 'the bastard son of a wayward southern bluesman.' He always said he wanted to create the home life that he didn't have in his youth. Complete with three sons. He'd always say, 'Give me three boys, mama.' Well, he found it, in the club, in between sets, with me. We created a life and a home for the girls and you and your brothers here in Jamaica, Queens. And your Gramps bought the house here because it reminded him of his home in Kingston."

Our cozy house is on the border of Jamaica and a charming hamlet called St. Albans, at the crossroads of Merrick and Linden Boulevards, two major Long Island thoroughfares. St. Albans was initially farmland that was developed in the 1920s and '30s. It was here in the 1940s that a great migration of wealthy Negro luminaries and entertainers, predominantly in the jazz arena, bought homes and built a vibrant community.

"That's the house that Count Basie lived in," Mom says, beaming with pride, pointing out a big house during our long stroll. "And over there was Lena Horne."

While these manses are resplendent, no one could ever mistake the home of the Godfather of Soul, James Brown, who announced his arrival to the upper crust of Queens Negro High Society by building a moat around his house, twisting a gothic *J.B.* into the wrought-iron fence around the property.

Fats Waller, Ella Fitzgerald, Jackie Robinson, and many more. These dimmed but never forgotten flames burn bright in my heart as Mom regales me with the glory days of the neighborhood, instilling provincial pride in knowing they walked the same sidewalks as I. And then there are the lesser-known but equally essential sidemen who still live there, of which my father and his friends can be counted. Living in what was once the hippest neighborhood in New York City, second only to Harlem.

Mom lets my hand go and I play cowboys and Indians with the other musicians' kids while she slowly strolls through our front gate, stopping to inspect and attend to her outdoor plants, riding out her high.

EVERYONE USUALLY HAS A ROLE IN THE FAMILY. I become the straight-laced brooding prodigy, not partaking in the weed, hunched over my drawing table while everyone else in the small dwelling on Linden Boulevard rolls it up, smokes it up, and whoops it up. I hear them all as I sketch and doodle: Mom, Dad, Lauren, Carol, Smiley, and Kal giggle and guffaw, lay down their rap and slap five, engaging in a form of connoisseurship, extolling the virtues of different gradations, the splendor in the grass.

My family's pot smoking make us local heroes within the neighborhood; revered, respected, protected by all the hip people who indulge with us, and tolerated by those who don't. Our neighbors who might've been uptight about the loud parties, bleary eyes, and gossip of marijuana growing in our backyard know that we kids are fed, clothed, and in school, that the garbage is put out on time, and that the lawn is trimmed and impressively decorated, all thanks to Mom.

I notice that "Mom" is what everyone in the neighborhood calls her, as if she were *everybody's* mother. I feel proprietary whenever a neighbor walks by and calls her this, afraid someone will steal her away. Many sponge off her sweetness, successfully hitting her up for loose change or a spare buck or two, tomatoes from our garden, pears from the trees in our backyard. Mom often asks me to donate a couple of my comic books to passing mentally disabled kids or poorer teenagers who have just begun moving into the neighborhood. I always comply but not without giving the kids the once over, maybe even a little stink-eye, so they don't get too close.

Some stop and chat, looking forward to her friendly smile or an encouraging word when walking by the house, she in the front yard raking the leaves or watering her plants.

"Hey Mom, whatcha growing there?"

"Wouldn't you like to know," she says with a wink.

Playing on the lawn with my superhero dolls, I see by the wide grins and excited eyes that our neighbors are charmed by Mom, doing her gardening, blasting pop music from a transistor radio, wearing an eccentric, artsy outfit, with one of Dad's pipes in her mouth, inspiring some to even call her "Papa."

Mom burns not only weed with the best of them, but also her brassieres at feminist rallies in the early days of the women's lib movement. She and my sisters often sit around the dining table, lighting up, discussing feminist literature from Betty Friedan, Gloria Steinem, and Erica Jong.

"I've got no fear of flying," she says with a laugh. "I get high all the time."

Bella Abzug, Shirley Chisholm, Yoko Ono, all trailblazers in the news, in my mind are contemporaries of Mom. Some of her edgier artistic creations are gay and lesbian greeting cards, the best of which has two silhouetted female heads facing each other, about to kiss, emblazoned with the banner, *"Lez be friends."* The cloud of libertinism looms as low as the marijuana smoke in my home. I stumble on a copy of *The Joy of Sex* and overhear many reefer-drenched references to taboo cinema, with enigmatic titles like *Last Tango* and *Deep Throat.*

6

EVERYONE HERE IS DEEP IN DENIAL. Most of them still use and then get up and profess many months and years of clean time. It's laughable yet also disturbing because the rampant drug use on a unit chock-full of addicts makes me feel like I'm on a ward where no one is in control. It feels like the addicts have a pecking order and the top men run the house. The top dog here on ward 6-A, or "King" as he is often called, is Bayou. He's an insanity plea patient and Vietnam vet who developed a poly-substance habit "in country," nursed it once he came back home, and eventually bugged out and raped his eighty-year-old landlady. Bayou uses his considerable monthly military checks to engage in a wicked usury and loan shark operation that has most of Building 40's patients and even some staff in his clutches. He also has his brother Easy visit bimonthly to collect a knot of cash, the profits of his illegal activity, while sneaking substantial quantities of reefer and crack hidden within the lettuce of two enormous hero sandwiches. I wouldn't believe it if I hadn't seen it unfold before me on the visitor's room table while receiving a call from Taylor, a high school friend who, upon discovering I was locked up, came to offer support while also suggesting he and I become an item. Figuring he was looking forward less to cementing our cursory friendship and more to wild just-got-out-of-the-joint sex whenever I *did* get out, I politely declined.

Bayou is in his mid-forties and can't read or write but he sure can count money. More than once he beat me with a slick "got change of a five?" bait-and-switch con that always had me losing at least two dollars, aided by his impatiently barking, "Cain't youse count, boy?" and other rambling ruses served up in his impenetrable backwoodsy Louisiana accent. He's surly and watchful, constantly appraising his environment, always looking for new ways to get over. When not resting on his "designated" dayroom couch, snoring like a fearsome crocodile, he is in his bedroom getting stoned, blasting southern Baptist revivalist radio, screaming "Hallelujah, Jesus!" at the top of his lungs.

Enduring periodic restrictions for intimidating patients who don't pay on time and for dropping crack pipes during treatment team meetings, he eventually regains his privileges and again prowls the grounds and beyond for money and new victims to hook. You know when Bayou is set to return to the ward by the anticipatory shuffling of the addicts who gave him their allowance to pick up whatever specialty drug or paraphernalia he couldn't offer from his own supply. Once the bell is rung from the outside announcing someone's at the door, fifteen to twenty of the thirty inpatients get excited and run like Pavlovian dogs, all eager to be first to get their drugs, catch a free toke or two for emphatic promises, or suck the dregs out of Bayou's pipe after he sits on his toilet throne and beams himself up to a galaxy far, far way. It's good to be the king.

It's a bit of Rikers all over again, very depressing and scary, only more so because the staff carry on as if everything's fine. As if they don't smell the crack and grass wafting up and down the hallway from the lavatory and laundry room, as if they don't see the dealing and bleary eyes, as if they don't smell the liquor on the breath of the few who are allowed out. Thank God I've got my art. I'd lose my mind for sure (for good?) if I didn't have it. It keeps me busy, keeps me alive and in touch with my past, my roots, and my estranged family. Mom is with me when I draw or paint. I do so constantly to pass the time, heal myself, and do my bid.

Eventually I am asked, in the typical circular group confessional, to explain why I'm here. I talk about the drugs and the breakdown but I am careful to avoid mentioning Mom, which is the crucial reason. I don't want to give anybody here anything to throw at me later. I'd heard and feared enough of that in Rikers. It's challenging to let my guard down and to heal properly when I am constantly under internal pressure to keep my offense to myself, for fear of being humiliated and shunned, or worse. No one must know what I did. I fear what would happen to me if any of these unsavory characters find out. It is an institution and even here there is a perverted version of jailhouse justice. A part of me wants to die and yet another part of me fears death in this haunted tower at the hands of these madmen and fiends.

7

WORKING FOR LARRY SHERMAN ORCHESTRAS isn't the worst thing that can happen to a musician. Plenty of talented guns, after cutting their teeth playing in gymnasiums and bars—or the no man's land of Greenwich Village afterhours joints, as my father did—are ready to cut their hair and shave their beards and get respectable. It doesn't matter that these one-time starry-eyed studs get married, have kids, and trade in their eleven-minute solos during "In-A-Gadda-Da-Vida" or "A Love Supreme" for sing-alongs to Devo's "Whip It." It is good and, more important, steady money.

My dad is a talented man. He plays almost any musical instrument you put before him. But don't think him some chitlin circuit show-off. He is a studied musician, composing various types of short musical stories, specializing in *Peter and the Wolf*–type children's fare, which he also illustrates. Being a tall, lean intellectual with charm only adds to his cache. There is just one problem: he is as brown as a Hershey bar. This does not go over well in the 1950s, '60s, *or* '70s.

My father is the only black person employed by Larry Sherman Orchestras during the 1970s and '80s. While my parents are having their umpteenth heated discussion over Larry's cheapness and stingy scheduling, I ask my dad in my precocious way, "Are you a token?" I am about ten years old.

Do ten-year-olds even *know* what that is or implies? I may have heard it on television. Maybe on one of the token network shows that my family loves to watch. Perhaps *Room 222*, or *The Flip Wilson Show*, more probably *That's My Mama*. *My* mama winces at first, empathizing with the pain and embarrassment Dad must feel, but then smiles at my apparent accuracy and plaintive challenge to the household's primary breadwinner. She loves a good intellectual scrap, especially when her astute baby son throws the first blow. Dad gives my question a thoughtful and painful moment to digest then follows with his patented rationalizations, intellectualizations, and bullshit.

"Iss, there are things that men, and as people, we all feel we have to do, or need to do. To survive, to satisfy our desires for legitimacy, and to unselfishly provide for our loved ones, a man's partner and, yes, his progeny, of which you, son, would be considered . . ."

I don't understand a word after a while. I guess I deserve to be addressed over my head by a man with wounded pride were I to dare use pointed words and concepts that I could barely comprehend.

Though he finally reluctantly admits that he is indeed a token in the enterprise, Dad gets along with the other musicians in the orchestra. He speaks well of these fellows whom he shares jokes and good times playing with, knowing that they, like he, paid their dues and are the tightest and most intuitive players they can be, or can be found on a suburban New Jersey weekend.

Because he only works the weekend, Dad usually sleeps the week away, waking up at around two or three in the afternoon. I guess he needs his rest due to the exhausting schedule of rehearsing new material during the evenings, one full gig on Friday night, two on Saturday, and then two on Sunday. These are four-hour affairs held at The Manor in West Orange, New Jersey, a glorified catering hall where the moneyed suburbanites organize teenage birthday parties, bar mitzvahs, and weddings. Dad plays electric bass guitar throughout most of the gigs but Larry Sherman knows he has a secret weapon. Toward the end of the evening my father will use his deep, sonorous, baritone voice to serenade the ladies with the very '70s ballads "I Believe in You and Me" and "One in a Million You." Oh, how the white middle-aged mothers swoon when he lets these two out of the box. That he is tall, dark, and handsome only enhances the fan factor. The husbands skulk around, scowling about this flashy, uppity nigger getting their wives all hot. These same men will probably get neurotic while fucking them that night, fearing that their women are imagining Dad's face singing to them as they pump it home. Rather they should thank my dad for inspiring their semiannual bang.

It is a routine that Dad has and we grow used to, him rising from a deep slumber to shit, shower, and shave while Mom irons that night's dress shirt. He splashes on strong and attractive cologne, which seems unattainably adult. He sips on a cup of fresh brewed black coffee and smokes his More cigarettes. Walking about the house in black dress socks, dress shirt, and undies, Dad runs through a series of vocal exercises and scales, getting his voice in shape for the night's serenade. Sometimes his voice fails during these exercises, and he chastises himself when he can't reach a high note—"Dad blast!" The best part comes when he slips on the elegant full tuxedo, of which he has maybe three. Then, before he leaves, he allows Mom to give him one last inspection and loads up the car with his electric bass, mike stand, and God-awfully heavy and cumbersome amplifier. My dad is a professional musician on his way to slay them in New Jersey. Even though he has gone from playing challenging jazz in trios to Top 40 for the kids and cheesy love songs for the housewives, he is still super cool.

As I get older and start to miss him, I grow curious about my dad and his work. His suiting up for battle, going away in his chariot to slay the dragon and romance the muses, and then the return, at 2 or 3 AM. Hearing the car back into the driveway, the red tail lights illuminating the rear bedrooms, his weary entrance back into the house, then him fixing up a large plate of leftovers while the sounds of *The Late, Late Show* emanate from the kitchen. I reach the age where I want to see him slay that dark, hungry beast. I ask if I can come along and watch him perform. He is pleased to take me, if only to reclaim his baby son from his wife, who he fears may be turning me into a sissy.

While the Jersey bandstand crowds are respectable, it is on the last few jaunts with him I see firsthand how his wicked bass playing and deep, rich, expressive voice affect women. Seated in the first row center of this mid-sized catering hall I watch him sing as several women swoon, scream, and talk to him suggestively from the audience.

One thirtyish, lean black woman squeezes up next to me, exclaiming, "Is *that* your daddy? You're his baby, right? OK, good, I'm gonna sit right here next to *YOU!*"

Then she embraces me while screaming out, "Sing that song, Papa!"

Dad leaves me after the show for a spell, disappearing with the female fan. As the crowd disperses, the band packs up their gear, and I wait for Dad to return, the keyboard player and I sit at the piano and we play and sing numerous rounds of "Heart and Soul."

8

I SIT AND SKETCH IN MY WATERCOLOR PAD, occasionally flipping through to review some of the recent paintings I've done. After the morning therapeutic community meeting Mrs. Sapros comes over to the small table in the dayroom where I've set up my workstation and asks to see them. The elderly ward social worker has smiled at me often and with approval since I arrived, because I avoid trouble and show self-motivation. Our contact has been cursory up till now. When she asks what the new piece means I ask, "What do you see?"

She laughs, recognizing that I put her on the spot, but recovers nicely, saying, "Well, I'm a New York State licensed clinical social worker, not an art therapist, but I *can* say that it looks like you've been through a lot and held it all in, voicing it through your art, which is great. Some speak of rage, distortion, and have a hint of violence. There's a lot of forward motion in the lines and figures, like you wish to keep moving, but the backgrounds in your paintings are all dark and murky. Not as clearly defined and detailed as the main figure."

"I guess I'm trying to bring out the foreground. That's the selling point, y'know?" I respond. "That's what the picture's all about. So I put a lot into that. Work it so it shines, so it stands out."

"And if the central figure were you, with all the detail and intensive crafting, what do you think it would say about you?"

"Well, I just wanna be the best that I can be. I mean, I've already been the worst. Some people would say I'll always be screwed up, tainted, y'know?"

"Maybe it's good that you have a focus."

"Yeah. Discharge."

"Right. Of course. But don't neglect the background, the past, *your* past, and your trauma in your relentless pursuit of perfection or harmony because your trauma, your grief, your struggle will always be there. And better to embrace it, work through it, resolve it, and understand it. Then you'll find that health and wellness and wholeness will be right there with you. And you won't have to chase it. It will come to you."

As much as I'm open to healing I already recognize a propensity for platitudes and psychobabble in this hospital. I'm always on guard and assume I'm getting more of the same from the social worker, but I stop thinking about what Mrs. Sapros is saying and focus on how she is saying it. The quiet tone. The warmth in her voice. I feel vulnerable. My defenses drop and my heart melts a little. It sounds like home. It sounds like Mom. It sounds like love.

9

DESPITE THE MINOR SUCCESSES ON THE WARD I am still tied down to the hospital and must abide by their rules, more or less. Make those baby steps up the privilege ladder, from escorted to unescorted to furloughs to discharge. The Mahatas already recognize me as an artist of note, and the treatment team has observed me, sitting and drawing for hours in the dayroom. They all agree on what would be the best rehab placement for me. After six weeks on the ward I acquire escorted-on-grounds privileges to attend programming at the jewel in the Department of Rehab's crown, the Living Museum.

"Creedmoor used to be its own world," Mr. Ding boasts. He's an old-timer and generational employee, one of many family dynasties having younger relatives currently employed as Mahatas in addition to aunts, uncles, and parents who ushered them in. Mr. Ding schools me, whom he calls a "new Jack," on hospital history during my first escorted walk. With a small collection of my art work under my arm, I walk with him from the locked ward in the main building across the massive campus tucked away on three hundred acres of former farmland to my program on the other side of the grounds.

"Did you know we had more than six thousand patients here at one time? The ward staff roster was so many that we got our own name. We made that shit up . . . and it stuck."

It feels good to get fresh air and sunlight again after being locked on the ward for most of the summer. I don't want our walk to end, especially when we approach the dilapidated building that houses my program. But then I walk inside.

Stepping from the green and tranquil grounds into the decommis-

sioned remains of this food preparation/dining facility, I have no idea
what to expect. I just hope it will be a step up from the popsicle sticks
and *Cosmo* magazine collages that overrun the art programs back on
the ward. Mr. Ding says the building was abandoned for years after the
late 1960s. "Governor Rockefeller created more better policies aiding
and feeding the mentally ill. Creedmoor lost the farms. This building
closed and they had the patients eat on the wards. No homegrown
foods, now pre-fab meals like TV dinners or airplane food. That was a
fucked up move on the state's part, if ya ask me. But some a y'all should
be happy you're eatin' at all."

The building had been a squirrel-and-pigeon-infested storage facility until taken over in the early 1980s by two ambitious Europeans,
one of whom greets me. "Good morning. Come, sign in, make our
statistics," he says with a twinkle in his eyes and a lit cigarette dangling
from his mouth, motioning to the attendance sheet. "Welcome to the
Living Museum. Go on, you can take a look around. There'll be a test
afterwards."

It has a leaky roof and peeling paint, and I worry about asbestos
exposure. But it's an ideal artist's studio. The space is immense, with
plenty of good light streaming down from large transom windows set
just below the ceiling. Alongside those who are heavily medicated,
doodling and drooling, are manic mavericks who invert convention on
a whim. The common thread these talented artists wear is the unfor-
tunate pattern of the straitjacket.

This Living Museum has over twenty years become the largest open
art studio program dedicated to the painting, sculpture, and writing of
the mentally ill in America. Everything within the forty-thousand-
square-foot, two-tiered space grabs my attention, with paintings and
sculpture peeking out of the strangest corners. The main studio space
is on the second floor, with a catwalk overlooking the first floor. "The
administration just gave them permission to use the entire building,"
Mr. Ding tells me. "They gotta really clean this shit up, though." Coming up the stairs, following a "stream of consciousness" painted on the
floor and steps, I find the Garden of Heaven, a beautiful and bountiful

indoor greenhouse that is tended to with the utmost care. Then I enter the "battlefields" of life and, in this community's case, of the mind: the four primary stations of existence. In the building's corners are thematic rooms indicating the experience of leaving the womb, or Eden.

First is the Hospital, white-walled, ascetic, displaying a creepy, vintage 1940s dentist's chair and an immense eight-foot waste paper basket dedicated to actual Creedmoor memos. Then there is the strength, sanctity, and multi-theism of the Church, soothing for patients like myself with religious preoccupations, with a huge altar and stacks of multidenominational Bibles. The Workplace features a wall of Big Brotheresque TV monitors brandishing slogans of revolution, from the sarcastic to the sincere. Finally, I discover the comforts of the Home, complete with plush couches for a father to sit on, a stereo with hundreds of LPs for the kids to groove to, and a refrigerator obsessively scrawled and painted on, possibly by a mad housewife. Traveling in that stream becomes a moving experience of nature, faith, purpose, and finally healing and grace, delivered by the detritus of humanity living on the margins of society. And now I am one of them. And never before did I want so much to be here, with them.

Walking through the museum brings me back to my family home. Mom decorating it with artistic flair, itself a bit of a museum, with its palm plants and creeping vines, jungle décor, multiple mirrors, murals, sidewalk finds, well-placed trinkets, tchotchkes, and gewgaws. I can't hold back the sadness and longing for my childhood, my family. I excuse myself from Mr. Ding, step into the nearest bathroom, and cry like a baby.

The Living Museum is the brainchild of Polish artist/actor Bolek Greczynski, the European who greeted me and who handles day-to-day directorial duties, and Austro-Hungarian filmmaker/philosopher Janos Marton, who pops in from time to time, beautifying the space with dried flowers and abandoned greenery. Taking cues from the artist colony at the Maria Gugging Psychiatric Clinic in Vienna, this museum celebrates idiosyncrasies and creativity, providing a nurturing environment where people diagnosed with a wide range of mental illnesses create art. I sit before Bolek awestruck, while he lights up another cigarette from behind his paper-strewn desk.

"This is a sanctuary," Bolek announces with flair in his Polish accent as my orientation, "for the fragile, vulnerable, traumatized, you know, the real talent. We allow the afflicted individual to create without boundaries, identifying him or herself as an artist and not as a mental patient. This identity change allows the artists to see themselves as productive members of society, leaving behind the stigmas that are often associated with mental illness. But make no mistake, we are really only here to make straight up art, you know. So get comfortable and get started."

A lovable curmudgeon with a wry wit and droopy moustache, Bolek is pleasant enough even while battling what I later discover are the end stages of AIDS. After reviewing my watercolor pad and two medium-sized oil paintings, and seeing my talent and desire to work in a larger format, he gives me his appraisal and blessing.

"Ah, I see, cartoons, comic books, sci-fi. America!" he laughs. "You are red-blooded American boy. But you see it differently, no? Being black man, yes? No, what you have to say is good. And your work is good. You are a great artist. I cannot teach you anything. Go do what you want to do."

JUST COMING FROM A LOCKED WARD where I cannot move freely beyond the smoke-filled walls or paint uninterrupted, Bolek's respect and trust in me has a profound effect. I quickly recognize the Living Museum as a refuge and my new artistic base of operations. Over the ensuing months, with Bolek present, and later, when he's out on sick leave, I rise to the challenge of all this wall space and unlimited resources by painting large murals, which soon spread into much of the as-yet-untouched downstairs area. These include homages to the twentieth-century civil rights struggle, the space race, and great minds like James Joyce and Albert Einstein. Garnering praise for these works, I put my all into painting my freedom in the main reception room, a mural of an expansive blue sky with cumulus clouds depicting the majesty of Heaven. I gaze upon this sky daily, as a balm for having to spend most of my time on a locked ward in Building 40.

The freedom that Bolek gives me, anointed as the official tour guide and "new face of the Living Museum," affords me some rewards, including chatting up the more attractive visitors who are impressed with my work. Because I present well with no discernible illness, many flirtatious young female visitors assume I am a staff member, and thus a "safe" receptor for their attentions. I don't rush to correct them.

Then, a year after Bolek's prolonged illness and death, the museum comes under new management. His directorial replacement, Dr. Marton, was a one-time ward psychologist in the hospital who did a lot of the behind-the-scenes Living Museum budgetary and bureaucratic wrangling with the administration. He is also a benevolent libertarian and starts planting seeds of freedom. "You should try to get out of here," he tells me. "Do you have a lawyer?"

"Just Barry Newfeld at MHLS."

"No, I mean a good one?"

"Nah, he's all I've got. Besides, I just got here as far as the hospital's concerned. And I've got a pretty serious case."

"That shouldn't matter. You are fine now, no? Fight, fight, fight."

10

GLUED TO THE TELEVISION, I am more than peripherally aware of the fallout of the Summer of Love, the double whammy of the King and Bobby Kennedy assassinations, the Democratic National Convention protests, man's first walk on the moon, Woodstock, and the break-up of the Beatles. That last milestone has had quite an impact on me as I was born into a Beatle-loving household.

My spiritual Beatle is Paul. I find him adorable, and his melodies and singing voice move me like no other musician's. To make the connection complete, my sister Lauren informs me his birthday, June 18, is a day before mine.

Mom and I are watching the 1971 Grammys. We see Paul rush onstage with his new wife, Linda, to accept an award for the group, wearing a fine tailored suit and white running shoes with a black stripe down the sides. Well, of course I bug Mom to buy me a pair of white sneakers with a black stripe down the side "just like Paul McCartney." I think I end up with PF Flyers, but that isn't the point. Thing of it is, I have a Beatle jones that will not be quelled by their break-up, their less-than-spectacular solo careers (compared to the group output), their deaths, or my getting old.

In the family home the sleeping arrangement is pretty solid. In the 1960s and into the '70s my parents inhabit the rear downstairs bedroom. My older brothers Smiley and Kal have bunk beds in the room next to it. I sleep with my parents until I get too big, and then I am moved in with my brothers where I sleep in a hand-me-down crib until I am about five years old. This makes me a target for their taunting.

Arthur Phipps, Mom's father, affectionately known as Gramps, stays in the front bedroom upstairs and my two older sisters have rooms further down that hall past a small kitchenette. I am always up there seeking my teenage sisters' attention. Despite periodic digs, they are very kind, especially Lauren, who shares and fosters my interest in fantasy and science fiction, letting me stay up late with her watching reruns of *Star Trek*. She is a dedicated first-generation Trekkie and we delight in the camp of Captain Kirk. They also have great friends who don't mind my bouncing around—hippies and students often getting high on grass and other substances, which I see them ingest but know nothing about. The teenagers are amused by my antics. I probably intensify their high as I ramble on about how Batman dances the twist with Godzilla on the top of the Empire State Building. They prod me for more, wondering who is freakier than whom.

I enjoy going upstairs to Lauren's room, asking her to play *Sgt. Pepper* for me. There in the light of her lava lamp I listen, studying the wondrous sounds emanating from the phonograph's speakers and the colorful faces staring back at me from the cover. I love the first side of the record but grow terrified of the last song on it, "Being for the Benefit of Mr. Kite." Its deranged circus noises whirling and building to its conclusion conjure the burning of a carnival funhouse, among other frightening things. This song is too psychedelic for my innocent mind. I often run out of the room screaming for Lauren to put the record on side two where, after George's Indian indulgence, I can be soothed by Paul crooning about getting old.

One Sunday afternoon, while Lauren and Carol, some of their stoner friends, and I sit around enjoying the first side, drinking Kool-Aid and eating potato chips, I get very frightened. The song playing is "Fixing a Hole," sung by my favorite Beatle, but his voice is distant and then lost. The music echoes and mocks my anguish as this foreign malady sweeps over me. The drums match my heartbeat, the bass guitar becomes the blood rushing through my veins, and the trebly guitar and keyboard are my eyelashes as I blink, the saliva in my mouth as I began to gasp for air, the gnashing of my teeth. I feel sick and terrified, and not because of "Mr. Kite" this time. I run out before the song ends, before the side closes, not running for Lauren to flip the record over, but running screaming for Mom to save me from this unknown, dreadful, creeping terror.

Bounding down the stairs, not like I did with a towel pinned to my shirt, playing Superman, I scream and cry, looking to escape, looking to be saved. My sisters follow me, past the foyer and through the living room. They are attempting to calm me, soothe me, and stop me from reaching our mother. As Mom rushes up the hall, catching me in the kitchen, I collapse in her embrace, wrapping my arms around her waist, burying my head in her lap.

My sisters are anxious, worried not for me but rather themselves. Carol quietly hangs back and watches, giving me the side-eye, waiting for the truth to spill and the shoe to drop. Lauren is more proactive, rambling a colorful and convenient excuse that doesn't explain why I am frantic, but absolves the two and their friends upstairs of any wrongdoing. I cry fitfully in Mom's embrace, holding onto her for dear life. While my sisters engage in damage control I think it can't get any worse . . . but it does.

"Relax, honey. Relax. Breathe, Iss. OK? Now tell me, what's wrong? What's the matter? What's bothering you?"

As Mom consoles me I look over her shoulder through tearing eyes. On the back of one of the French doors that separates the kitchen from the living room I see a huge, brilliant orange, undulating crab-like creature. Its body is at least three feet in diameter and certainly big enough to make a meal of little me. It is hanging there, like a living, creeping old coat.

Mom and my sisters have become armchair astrologists and tarot readers since the dawning of the Age of Aquarius, and in this house the knowledge of our star signs has become as prevalent as knowing our middle names. I see the frightful giant crab lurking behind the door as a direct link to Mom's star sign, Cancer. This creature is an embodiment of my mom—a part of her that she can shed, hang on the back of a door, until she feels free enough to wear it, *become* it again. Suddenly I am even more terrified, afraid to be embraced, held, captured by the monster in its mommy-form. I release a shrill, girlish, high-pitched shriek. Fearing being rent by the innumerable legs and pincers, devoured by the Cancer creature, while its demonic daughters look on, satisfied that they have delivered mommy monster its meal, I lapse into unconsciousness, spent by my running, screaming, crying, and palpitations.

The drug culture of the day saw plenty of bored, errant, mischievous teenagers misusing various substances to their amusement and occasional detriment. So it's inevitable that between my sisters and their friends, either intentionally or by accident, the busybody bratty baby brother would eventually get dosed.

I wake again hours later, lying in bed, tucked into Mom's warm embrace. She is stroking my hair, daubing my forehead with a cool, damp washcloth, whispering soothing affirmations to me. Gently jostled by Mom's laughter as she watches Señor Wences on *The Ed Sullivan Show*, Mom notices I am conscious and smiles.

"Look, Iss. It's the man in the box. Can you see him?"

"Yes," I answer in a small quiet voice.

"You must've had a fever. Are you feeling better?"

"Yes."

"S'alright?" Mom asks, playfully mimicking the ventriloquist on television.

"S'alright," I parrot back.

11

"HELLO?"

"Hello, Clu? This is Issa. I need your help."

"What's the matter?"

"I'm in a bad way. There's so much more I want to tell you but I've only got five minutes on this phone."

"Where are you?"

"I'm at King's County Hospital in Brooklyn. The psych ward. Do you think you can come see me?"

Clu is quiet for a moment then says, "Yes."

Clu Turner is the last person I thought I'd ever contact in an emergency. But the Art Students League's phone number is one of the few I remember, and she just happens to be in the office when I, delusional and desperate, call. She's always harbored a crush on me, developed when I modeled nude at the league, where she is a portly and bespectacled class monitor. She rushes to my aid.

Within a few weeks Clu brings me a change of clothes, several art history books, and drawing materials. She comes to visit often and I am very fortunate to have her support. While I knew before my psychotic breakdown that Clu was into me, I simply ignored her attraction and advances. I needed her then not as a girlfriend but as a sounding board, a crutch, a human shield in case the aliens decided to attack. Now I see she may be expecting something more. I deduce this from her hungry eyes and sexually explicit descriptions of various provocative art exhibits she attends during the week. Realizing that we are always in small rooms either alone or with only a few other visitors and little or no supervision, I take a chance and ask Clu if she wants to touch me.

"Oh, Issa, I thought you'd never ask," she says, looking over both shoulders to ensure discretion, then sliding her hands under the table.

"You see that?" the uptight sister of a fellow patient sitting across from us whispers to her sibling.

"Yeah," he guffaws.

OUR UNION SOLIDIFIED, Clu makes the long, exhausting trip from her parents' home in the Bronx to visit me wherever I am housed, including a mercifully brief stint back on Rikers Island after discharge from King's County. Remembering the endless detainees' bus ride from court, through Queens, over the narrow Francis Buono Memorial Bridge, and then the draining wait in the bullpen before getting escorted back to the unit, I can just imagine the exasperating mass transit process that Clu describes. She is quick to point out the various blind spots in Rikers' visitor's room, despite a center structure filled with correction officers and the occasional guard making rounds. We're not seen as a threat by these sentries who, satisfied no contraband is being passed, allow us to masturbate each other.

I garner much respect from the other inmates and detainees that spy my makeshift trysts with Clu. Those who don't get to see our sex play are treated to repeated telling of the exploits by the other inmates, which make the rounds quite quickly, while others opt to live vicariously through the smell of Clu's sex on my hand.

12

Now that I'm in Creedmoor, Clu grows sick of my touting the kindness and compassion of Gaia Sapros, the ward social worker. "She's sweet, Clu. Gives me paper to draw, pencils, watercolor paints."

"And don't I give you that?"

"Uh, yeah, you do. I'm just saying she's really nice to me. And really kind, for this place."

"Well, seeing as you've found someone else to take care of you, I guess you don't need me anymore."

Following a jealousy-tinged rant directed at Gaia, Clu stops visiting, refuses my calls, and disappears from my life. This leaves me sad, alone, and vulnerable, with no outlet for affection and intimacy.

For three years, from King's County Hospital, to Rikers, to Mid-Hudson Psychiatric Center, and now finally Creedmoor, Clu took me warts and all. She knew of my transgression and the guilt I felt but never judged me. Clu showed me that I could formulate and maintain a meaningful relationship with a woman in this locked down environment. It was challenging but we hung in there. I feel bad that I said the wrong things, hurt her feelings, and lost her forever.

I wish to hook up with someone again but how do I explain the total absence of family, what's kept me in all these years, and other sure-to-be-asked questions? I don't want to begin a new relationship on a foundation of lies, half-truths, and sins of omission. Clu's friendship and willing sexual attention was a welcome diversion and relaxant, in addition to earning me respect and protecting me from the criminal-minded booty bandits and down-low brothers found in institutions. Now, in this den of insanity, once these characters recognize that Clu is no longer in my life, they see an opening they can hopefully slide up into.

For the most part homosexuality in Creedmoor is not as violent as it is in jail, with the rape-you-for-your-commissary-and-protection dynamic. The guys here tend to horseplay during the day, running up and down the halls, expending all of their manic energies, until the evening, when they pair up, make love, and then spoon, childlike, on beds in the dorm. However, Darrell would annoy even the most open-minded libertarian. He makes it a point to haunt the shower room, pulling back the flimsy vinyl curtain just when I'm scrubbing my balls to inquire sincerely, "Do you need any help?" That he's a psychotic, burly six-footer known to punch out doctors keeps my tone measured and even friendly. I often answer, "No thanks, Darrell, I got this."

An absurd exchange would follow to keep him calm and keep me safe, him reiterating, "You sure now?"

"Nah, man. Maybe next time."

Don, a fellow insanity plea patient and real ornery dude, puts up the front of I-don't-take-no-mess. But I get to see his level of desperation when I take a call for him on the ward payphone and open his door without knocking. "Close the fuckin' door!" he screams, dick deep in Roger, another surly tough guy. Roger winces, drawing gusts of air through gritted teeth, but takes it like a champ.

Then there is Lloyd, who is tormented by his homosexuality. He's known to go on screaming rampages that can be heard throughout the ward, taking on the voices of his community, his family, his mother. "Sissy!" "Homo!" "Faggot!" "Cocksucker!"

Rushing into the bathroom to use the commode and running into interference, then a full-on bottleneck, I find myself doing the I-gotta-pee two-step as the entire ward is huddled around the center stall. Pushing my way through, assuming it is Bayou finishing a few particularly potent crumbs of crack, I discover two men in there putting on an inspired floor show. While Eli sits on the toilet engaged in spirited fellatio, Lloyd stands before him, his eyes shut tight. With fingers in his ears he is struggling to keep the internal inquisition from attacking at this vulnerable time, with him in the midst of this damning episode.

With all the rampant gay play going on in the lavatory and dorms it is inevitable that I succumb. In the bed next to mine, for the third night in a row, Lowell is working Timiteo fervently from behind. But due to Lowell's penchant for habitual masturbation, and the sexual dysfunction of the meds, these hours-long stroke sessions yield only frustration, fraught with hissed curses, at Tim and himself, bearing no fruit. With a magnanimous gesture that speaks more for my wanting the sex to stop, I call over to Lowell and Timiteo, "Do you need a stiff dick?"

I can feel Lowell deflate in the darkness. Timiteo shouts, "Yeah!"

The blowjob I receive makes me feel dirty, even though it was of my own volition. Yes, Lowell was so shamed and intimidated that he never returned to fuck Timiteo, and yes, Timiteo begged me for another go 'round. But I decline his repeated offers and even confess to Gaia, who promptly has me moved out of the dorms and into one of the doubles down the hall, closer to her office.

13

THE SOCIAL WORKER doesn't seem to have much of a life. Barring obvious holidays and weekends she's always here. She sits at her desk writing progress notes in a stack of patient's charts. Other patients wander into her office out of boredom, groping the dish of candies on her bookshelf. When not painting in the dayroom I hang out there too, taking the opportunity to engage in hours-long conversation, disguised as more intensive therapy.

The other women on the ward, staff in their late twenties, appear jealous of my closeness with Gaia and her fondness for me. They're what you would call around-the-way girls, unsophisticated women from the neighborhood, all with at least one child and all without a steady man. Emjay, a squat, boisterous Mahata with a disagreeable disposition, puts herself out there for me. She pulls me several times into the staff lounge/locker room, her hideout, showing me nude Polaroid photos of herself in various arousing poses. I nervously flirt back, out of discomfort and fear, but my reply is a polite no thanks.

I am summoned from a midday nap in the dayroom by a lackey patient and told to meet the Mahatas in the staff lounge. There, holding court with coworkers Barbara and Donna, is Emjay, sitting up on the windowsill, her huge frame blotting out the summer sun.

"Come over here," she bullies, legs spread as if to envelop me into her ornery orifice. I dare not move. "You think you're the shit, don't you? You must got a gold dick." The other women whoop and "humph" in amusement but I am intimidated, frightened, and silent, still rubbing the sleep from my eyes.

"Is that it? You packin' something special down there? C'mon, let's see it," Emjay spits, clambering down off the windowsill, grabbing at my pants, undoing my belt, unzipping my fly. Emjay stops just short of pulling me out, perhaps hoping that I will follow through. I just stand there with my back against the lounge door, wearing the small wounded look of a molested child.

"Awww, Issa's shy," Barbara pouts, as I slowly zip up and rebuckle my belt, lowering my head, averting my eyes, feeling ashamed and humiliated. Their taunts continue as I exit their lair.

"Next time you wanna talk shit remember how you showed your ass and chickened out!" Emjay calls after me.

"It's OK," Barbara stage-whispers, "I'd still sleep with you."

"Yeah, Issa. I'd sleep with you too, but I wouldn't *fall asleep* with you," Donna quips, to uproarious laughter.

I tell Gaia about this in our next session. She listens intently at first, with a dour look on her face that I have never seen before. Then she exhales, as if she were holding her breath all throughout my telling of the incident.

"So what do you want to do about it?"

"I dunno."

"How do you feel?"

"It makes me feel bad. Dirty. Used. Embarrassed. Ashamed."

"OK. Listen to me very carefully, Issa. I'm going to ask you something that you really need to think about before you answer, because once it's started it can't be undone. And once it gets going it may get very hot for you but I'll see to it that you are safe, OK? Do you understand?"

"Uh, yeah, I guess," I reply, but already I'm getting nervous.

"OK. Issa, would you like me to file an incident report?"

"Oh, I dunno. That means they'll get in trouble."

"Yes, they will."

"They may even get fired."

"That's right!" Gaia intones, as if relishing the thought.

"I dunno, I mean other staff might get pissed off too, right?"

"You better believe it. You'd probably have to be transferred to another ward, and I wouldn't like that because we've come so far, *you've* come so far, and it would be a shame to disrupt that progress. But you're very smart. You've seen how this place works and you know this would not be a good environment for you once they were reported. Hell, I don't know *where* you would be safe in this building, in this hospital. That's why you need to seriously give it some thought."

"Forget it," I say. "Just forget it."

14

My FAMILY HAS A SILVERY BLUE DODGE station wagon with faux wood paneling on the sides. We all pile in and ride out at various times of the year to visit well-to-do family friends in Sag Harbor, an upscale black enclave out on northeastern Long Island. I take my favorite spot at the back window staring wondrously, like watching live television, taking in where we've been and making faces at the cars lagging behind.

This familial unity does not last. By the early 1970s we become a two-car family. Cars are affordable and we're doing well. Dad needs one for his gigs and Mom uses the other to run errands and shop for us. This also makes it easier for Dad to do his gallivanting. Mom catches on and follows, often with little me in tow.

On a low speed chase, Dad wise to Mom's tail, making turn after turn, trying to shake her, we circle the neighborhood, slowing to a crawl, like a rhumba down the roadway. After one of Dad's abrupt stops with Mom close behind, the two cars collide. Mom throws a shielding arm across my body to keep me from flying into the dashboard. After ensuring I am unharmed, Mom bellows, "Stay in the car!" She gets out, screaming at Dad in the middle of the street. Seems Dad has to find a better sausage delivery system. It doesn't take long.

Dad thinks he's slick. He has taken to announcing that he has some errands to run: post office and hardware store. Scooping me up, Dad takes me with him, as if this will assuage Mom's suspicion—I mean, really, would he take the baby son with him while he goes catting? Well . . . yeah.

We do indeed run errands, buying stamps at the post office, screws from the hardware store. We even visit the Sweet Shop, where he lets me pick out three or four comic books and some candy. Then we wind up in one of his girlfriend's houses. While I am preoccupied with Spider-Man and the Fantastic Four, Clark bars and Bazooka Joe, Dad gets off a quick one in the upstairs bedroom. He tosses off, "Don't tell your mother where we were" as we drive back home. Somehow the superheroes and sugar rush cloud my brain, for I never do tell Mom about our little pit stops.

Mom knows anyway. Dad usually tells her. He isn't good at hiding his indiscretions, like he wants to get caught. One of Dad's major flames, burning for several years, is Rose. We've been to her house often and it always seems to be under construction. Numerous times I nearly fall through the floor attempting to use her bathroom, the din of sawing wood, banging hammers, workmen all about the place, while Dad sneaks into her upstairs bedroom. Rose always appears to be sickly as Dad escorts me in to sit with her for a spell before we leave. She just lies in bed, exhausted, her smooth, milky skin peeking seductively out of a fraying, sky blue terry cloth bathrobe.

"You took my son with you to see that fat white cow!" Mom rages, offended that Dad runs into the arms of a white woman, even though Mom is damn near white herself. But I guess, for Dad, not white enough.

I know that I am growing under Dad's influence when on one of our last trips to see Rose I find myself noticing her daughter for the first time. The pretty, precocious, pre-teen mulatto girl introduces herself as Cookie. While I am known at home and in school for having a quick wit and smart mouth, I shock Dad, Rose, and myself by blurting, "I'd like to take a bite outta *that* cookie!"

"HA! You are definitely your father's son!" Rose shrieks with delight. Cookie's eyes light up, sizing me up as her new little boy toy. Dad gets me out of this house after he gets his nut, but he never takes me there again, and I never get to taste that cookie. As a prepubescent I am not ready, but it is surprising and exciting to dip my toe in those waters.

There are numerous other women my Dad attaches himself to, but

I realize that, though his longtime lover Rose is white, her daughter is half black. I often wonder why he never took me back, wonder if Cookie is his child, wonder if I have half-siblings from Queens all the way to New Jersey.

MOM AND DAD GIVE MY BROTHERS AND ME a small black-and-white TV for our room, and I find myself staying up later and later to watch. My favorite programs are the horror movies. I love catching a good austere scare from Universal Studios or England's Hammer Films, but for the real primo nailbiters I stay up on the weekend with Smiley, Kal, Carol, and Lauren and take in *Creature Features* and *Chiller Theater*. These local fright shows with the goofy gothic hosts feed our young minds with the trashiest, scariest, freakiest Grade-B horror movies ever made. After watching these movies I draw the lead creature, usually hosting a variety show or singing on *American Bandstand*.

But the relative innocence and safety that I feel within the home gives way to uneasiness at my first cinema experience, *True Grit* on a double bill with *Yellow Submarine*. Though I bug Mom and Dad strictly to see my beloved mop tops, I am frightened by images of a totemic John Wayne riding his horse like hell with guns blazing. It is a pretty loud and unfriendly picture. Sometimes the family drives into Forest Hills to the Midway Theater to see disaster films like *The Poseidon Adventure* or *The Towering Inferno*, but everyone I recognize in these films from other movies and TV gets killed off. It is a real downer. I feel sad and mourn for all the stars that meet their fates in these films. But there is one film that Mom takes me to that will play like a rerun from hell in my life more than a decade later.

It's my eighth birthday and there is a new film out that's getting a lot of buzz. The TV ads are creepy with spooky tinkling keyboards on the soundtrack and all of my sisters' friends are talking about it. It is a horror flick that Mom wants to see and she takes me along, as she can't leave me home and she assumes I'll enjoy it. After all, I am the child aficionado of science fiction and horror.

William Friedkin's *The Exorcist* thoroughly fucks up my mind. From the first strobe-like flashes of the demonic skull face, red-rimmed eyes peering deep into my soul, reigniting the flames of fear that I had tamped down since my discovery of the Cancer creature, to the deep, wicked, mannish voice emanating from the damned child's mouth spewing unfathomable profanity and green vomit, I am awestruck and terrified. I read later that subliminal flashes of frightening images were spliced in at key moments, no doubt to increase the fear factor. Subliminals were a common practice in Hollywood, introduced in the 1950s by theater management splicing the words "drink Coke" and "eat popcorn" into a film to maximize profits at the concession stands. It seems Mr. Friedkin had flashed "scared shitless" and "irreparable damage" into my head.

The assault of this film is so strong, and the visuals so compelling, that I cover my eyes throughout the last half of the picture, leaving only the frightening, cacophonous audio to work its spell. All the while Mom tugs at my hands, playfully chiding me, "C'mon son, watch the movie. You like scary movies, don't you?"

I am beaten at my own game. I can rattle off the names and year of introduction of the entire Universal Studios family of surreal monsters, reveling in Boris, Bela, Lon Chaney, and even Dwight Frye, and spin yarns about all the giant nuclear age insects, mutants, and behemoths. But I cannot handle the very real tale of a little girl, not much older than myself, inhabited by an evil spirit, a demon, hell—Satan himself! What the *fuck!*

The concept of God and the Devil, good and evil, is too abstract for me at this time. We are basically a secular household. Yes, my sisters went to Catholic school, but they were high schoolers in the age of hippie unrest and disillusionment, the age of *Time* magazine asking "Is God Dead?" and of their friends and classmates claiming to actually *see* God during stirring guitar solos from Eric Clapton or Jerry Garcia while tripping on acid. My brothers and I snicker while Dad sends us to bed with Arabic prayers, not understanding a word and mystified when he closes the sermon with nods to the invisible angels on either side of him.

Though Dad is a proud Muslim he fell away when Malcolm X died, amidst the Nation of Islam's ugly infighting and fracturing of the brotherhood. I come up with a cursory understanding of Islam, Mom's tenuous attachment to Catholicism, and a strange name that brings unwanted attention and anticipation. With it constantly mangled by teachers and students, I am teased in school, on the playground, and even at home by my siblings when they need comic relief, the worst malaprops being Kisser, Pisser, and Sissy.

I do not have a firm understanding of God or Jesus, my namesake, through much of my early life. All I know is the evening prayers Mom serenades me with. Sing-songy lullabies with an air of dread that God somehow makes all right . . .

Now I lay me down to sleep,
I pray the Lord my soul to keep.
And if I die before I wake,
may God in Heaven my soul to take . . .

With Mom kneeling beside my bed, sentient and protective, we end with respectful family shout-outs and "God Bless," starting with the Grands and ending with my nieces and nephews, the new editions. I get excited when my name is mentioned, like I'm special in God's eyes . . . and maybe I *am*.

15

"**Y**OU HAVE TO REMEMBER, you are still a patient," I'm told by Creedmoor's rehab staff in response to my demands for a raise.

Thanks to the good notices from my mural work at the Living Museum, I am given a job in Creedmoor's Department of Rehabilitation patient employment program to beautify various buildings. But I'm being paid far less than minimum wage while single-handedly, and quite quickly, covering the various walls of the hospital's activity center with professional quality murals (bowling, basketball, weight-lifting, billiards). I ask for more than the $2.50 an hour that is customary starting pay for patient employment jobs.

"You feel ripped off. And you're right, you *are* being ripped off," Enya Face, the director of rehab says, as a curious means of consolation. "But this is the most we can give you. You can talk with your rehab supervisor about periodic increases, which you are entitled to receive after performance review, but basically this is it."

"But what about that state-funded artist-in-residence position . . ."

"That's never gonna happen. Like I told you, that money, and allocated creative arts funds in the rehab budget, all go to inpatient services and the Living Museum. And you go to the museum, don't you? And you like it there, right? You don't want it to get shut down because we can't afford to keep it going, do you?"

Checkmate. I feel exploited and it hurts. Not only do I feel abused but I am also trapped. If I quit I would get no money *and* a bad note in my chart for dropping out of the program. I protest by not going in for a week, feigning illness. I spend this time in Gaia's office, painting, fuming, and strategizing. She is also angry and encourages me to seek representation for my artwork. "If Creedmoor refuses to sponsor your talents then we will find someone who will see whatever value there is in them and you and not exploit you," Gaia says. "This means you taking an even more active role in promoting your work, and all this from behind the walls of this hospital. Can you handle that? Because I believe in you, so I'll help in whatever way I can. Here's my Rolodex and there's the phone. Use it!"

Licking my wounds, I return to my employment program, but Gaia keeps me focused on the bigger picture. At Christmas she presents me with a 35 mm camera and I start snapping rolls and rolls of film of my growing body of work. "I figured you'd need it," she says. "Of course this is between you and me, OK?"

With appropriate prints and slides, Gaia and I do research and use Creedmoor's post office to send many mailings to various state-funded art agencies and independent galleries focusing on self-taught and outsider art. This genre is growing in popularity and, by virtue of my psych history and current status, is pretty much the only niche that I fit into right now. I receive many positive responses, some asking for work to be displayed. Gaia happily agrees to transport the work to the various venues. "How else will it get there?" she smiles. "If it fits in my car it'll be in the show."

Throughout the state my work is being requested in a slow but steady process of discovery. This would not be possible without Gaia financing and sponsoring me. I appreciate this kind of close and productive social work from her, even though I know that it is an anomaly.

With Gaia's guidance I decide to apply for a grant with the New York State Council of the Arts. Within eight months I am selected as a recipient of an individual artist's fund and receive a respectable award of $1,500 to mount at least one show that will benefit the community. I choose a small gallery operating out of a mental health drop-in center in my hometown of Jamaica, Queens. Following a vigorous letter-writing campaign from various art supporters, community organizers, and disability advocates, the hospital forensic committee allows me to attend my opening.

My one-man show, *The Diversified Mind*, is a modest success. A serendipitous viewing by representatives from the National Artists for Mental Health, an influential Albany-based outreach organization, appreciating my versatility and message, results in their sponsoring my show. This affords me the opportunity to display my work in various galleries up and down the state of New York. This is fortuitous and problematic, as I am asked by the public to attend these openings and, after forensic committee review, usually granted the privilege. However, I can only leave the hospital on two-to-one male-only Mahata-escorted day passes. Meaning I am to be no more than one arm's length from both male staff at all times, while receiving guests, performing a small set of original songs on a borrowed guitar, and reading some of my poetry. To quell the embarrassment of these restrictions, I often refer to the escorts as "roadies" and "my entourage." One charmed patron of the arts has taken to calling me "the renaissance man." I feel more like a celebrated freak.

16

APPRECIATE TAKING OCCASIONAL BREAKS from my artwork, walking down the hall and sitting with Gaia in her office for a spell. She is genuinely concerned about all of us, from the wackiest bugout to the craftiest sociopath. She knows when you're bullshitting and calls you on it, but then flashes a forgiving, grandmotherly smile that calms the fears of the nervous psychotics and melts the defenses of the crazy con artists. Even Bayou is protective of her. "I loves you, Miss Gaia," he gushes. "My word to God, if any a dees muhfuckas try ta disrespect you I'd kill 'em. Pardon my mouf."

Not only a model patient on the ward and shining star at the Living Museum, I have become Gaia's favorite patient. The other patients notice but say nothing. It becomes a sad joke among the staff, thinking this robust, handsome, and talented young mental patient with no family support could benefit from the extra kindness and attentive caring of the mother figure. I am seen as the super polite and insightful patient with a scary history, always deferring to Gaia, respectful and trustworthy, although inside I bristle when more than once I am referred to as "a good boy."

Gaia surprises me with the gift of a laptop computer as a birthday present. "I've seen you scribbling in your mountain of composition notebooks. You must have something to say, so why not do it properly? Let this be our little secret. Write a book about your life, about this goddamn place. Just don't forget to thank me in the credits."

I am an oddity here in Creedmoor, an inpatient with a laptop where most employees don't even own home computers. The Mahatas look at me curiously, tapping out my thoughts, dreams, and desires.

Some of the bolder brothers and around-the-way girls disturb my flow, wanting to know, "Just what the fuck do *you* have to write about?"

In the summer, on a whim, Gaia starts taking me for short jaunts off the grounds in her car. "It's a beautiful day. Let's go for a drive. Get out of this stuffy office. How does Flushing Meadows sound to you?"

"Oh man, I'd love that! Is it OK?"

"Sure. You're with me."

I revel in this like a dog with his head out the window. These excursions allow me to enjoy the summer off the ward and miles away from the program. These are my first tastes of real freedom since my arrest three years previously. And though Gaia is escorting me, it is against official hospital protocol. I see it as a reclamation of normalcy. Though illegal, and I'm sure she knows, it seems a shame to waste all that blue sky, sunshine, and fresh air. Over time our drives take us farther and farther, lasting most of the day. We often play a game of "If They Saw." Calling out names of various Creedmoor employees, from the janitors to the administrators, wondering aloud what they'd say or do if they saw us together, away from the hospital, strolling through the park, eating ice cream, linking arms. It is a fun distraction. I enjoy my daily escapes from "the bubble city," re-experiencing the world with a woman, even if it is my sixty-five-year-old social worker.

17

Before Dad's drive from Jamaica through Manhattan to gig in
the Garden State, he is required to make a quick stop in Bayside,
Queens, to pick up a fellow traveler. He is partnered with Dennis
Sloan, a drummer who's been carpooling with Dad for years. How they
squeeze Dennis's kit into the Dodge Valiant with all of Dad's gear I'll
never know. I also don't know what goes wrong one late spring Saturday evening when my Dad disappears for several hours. It is unsettling
when an hour and a half after Dad leaves for work Mom gets a call. It
is Dennis. Dad hasn't arrived.

"I don't know where he is."

"He should have . . . yes."

"I know he was supposed to pick you up."

"Yes. I know, Dennis. He should have . . ."

"I don't know where he is, Dennis!"

The calls from Dennis are at first intermittent and then constant.
He is angry. This is his job being fucked with. Mom is frantic and
scared. Her panic is spreading. Smiley and Kal start asking Mom a host
of questions, ratcheting up the emotion. I stay silent, knowing Mom
doesn't need another excitable chatterbox to pluck her fraying nerves,
but I am scared, too. Dennis is calling every couple of minutes, not satisfied that Mom knows nothing about Dad's whereabouts. This annoying
suspicion doesn't help the worry—perhaps Dad is wrapped around a
telephone pole, steering column embedded in his chest, drowning in his
own blood, sandwiched in the Wreck of the Valiant. Mom is thinking
the worst during these desperate hours of silence, elevated by Dennis's
aggression, and I am right there with her. It is a relief when Dennis

stops calling, right around eight o'clock, when he and Dad were slated to launch into their first number with the rest of the orchestra.

Dad is greeted to a round of questioning when he walks into the house an hour or so later. He looks beat, but there is an odd look to him other than exhaustion. His face is drawn, his mood sullen. He is angry, maybe at Mom or my brothers and me for being so concerned, as if we shouldn't have rushed him, demanding answers, expecting something more than his now typical moody routine. Dad sits in the kitchen for a long while, smoldering, and maybe a little embarrassed. He doesn't speak much. Doesn't give a sufficient answer to where he went or why he didn't pick up Dennis. He doesn't give a shit about Dennis, or Mom, or us kids. In my little preadolescent mind I develop a fairly rational scenario as to where my Dad went for those lost hours.

Pussy. He did it all for pussy. I understand enough about my father by this time to know he would screw his friend, blow a night's gig, betray his wife, and dismiss his children all for a little pussy. That explains the anger at having to come back to the old ball and chain and embarrassment at being caught out there without a reasonable excuse.

Dennis Sloan stops being friends with Dad. After losing a night's wages and recognizing that on a whim it can happen again he can't trust him. Who would? Dennis even gets hostile at gigs, calling out from behind his drum kit, "Try to keep in time, nigger. You're good at that, right?"

Larry Sherman punitively docks two of Dad's paychecks to reimburse Dennis for his lost hours and teach Dad a lesson. Mom doesn't like that but Dad doesn't seem to care. What is up with him? Where did he go? What did he do? Was the pussy *that* good? No one knows where my Dad went that late spring Saturday evening, and he never tells.

I'VE GROWN DISTANT FROM DAD, disappointed by his flagrant indiscretions and him rarely being present due to constant gigging. Mom is also disenchanted.

"Your father thinks being Muslim is about having a bunch of

women, but he's a phony," Mom says to me while Dad's away. "Muslim? With his coffee, cigarettes, and reefer? He forgets that it was *my* father who paid for this house. He forgets that I invited him here and I can put him out at any time. If it wasn't for me he wouldn't survive in this town. Probably be singing on street corners, trying to hustle up bus fare back to Tampa."

I grow up intrigued but still embarrassed by Dad's Arabic prayers, spoken with vehemence in that strange tongue. Eventually, I do not answer when Dad greets or departs with his customary salutation, "As-Salaam Alaikum." He stands firm, repeating the phrase with emphasis, refusing to leave unless I respond.

"Wa-Alaikum Salaam," I mumble, just to get rid of him.

18

Doing so well under Gaia's tutelage, I've been asked to participate in an individual therapeutic forum/training session with Dr. Ray Gillespie. He's a media savvy cable-access psychologist currently riding the wave of a successful series of books he's written about the MICA patient. This is an acronym for mentally ill chemical abuser, and as a result of my documented pot abuse and resulting circumstances I've been given that classification.

"The MICA patient is a growing community following the rise of this damned crack epidemic," Gaia explains. "Dr. Gillespie's proposed revolutionary therapeutic technique breaks down the acknowledged barriers of denial and noncompliance commonly found in these patients." I agree to sit for the hour-long one-on-one individual therapy session to be videotaped in the hospital's activity center auditorium and attended by every professional staff member in Creedmoor.

After a brief introduction by Gaia, I step out of the wings and take my seat on the stage across from Gillespie. He's beefy, haughty, and preoccupied with the microphone clipped to his sport jacket lapel, fiddling with it through most of our session. Though I am nervous sitting before the auditorium of rapt, scrutinizing faces I eventually relax, looking down to where Gaia is sitting, smiling with pride, giving me strength.

Dr. Gillespie's revolutionary therapy is actually pretty pedestrian, and he's more interested in pressing the flesh and selling autographed copies of his book than the fumbling emotional bloodletting on stage that leaves me vulnerable. I'm set to receive a patient recognition award after the presentation, maybe as a consolation prize from the Department of Rehab for their high-handed handling of me at my PEP job.

Gaia nominated me and says I deserve it. I wonder if there'll also be categories like Most Likely Not to Drool or Least Resistant During a Takedown.

"It's good for morale," Gaia whispers to me just before they call my name.

"Yeah, whatever," I mumble, seeing it as too little too late, just wanting to collect the certificate and eagerly exit this auditorium of curious glances and pitying stares.

Gaia and I go out for a longer drive than usual after the award ceremony. Parked at Jones Beach, watching the sunset, I take her hand in mine. She rests her head on my shoulder, and we hold on to each other without saying a word.

Back on the ward, as she packs to leave for the evening, I move past her in her office and our bodies engage in a tentative dance of attraction. "Thanks, Gaia," I smile.

"For what?"

"For the award, the ride to the beach, the freedom. For everything."

"My pleasure, Issa. Anytime."

I bend to kiss her cheek. She turns her face and nearly kisses me on the mouth. We linger with this magnet-like attraction holding our faces in place for what seems like a few minutes although it is probably only a millisecond or two. The scene and feeling stay with me all weekend. Until we meet again on Monday morning, when she calls me into her office, closes the door, and we kiss like high schoolers in the balcony of a dark, seedy cinema.

I HAVE BEEN NOTICING GAIA MORE FULLY, perhaps as an appraisal. She's thirty-seven years older than I am. With her short grey coiffure done up and sprayed like a Queens housewife she might be overlooked, but there is a subtle sensuality about her. She's elegant, but with a knowing look in her eyes that is suggestive and even sexy behind her bifocals. Her jaws are slightly jowled, from a mouth turned down with grief, mourning her youth. Her lips are tight, like she's not used to smiling.

When she does it's brilliant, even if she is flashing false teeth.

Though it is odd and inappropriate that my therapist and I are engaged in deep kissing and heavy petting, inevitably it gets hotter. We are often looked in on even with her door partly closed (which comes to mean "Do not disturb—Issa in session"). Tired of sneaking kisses while one or both of us keep an eye on the three-by-three-inch window on her closed door, Gaia has taken to taping up a decorative cover for the porthole. This allows us time away from prying eyes. Gaia knows it goes against policy, as does our affair, but she doesn't seem to care.

The papered window becomes a regular thing. When nosey staff and patients knock, Gaia simply nudges open the door a bit further with her orthopedic sandaled foot. Her excuse to her supervisors and staff is, "the therapy is intensive at this point and requires unencumbered concentration from both patient and therapist."

Eventually, she takes it upon herself to prevent any further interruptions. All it takes is the turn of her key and Gaia's office door is locked with me, a patient, inside with her, a major taboo in this or any psychiatric institution. Noticing the ponderous silence after the definitive click, I gently sing, "I think we're alone now . . ." Gaia prefers Tom Jones to Tommy James and many such appropriate allusions are lost on her. Without explaining the '60s pop reference she gets the gist, blushes, and says, "Yeah, I guess we are. So what do you want to do about it?"

I come around her desk and we kiss, but with more passion than before. I nuzzle her neck, lined by age. I unbutton her blouse and see for the first time her supple breasts and concave stomach moving to a quickened nervous rhythm. She's been hiding herself beneath her outdated polyester wardrobe. Hiding her un-sunned but ripened form, embarrassed by its telling scars following childbirth, hernias, and a hysterectomy.

She lies on her desk and we make love, and we do so all afternoon, against her bookshelf, on her couch, in her chair, and in the windowsill. I am hypervigilant throughout our spirited sex, always checking the light beneath the door for shadows. Gaia is miles away, perhaps years. She cries, as if a virgin taken for the first time.

GETTING INTIMATE WITH GAIA I have now become privy to the incestuous inner workings of Creedmoor Psychiatric Center. It seems everyone is fucking everybody else. Not only does Gaia volunteer who's doing whom, but I can also see it. It feels similar to when vampire Tom Cruise infects Brad Pitt and Brad soon experiences a whole other world within the world he knew. And though it's frowned upon, sometimes a cool, cogent, and capable patient is let in on the action. I have gained access to the wanton and wicked world of the employees here and the overall vibe gives credence to the old axiom regarding what happens to so-called normal people after spending too much time around the mentally insane.

I NOW HAVE WHAT COULD BE CONSIDERED the perfect schedule: program time all week away from the ward, from 8 AM till 4 PM with no return for lunch, weekends from 8 till 4, and the coveted evenings from 6 till 8 PM. I got all of this through Gaia's constant meetings with my new treating psychiatrist, Dr. Santi. She's a pleasant and fair-minded middle-aged Filipina who, truthfully, has not the slightest idea how I am doing let alone what I am doing. The doctors who write the privilege orders here don't know much about their patients and rely heavily on the opinions of the treatment team. I suppose I am very fortunate to have Gaia so deep in my corner.

The role of the ward social worker has been compromised with Gaia arranging increased off-ward privileges for me in exchange for sex. The question is, should I continue to act as boy sex toy to keep them? I don't feel that I have any other choice if I want to continue savoring the exquisite fruits of freedom while still living in this restrictive, locked-down existence.

I sometimes feel like I need Gaia now, not like a significant other but as a mother, the way I needed my mother. She buys me clothes, CDs, silly, loving little trinkets. Lets me know I am always on her mind. But what the hell am I doing for her besides giving my time and attention? I make hand-painted "just because" cards for her but even there I can't write inside the fold just how important she is to me. I can't even think about loving a married woman.

"The marriage died decades ago. I stayed for the kids. I don't blame them," she says softly in our therapy session, now more for her benefit than mine. She sounds bitter, like she doesn't want to admit it. "I blame myself more. The house is in my name, all the bills, too. But I couldn't bear to throw him out, leave the kids fatherless.

"It was a different time then," she says again and again, trailing off into moments of deep reflection. "Twenty years ago he suffered a series of heart attacks, but our intimacy ended before his heart problems. After my hysterectomy, which disgusted him, leaving me unable to produce more children, and in his mind unable to perform, he delivered the final slap, saying, 'You've got a sewn up hole. You're not even a woman anymore.'

"I just shut down. Being a devout Catholic prevented me from kicking the bastard out—especially after he was helpless. My religion also prevented me from fooling around—until now, and to be with you, so much younger, and so different from me. But maybe we're not so different at all."

Gaia boosts my ego and at the same time she's genuinely helping me, but can I trust her to do the right thing? What if I grow into my own man and decide one day it's time to leave? Would she anticipate this and build a fail-safe within me to prevent my straying? It was her job to clean me up, set me right, but how good of a job can she do if she's fucking me? And I am starting to notice cracks. Gaia gets very jealous, catching attitudes at silly things like my eyes lingering a bit too long at an attractive woman in a magazine.

"I don't blame you looking at the pretty women. After all, this *is* my last hurrah."

"C'mon now, don't say that." I try to reassure her and myself that it's not just a fling.

"Oh, just stop it, please. I'm a fool, a damn fool. An *old* fool! I see how your eyes light up when younger staff buzz around you."

"I'm not interested in anything with the Creedmoor stamp, besides you."

"Well, I'm waiting for that day when some sweet young thing comes along to steal your attentions and then your love away from me." As much as I protest this possibility, my proclamations of love sound like a lie.

I stay back on the ward while the other patients go into the dining hall for lunch, but I don't go hungry. Gaia brings in home cooked meals kept in Tupperware, heated up in the staff microwave. I stay in her office under the auspices of getting 'round the clock therapy. Once I'm counted and everyone is off ward we make love in her office.

"There's nothing wrong with a quickie," she smiles.

We breathe deeper, sweat more, and become more ambitious with our sexual menu. As an insanity plea patient locked up indefinitely and not allowed to have sex, I rationalize my involvement with Gaia not as patient abuse but as a whirlwind romance, pushing doubt from my mind. However, though she conducts herself with me as an equal, and even at times with hints of subservience, our true roles as they are and will be seen by her peers and society never escape my thoughts, no matter how close we get.

The female Mahatas, including the three who molested me, pull me into the staff lounge from time to time and disparage Gaia, railing against "them whiteys that wanna pick your brain, make you think you're crazy, and forget who you are."

"I'll try to keep my distance," I tell them, and then trot off for more sex in Gaia's office.

No one would ever figure us out. It almost doesn't make sense. She's small and frail, kind of square, and so much older. I'm treated like a trophy. "The kind of man every woman would want," or so Gaia tells me.

Gaia and I embark on a New Year's Eve head-trip as far as time will take us. Departing at 8 AM, we eat an excellent breakfast in a secluded restaurant in Westchester, make love for hours in a discreet motel in Yonkers, then ring it in right, toasting with some champagne, wrapping up in the backseat of her Mercury Grand Marquis Town Car. At ten minutes to four she and I drive up, as always, across the lot and down a ways from the entrance to Building 40. She hands me an envelope before I get out. I read her note walking back to the ward:

My love,

I want to do anything you want anytime you suggest. I don't care. I just can't suggest it myself. Coming from me, not going along with the times—it would be taboo to do it. If I hadn't locked myself away I would be different. I would not be afraid to say what I wanted to say and do what I wanted to do. I knew what was happening out there. I was not a part of it. I was locked up.

Locked out.

Locked away.

You unlocked the door.

19

Dad's signature song is Nilsson's wanderer anthem "Everybody's Talkin' at Me," and he's a bad motherfucker. Literally. Dad has girlfriends everywhere. This is the lure of playing music. It is a given that women will fall at your feet if you slay them with your ax, then you can croon them up to Heaven, which is usually their bedroom or some cheap motel for the night.

My mom is no slouch either. Even with the five kids she bore, many men in the neighborhood creep around, still vying to take her away from her errant husband, or at least offer to be second banana. She is loyal to Dad, though. He is packing and knows how to use it, and plainly, I think she's whipped. This is not to say that they don't entertain outside interests. It is the '70s, mind you, and the latest thing to hit the suburbs is swinging.

I realize that my parents are swingers using two deductions. First, I am a nosey kid, always digging around in everything. Nothing is private in my house as long as I have a half hour alone to dig in and discover. In their bedroom I find several magazines with pictures of naked white women and pithy paragraphs written by their husbands advertising all sorts of pleasures and depravity if you, dear reader, are so inclined. Swing magazines. That's even what some of them are called. Why would my parents have these magazines without an interest in meeting some of these white women and their husbands . . . to do God knows what?

My second indication is the appearance of "Bob" and "Marge." They're a married couple that are now over at our house constantly. They have a teenage son old enough to stay at home unattended. This couple and my parents become close, coming out of nowhere .

. . or maybe just picked out of a magazine. "Bob" resembles a devil-worshipping gnome, complete with Barnabas Collins hair-do dyed jet black, sculpted goatee, and curious gold medallions and miniature spoons swinging before an open, hairy chest. "Marge" is tall and affable, a bit doughy and suburban. I don't get what they see in each other, and maybe that is it—they see *nothing* in each other and instead agree to seek out other lovers. Enter Mom and Dad.

"Bob" and "Marge" and Dad and Mom smoke pot for hours in their private parties, laughing, talking—seemingly in another language, maybe even coded, foreign to my innocent ears listening in the dark from my bedroom down the hall, the door slightly ajar. I notice the parties my parents throw for their entertainment friends cease after a while in favor of these intimate reefer and red wine get-togethers with the new couple. They are inescapable. Yet I don't know what "Bob" does for a living or even their last name. It is probably "Smith."

I only visit their home once and it is too dark, wet, and winding an evening's drive for me to recognize and remember where we are, kind of like when Batman takes people to the Bat Cave. While the adults entertain themselves their son "Billy" gives me heavy doses of stink-eye and cold shoulder as we watch *All in the Family* and the *Movie of the Week*. Maybe he is just going through those teenage changes. Or maybe he is old enough to know the truth about his parents that I only glimpse of my own. Maybe he detests not only their swinging but also their shacking up with niggers.

As quickly as "Bob" and "Marge" enter our lives, so they depart. It is no major loss. There are plenty of other freaks that come to play in our sandbox. But Mom seems to undergo an awakening. She grows dissatisfied with Dad and her unfulfilled life as a Queens housewife, intent on cultivating and reinventing herself.

One day in the late '70s Mom calls me into the kitchen. "Son, your mother's on strike," she says. "I'm going to start school again soon. I'm taking art, horticulture, and business courses at Queensborough Community College."

I am proud of Mom becoming a student. Though she is garnering the knowledge and skills that will enable her to start her own small business, all I can remember are the bad things during this time—like Dad's cooking.

His cuisine consists only of cut up frankfurters in boiled cabbage with a dollop of ketchup for taste. He insists it's good for us. My brothers and I liken it to torture. Mom treated us to soul food, traditional American, and Jamaican flavored dishes. My favorites were her exquisitely prepared fried chicken and fish over rice and beans, seasoned steak with creamy mashed potatoes, various steamed vegetables, lovingly balanced salads, and especially her homemade carrot juice that was thick, sweet, and delicious. Dad gives us soggy, foul smelling, slimy leaves augmented by little pink bits of processed meat, of which I'd had my fill as a child on my trips to the market with Mom. I must admit that I've become a small tyrant, refusing to eat certain meals if I don't like the looks of them. Mom indulges me. Dad isn't as tolerant and watches me go hungry many nights during this period. I am filled with fear while Mom is pursuing her education. It is fear that Mom isn't taking evening classes at all and is actually planning to leave us. Leave *me*, to make the best of life without my mother and to learn to eat and enjoy cabbage and hotdogs.

Mom doesn't leave us, but she's laying the foundation for a Canadian dream suite. A place we can escape to several times a year, where she can paint and create free from the now spoiling Big Apple. She discovers that Toronto has a burgeoning West Indian community. Many Jamaicans, including relatives of my maternal Grands Arthur and Mildred, are immigrating to Toronto, as have people of many other cultures, making it a tolerant and progressive cosmopolitan city. Our newfound kin invite us up every summer and Mom realizes there is a place just as bustling as her native New York yet considerably cleaner and more civilized.

But after embracing hitherto unknown relatives, inspired by Alex Haley's *Roots* phenomenon, it is inevitable that we see rotten fruit in the bunch. Cousin Tung is burly and fair-skinned with shifty eyes and a fondness for tight polyester. As I watch with disinterest a parade of "new" family welcomed into our home, I fail to realize that Tung, married with kids my age, also has a fondness for young boys. I discover this when he creeps into my back bedroom, closes the door behind him, and deftly slides his cold, hammy hands up my T-shirt, rubbing, cupping, and squeezing my chest.

"What are you? Are you a boy or a girl? Tell me—are you a boy or a girl?" I hear him breathing in my ear from behind.

I've been plagued by this phrase at other times in the neighborhood. I've always been chubby with a cherubic face and loose curly hair. In my tweens I am somewhat androgynous and my artsy, dreamy ways come off as girlish to concerned family, friends, and neighbors. They see me skipping down the street, humming to myself with a bag of candy and comic books in hand, and call after me, "Hey kid, are you a boy or a girl?" I don't pay it much mind as it happens coming back from the Sweet Shop, but it is extremely troubling at my bedroom drawing table with a man's hand up my shirt.

"I'm a boy!" I answer, frightened but firm. However, Tung isn't looking for a discussion. I squirm and shrug him away.

I tell Mom about Tung's molestation but she refuses to believe me. I suppose her being an only child and now discovering the family she always wished she had, it is more important to maintain this connection than believe and defend her baby son. He comes back a week or so later with the same routine.

After Tung's second visit to my room I tell Mom again and this time, after emphatic questioning, to be completely sure I am telling the truth, she confronts her cousin and banishes him from the house. I should feel good about this but the damage and the compound injury is done. I'm twelve years old, in middle school, and I shut down. What had been a promising honor society academic path suddenly crashes and burns. I go on to fail seventh grade math class.

20

OUTSIDE OF STEALING THE OCCASIONAL KISS or two in grade school, only to hear, "Ewww, you kissed *him*? He's so weird," I don't care much for girls. I am usually too shy to approach the ones that I find pretty and too caught up in rock and roll, horror films, science fiction, comic books, and painting my approximations of the same. While most of the boys in my neighborhood were boasting of credible sexual experiences as early as age thirteen, it seems that I am a late bloomer. It does not help that Tung's molestation has produced immense sexual shame and guilt. In order to not feel those bad feelings, I choose to not feel at all. Still, I cannot deny the stirrings of adolescence and young manhood.

One young girl of my age catches my eye. I see her periodically in my middle school and she also lives right around the block. Jewel and her younger sisters, Nikki and Candy, are all named like strippers, which should come as no surprise considering their mom, Queenie, is a former stripper and neighborhood bon vivant.

Jewel appears troubled and moody, like all of Queenie's daughters, as if they had endured some form of abuse and were now just riding it out. I feel a kinship with her because of this. She is the child of her mother's first marriage to a white man and so Jewel has emerged as a beautiful café au lait princess with auburn hair and dazzling green eyes.

For most of middle school I vie for her attention, and she seems to like me back, waiting patiently for me to make the first move. Unfortunately, I stumble and guffaw through every encounter, sometimes outright insulting her, causing us to come to kiddie blows. I have a rival in school chum Dwayne Harrod, who is a beefy kid from the Caribbean and very principled, proper, confident, and clean. He carries his books in a valise and sports some variation of a suit every single school day. Though I feel I can't compete with this guy I do so, if only because I realize he's a blowhard who hates to lose. We both buzz around Jewel, a true gem with a bouncy booty that has even the older men stopping to honk their horn. What I fail to realize is that her mom prefers me over Dwayne, whom she considers a "corny hayseed," and wishes to get Jewel hooked up with me. This is a trump card in Queenie's own rivalry with my mom.

After we both graduate junior high, Jewel offers to give me some; the fumbling escapade in my dark closet, where I fail to penetrate as we stand face-to-face, lets me know she likes me enough to engage. But perhaps I should study my parents' *Joy of Sex* handbook to be better prepared if there will be a next time.

A year later, at one of Mom and Dad's house parties, Queenie arrives with Jewel and displays her like a china doll. I am not the only one who ogles her. While all the adults get progressively high, Jewel moves closer and closer, with me studying the doo-wop on the living room stereo. I cannot make out what she is saying and she appears frustrated by this, finally shouting in my ear, "Let's go to your room."

I usher her from the living room, through the kitchen, past numerous party people all stoned and oblivious, into my rear bedroom. She pads around my room, playing with my horror movie monster dolls and giggling at my homemade Beatle posters. Her desire is so obvious that within no time she moves close to me and we start tongue kissing. She watches as I undo her tight jeans. While I try to be smooth, our failed encounter from last year reverberates in my head. I want to make all the right moves this time.

Pausing for a moment to sift through candy bars, Bubble Yum, plastic army men, and Duncan Yo-Yos, I fetch a condom from my headboard. Never having done this before, it goes on with some effort. I sink easily and deep into her warm flesh. No sooner have I entered her, after a few enthusiastic pumps, then the condom I'm wearing busts. Very conscious of the possibility of an unwanted pregnancy I quickly, but begrudgingly, withdraw. Seeing my disappointment and also wanting more, Jewel says, "You can put it in my ass."

It's amazing how quickly and easily she takes me. We carry on for quite a while, feces and shredded condom flailing between us, before Jewel jumps out from under me, exclaiming, "I think I'm gonna be sick." I am left standing there, penis bobbing boldly, practically begging her to come back so I can bust a nut. She slips on her jeans, gets up, and pats my butt while playfully pinching her nose and scrunching up her face, saying "Ewww, shitty dickie," as she helps me tuck my member back in my pants. All the better, for almost immediately after I zip up, my brother Kal bursts in, screaming "Ah-HA!" brandishing a cheap instamatic camera, taking mock photos of "the scene of the crime."

Jewel laughs as she leaves, working her way up to the busy kitchen. I stay behind, annoyed at my brother, and at my not being allowed to continue and come, but also gratified at my first "piece." I am also grateful to have been deflowered by such a willing, knowledgeable, and experienced partner. I wind down the evening eating a Three Musketeers while watching Bigfoot battle the Six Million Dollar Man.

21

I START TO FEEL LIKE I DON'T FIT in my home. And I am jealous and resentful because I realize there is a presence there that my family loves more than me. She's called Mary Jane.

At thirteen I invite a neighborhood friend over to swap comic books in my living room. My family starts rolling and smoking, whooping it up at the dining table in the next room. My friend can smell the pot smoke wafting in—I can see it in his face. We sit there for a long time in silence, pot smoke everywhere, while they laugh and joke, talking about Hawaiian this and Acapulco that. Eventually I just get up, walk through the kitchen where they're carrying on, and retreat into my bedroom, leaving my friend in the living room. I just leave him there. I don't care. I guess Mom sends him home after awhile. I'm so damn embarrassed that I can't face him, him knowing that my parents, my family, are pot smokers.

Starting puberty, feeling my teenage oats and my balls tingle with the onset of manly defiance, I decide to take a stand. My family are all sitting around the dining table, smoking pot as usual. "Hey, Iss. What's up?" they ask, as I enter the kitchen, mixing up a glass of chocolate milk.

"I don't like it when you smoke that stuff," I declare. "I think it's wrong! I hate it!"

"Why?" they all ask in unison, shocked.

"I don't like it when you're all spaced out. It doesn't feel right. Y'all're always laughing, getting loud, and acting weird. Or doped up, dragging around, like you're sleepwalking. And always after you smoke." I try to articulate my alienation. My feeling that my family, and especially my parents, are not in proper contact with me, most of the time lost in their own heads. Mom shushes the others with an excited smile. If she only knew the full extent of my disappointment, shame, humiliation, and helplessness. Dad listens as I continue complaining, and seethes quietly for a while before finally interrupting, "Well, *I* don't like being dictated to by a thirteen year old."

Dad's dismissive comment makes me scared and angry.

"Iss, you just don't understand," he says. "You're uninformed. Let me tell you about the healing properties of marijuana, and the plant's history. The Native Americans smoked it. The founding fathers grew it and smoked it. Our people have been smoking it for generations." And on and on he goes, extolling the virtues of reefer with the emphasis of a statesman. Like he did when he had an audience of stoned has-been entertainers, making excuses for him and his brood to stay high, while they roll and smoke well into the evening. I feel put down, like my feelings aren't being considered, a clean kid in a house full of stoners, an oddball.

As the baby of the family, and the light in Mom's eye, I have become the eight hundred pound gorilla—spoiled rotten and accustomed to getting what I want. But in the unspoken choice between my desperate feelings of alienation and their getting high, I lose out. I have no other recourse but to withdraw into myself. By the time I poke my head back out, everyone and everything has gone to blazes.

For years I never invite anybody else over to my house. Finally, well past my teens, I bring in girlfriends whom I'm going to have sex with, quickly taking them into my room. I sneak them in not for fear of getting caught by Mom or Dad—it's cool with my folks—but to avoid them meeting my family, my parents, and maybe my getting ambushed again. Have them light up and get giddy and loud, and maybe have a girlfriend realize that my family are all on drugs.

Art and music are no longer my refuge, corrupted by Tung's advances at my art table and the senseless shooting of John Lennon during my first winter in high school. Soon after that tragedy, the disillusion of the Beatle dream, I cease playing guitar, not picking up the instrument for another fifteen years. Toward the end of my time at the High School of Art and Design I simply give up and peter out. I am lucky to graduate with a piece of paper that says, "Well, at least he showed up," and a steady girlfriend who, in a moment of candor, says, "I feel like I'm slumming."

Despite a wonderful open-ended excursion financed by Mom to stay with family in the UK, I return after several months, guilted by my girlfriend and disillusioned by the storied British art and music scene, which by this time is wall-to-wall Boy George and Haircut 100. My failure to receive a college scholarship, after my life up till this point being heralded as a visionary, leaves me confused and depressed. My math SAT scores are atrocious, regurgitating the pain and shame of Tung's molestation and its effect on my scholastic aptitude. I haven't the heart to attempt college and Mom and Dad don't seem too concerned. "You want to find yourself? Sure, go ahead. Just don't find yourself in our reefer stash like your brother Smiley."

I'm never properly educated about financial aid and am scared to death of student loans. My college attendance had been a given—or so everyone thought. I just don't give a damn. Before I know it I've grown into an aimless young man. I shed my baby fat and become lean and angular, much like my father. Whatever potential I may have had grows more distant, much like my father. I forego further schooling and abandon the arts in exchange for a job as a salesman in a city record store.

22

"O. J. SIMPSON IS ON THE RUN!" The whole ward, patients and staff alike, are transfixed and energized, united in watching the low speed police chase on TV in the dayroom.

"Ai, Dios! I want to see!" the new evening shift nurse exclaims, as if a prisoner of her treatment room, holding on to the half-door like an inmate grabs his bars. With the entire ward huddled in the dayroom, and the three Mahata staff abandoning their stations assigned to provide maximum oversight and maintain control, the nurse realizes she must stay put. "But I can't see," she pouts, "I have to stay here." This look is both sexy and comical.

"I can bring my little TV out, if it's OK?"

"Yes. Plug it in over here, in the treatment room. You have to stand on the other side of the door. But we can watch together."

This media spectacle begets a burgeoning romance with the evening shift nurse at lights out, when the patients are put to sleep and the Mahatas plant themselves in makeshift recliners in front of the dayroom TV. The night nurse, Bella De LaPuta, is an immigrant from El Salvador. "Yes, I come to this country across a river," she says by way of an odd introduction. "Holding my children close to me, hoping them and me don't drown. But, please, don't call me 'wet back.'"

This proud, ambitious, thirty-eight-year-old mother of three projects the façade of a health care professional, yet she seems unable to recognize boundaries or filter her ebullient sensuality. At times I am not sure if it is a cultural or language barrier, but eventually I realize, after many trips planted at her station, that this woman is trying to seduce me.

Pale skin on a moon face, with sexy almond eyes and juicy lips turned up in a perpetual smile, Bella says, "My husband used to sing the song 'Mujer Pequeña' to me. 'Little woman,' that is me. Well, some of me is small. And other parts are very, how you say, accommodating? I have had three children."

"Oh really?"

"Oh yes."

"Damn. OK. Well, you *are* a hottie."

"I try," she smiles. "I like to drink beer, but not too much. My stomach is get a little big. My husband say I'm fat. But I eat good and make sure my figure stay the same. My stomach get big, but my breast, my thighs. My . . . culo? How you say, my ass? Yes, it stay same since many year. Look at it. It still round, firm, sexy, no?" In street vernacular she's what one would call a MILF.

Bella expresses an interest in buying a home computer for her kids after noticing my laptop. "The computer is good, no? I will use it too when I buy. It is good for learning. I admire your articulateness, and impressive vocabulary, and command of the language English. I want, and need, to learn to speak better English. Would you help me?"

I accept, not thinking our flirtations or her seduction will amount to anything. "Don't worry, I think I can find time to teach you little things that should enhance and improve what you already know."

"Yes, I would like for you to show me something I can wrap my tongue around," she says with a wink and a smile.

Soon, repeated visits to her nursing station for health counseling become treatment room foot rubs, which develop into frequent kissing sessions. We don't engage in this kind of close contact often because patients aren't allowed to be alone with the nursing staff in the treatment room for more than fifteen minutes, other than for extended periods usually justified by a medical procedure. Our kissing continues, however, if only as one or both of us has one eye open, on the lookout for patients and staff, while separated by the half-door of her station. As the days progress we kiss deeper and deeper, mindful of the staff and patients who probably all know what is going on but say and do nothing. We are just an insignificant blip on a wide-sweeping screen overwhelmed by homosexual sex, violence, drugs, staff unprofessionalism, and administrative ineptitude.

BELLA IS RELUCTANT, YET TEASINGLY SO, to make a definite date when we can be alone together. This creates a longing that, although frustrating, is also very exciting.

"We can't," Bella purrs, in her girlish, accented voice before coming close, breathing deeply and kissing my lips.

"It is impossible to get away without someone asking 'where' and 'why,'" she moans, then another kiss, slipping her tongue into my mouth.

"Aw, c'mon, Belle! We gotta hook up, baby."

"No! It is impossible. No! We can never be together," Bella says with drama, sliding her hands down her form, squeezing her breasts, engaging me in a compelling catch-me-fuck-me game.

"I'm scare," she pouts, then unbuttons her blouse just enough to reveal her pert, brown nipple, inviting me to suckle upon it. "You love me, yes?"

"Um hmm."

23

IT'S MOTHER'S DAY. Even locked up I can't escape the constant TV commercials pushing flowers, chocolates, and housewares or the ward radio's heavy rotation of the Intruders' musical profession, "I'll Always Love My Mama."

In Mid-Hudson Psychiatric Center, you could not progress unless you openly admitted to your offense, often in weekly group therapy sessions. But after many years here in Creedmoor, outside of the forensic committee meetings every two years where they ask you to reenact the crime, an insanity plea patient can almost forget what he's here for. Many do. I am not that heartless, though my heart does feel frozen, a cold stone sitting in the center of my chest. My means of forgetting is burying my head in Gaia's and Bella's flesh, but the truth keeps surfacing.

I lose myself in sexual activity in addition to whatever artistic success I can achieve. I save whatever monies I earn. But I often feel like a male prostitute accepting surplus funds and gratuities from Gaia and Bella, which I use for art supplies and buying scores of mail order CDs, re-creating my once-coveted LP collection, now lost and destroyed, along with my entire artistic output before 1990, at the hands of my angry and estranged family.

As I lie on my twin bed in Creedmoor, with plenty of time to think, I often wonder how my family is doing. They do not answer my letters, and I've been told to stop making calls to the house. Carol and Lauren are at each other's throats over administratrix rights to Mom's estate. And in my last phone conversation with Lauren's Trinidadian boyfriend and firewall Bichi, he said, "God would piss on you if He had a dick for what you did to your mother, and your family." I wholeheartedly concur.

I think a lot about my sister Carol, and the last hug she gave me . . .

IT'S RELATIVELY CALM on the Mental Observation Unit of Rikers Island, and most of the guys are civil. I'm lucky to have gotten some pens and pencils from a guy who gets commissary. I got them on "the juggle," the prison barter system, with some cigarettes I received as payment after helping one of the guys compose a letter to his mother. He figured I was a studious type. His hunch paid off. I'm not the college boy some of the inmates call me, as I failed trying to pull a degree out of my ass, but considering most of these guys can't read or write I must come off like a Rhodes scholar.

My smarts afford me some more luxuries. Soon I become the house scribe. I either help write, or write completely in my hand, the hopes, dreams, and desires of about thirty grown men. I am the voice of many who, if they could, would probably open their letters home with, "Yo bitch." I give them a little polish and when necessary inject some steamy romance into the standard "I'm-OK-how-are-you-send-me-some-money" letters from the joint. It makes me feel useful and I get cigarettes as payment for a job well done. I don't smoke cigarettes. Reefer is really my thing. I use my cigarettes to juggle for more books, paper, pens, and pencils, keeping a journal and sketching in my cell at night.

Though the MO Units on Rikers are more civilized than general population, this is still jail, and you'll find villains and opportunists no matter where you go in here. Most smaller or scared guys who get weekly goods from the commissary get ripped off, and bad. Heaven forbid you don't go down swinging. At least then you've got your dignity. If they take you without a fight you're a punk and you're sure to be somebody's chump before long. As a chump you're assumed not capable of handling yourself on the floor. You're then approached by someone (usually the creep who stole your shit) who will offer you protection in exchange for your mouth or asshole when he asks for it. So you get to keep your commissary (which you'll probably end up sharing with the guy) and you get to be his bitch. If you're a smooth talker you may end up just a maytag. That's a punk who doesn't get raped but is probably washing someone's nasty shorts and socks in the sink to be left alone. Knowing this now I'm grateful I initially came in here out of my fucking mind. Seems they're all afraid of that. Whether they know the awful truth or not I've got a reputation as a maniac. That I come off very sane and even cordial only confounds them more.

Even though everyone here is trying to cop out to the insanity plea, or at least buy time away from the hell of general population, most are bluffing—and those that aren't are very well medicated. I quickly earn slot time on the phone, though I rarely use it because I have no one who wants to talk to me. I get in good with the house gang, who are basically the unit trustees who do all the cleanup and meal serving, also doling out justice when necessary, making the correction officers' jobs easier in a you-wash-my-back-I-wash-yours affair. One of the nastier COs continually whistles "If I Only Had a Brain" as the sarcastic soundtrack to medication time.

There's a real cast of characters here with wild nicknames to match. They call me Izzy. It could be worse. There's some poor guy with no teeth and a lot of lip called Gumby. Then there's a big black guy who insists on being called China, though I never figure out why, and another huge, very dark guy called, appropriately enough, Black. One's called Dread (for his hair) and another Froggy (for his eyes). We've also got Shorty and Half-Pint, two slim guys named String Bean and Flaco (the Spanish "skinny" equivalent), and a host of names suggesting places of origin—Tex, Cuba, Panama, Dominica. Rounding out the rogue's gallery are Earl, Nelson, and Whispers, a rotating team of Island-employed inmates operating as suicide prevention aides. They are all patient, empathetic, and kind, providing better social work and support than the burnt out and paranoid mental health professionals who check in on us every couple of days, even though the SPAs do it mainly to keep food and cigarettes in their cells and credit on their commissary accounts.

The chow here on Rikers is inedible. Calling it slop would be a compliment. From the mystery meats to the gruel-like stews, I gave up on it long ago, right after I pulled a small metal lug nut out of a mouthful of Beefaroni. I've developed enough clout and clients from my letter-writing service to charge and collect up front, affording me plenty of supplies while allowing me to juggle for food. A lot can be said for commissary cuisine. A pepperoni sandwich with American cheese slices on soft egg bread rolls quells many an evening's grumbling stomach. A side of Fritos corn chips and house made Kool-Aid completes the meal. On chillier nights I make an instant coffee and cocoa mix that sets me straight.

My periodic unease with Islam intensifies when I witness the exploitation of this peaceful religion here on Rikers. While most inmates enter as Leroy Washington and transform into Malik Shabazz, recognizing a strong and respected gang to join, I came in as Issa Ibrahim. This was the cherry on my psycho sundae, making me a reluctant big man on campus among the Muslim contingent in this institution, where fear, respect, and reputation are currency.

"A slab o' bacon," the white COs joke, perverting the Islamic greeting while escorting me to Juma services, where all of Rikers' Muslims congregate to praise Allah and eat bean pies. These same COs watch me go hungry, repeatedly denying me Halal meals due to my name not being on the official list. Seems I was so bugged out when I first arrived that I blew what was apparently my only opportunity to register. I end up feeling more and more like Leroy Washington.

"Abraham! Eye-za Abraham! On the VI!"

I am roused one early afternoon by one of the COs telling me that I have a visit. Escorted sleepily out of the unit, down the long, twisting hallways, past other detainees walking with macho defiance and giving each other the screw-face, I catch only glimpses of the pale late winter's sunlight that bathes the saved yet taunts those of us who reside on the Island. There are loudly announced "Options" here, such as hourly cell openings allowing me to sleep in, and daily trips to the law library where I research the insanity plea, and recreation in the yard, though I never utilize the free time in the sun and air of the outside exercise court for fear of intermingling with the hardcore criminals of general population. With the disclosure of my offense reverberating in my mind, and possibly in others' thanks to a page-three headline in *New York Newsday* when I first arrived, I don't want to take any chances.

After stripping out of my regular clothes, putting them in a plastic basket, and donning a stiff grey jumpsuit and tan shower slippers, I step into a vast, heavily monitored space that looks to be a cafetorium, except the meals are humble pie, crow, and I-told-you-so served cold. Surveying the numerous other jumpsuited detainees visited by their family and friends at knee-high tables, I see my sister Carol, now somehow older, heavier, laden down with grief and the inconvenient responsibility of being an orphan.

She jumps up and embraces me, enveloping and tight, bawling repeatedly in my ear, "Did you do it? Was it you? Did you really do it?"

Her intense emotional outburst seems devoid of any inclusion of me. She is alone, weeping for Mom and herself, and I feel I could be anybody, a stranger. Seeing me devolve over the past three years, and having been treated to a special pot-drenched performance in California last summer, perhaps Carol already knew I was crazy.

"CAROL, YOU'VE GOTTA HELP ME. I don't know what's happening to me. I think I'm smoking too much pot," I confess, strapped to the passenger seat of Carol's SUV like it's a lie detector. But I still toke on the burning joint at my lips while rolling more from the bag I brought with me from New York. She and her kids and I drive through the Embarcadero, a gaudy tourist's paradise full of overpriced restaurants and novelty shops where visitors can buy their San Francisco key chains, bumper stickers, and T-shirts.

"Oh Issa, you are *so* cool," she says, sarcasm seeping from her mouth with the pot smoke. I can't handle the hand-over-fist, roll-and-smoke style Carol is into. After a few more pulls on the generously rolled bone, my vision grows bleary. My perceptions become distorted. The side and rearview mirrors all look at me looking at me.

"I think I need to see a doctor."

"What do you mean?" Carol probes.

"I think I need to seek help, a psychiatrist of some kind, I dunno . . . "

"Oh, what do you want? You want to be around crazy people? Do you want to be on all types of drugs and medications, doped up in a crazy house? Is that what you want? Doctors and strangers asking questions about your personal life? *I* should be the one seeing a doctor! I'm living with four kids, a full-time job and no man! You're just, what, Issa, twenty-four? Get your shit together, man. And pass that joint."

My ten-day stay in Oakland with my sister is spent in a daze, full of soaring highs and dragging lows. It's pleasant driving around high in the car with Carol and her jovial friend Yvette, whom I remember fondly from my childhood, and their respective children, a total of six kids and three adults, on outings to eat Mexican food in Berkeley. We also go to a drive-in theater to watch Tim Burton's *Batman* on a beautiful summer evening, reminiscent of childhood trips to the old Sunrise Drive-In out in Valley Stream, Long Island. I also enjoy several day trips into San Francisco, catching the BART, whose clean appearance and reliability put New York's subway system to shame. Once in the city I take walking tours of Haight-Ashbury and the financial district. The suffocating atmosphere of Chinatown alarms me, but I am amazed and aroused by the massive calves on an otherwise slender Asian beauty as she walks past. I suppose walking up and down these streets will do that for you.

The lows, by contrast, are terrifying, exemplified by my running many times into Carol's apartment bathroom to splash cold water on my face. I stare for hours into that bathroom mirror, alarmed by what I see.

Looking down from the second story apartment's window onto the poolside where my young nieces frolic in the water, I cringe as they call up to me, blowing my cover. "Uncle Issa! Uncle Issa! Come in the pool!"

I am too frightened to join them. I just stand up there and watch, fleshing out my role as their weird uncle from New York.

Now, AS THE ACCUSED, I feel I owe it to Carol to answer the only question she came back to New York, and here to Rikers Island, to ask. She has no interest in the why, if there is even a reasonable explanation, which there isn't at this juncture. She just wants to hear it from my own mouth. "Did you do it, Issa? Did you kill my mother?"

"Yes," I answer.

24

MY HOMETOWN OF JAMAICA, QUEENS, has always had a bad reputation with the rest of the borough, mainly because it is the suburban township most densely populated with black people. And no matter what anybody *says*, it seems *no one* wants to live around black people. We, like the other middle class black families in the neighborhood, also wish to maintain the bourgeois status quo. If only to preserve the hard-working, middle-class quality of life that we embraced when we moved here or, in my case, when I was born.

I must admit that, for a while, growing up in Jamaica was quite a joy. My family is like many other black families who embrace the suburbs, working hard to pay the mortgage, keeping our lawns green and trimmed. For us, Jamaica was Utopia in blackface. I grew up with not one but *two* large municipal parks in my immediate backyard. Everyone knew you and we all looked out for each other. So it was a typical suburban reaction when the undesirables arrived.

It's a very sunny afternoon sometime in the mid-1970s when the first welfare family moves in down our block. My brothers and I hop on our bikes and go to check them out. They're unkempt, seem uneducated; there look to be about fifty of them, all sitting out on their stoop, spilling onto the sidewalk, each uglier than the next. It's like a photo-op for some dark carnival of freaks and malcontents. I feel the quality of our serene suburban life will soon change.

The Davis clan is looked upon with great suspicion and, sure enough, they begin fighting, stealing, selling drugs, and creating mischief and disharmony in the neighborhood. What I don't expect is how alluring this all is to my brothers. Within no time Smiley and Kal welcome the Davis kids into the neighborhood and into our home, where they proceed to eat our food and steal my comic books. Smiley has never liked the familial pecking order in which I sit on the top of the heap, or at least before him. He has always wished to see me get my comeuppance, so this type of disrespect of his baby brother is not only tolerated but encouraged. It only gets worse, and my brothers are right in the thick of it. Eventually, Smiley takes to petty thievery and vandalism. He neglects his studies and tokes up before class until his behavior finds him suspended and then expelled.

Most of the Davis kids wind up in and out of jail, but other nefarious families come in their wake. By the late 1980s, all the decent folk have run indoors, afraid to linger too long in an unsafe community overrun by attitude, aggression, and desperate attempts to gain respect.

And then, of course, there's crack.

It comes virtually out of nowhere. It becomes ubiquitous in just about every black American neighborhood. An entire generation of black men are taken off the count, either to jail, the asylums, or the cemetery. What few are left shuffle sadly down their tarnished streets, homeless and hopeless, looking like the bastard sons of Mr. Bojangles. The crack-addicted women find shelter as concubines, until they became too dizzy, dirty, and undesirable, and wind up similarly institutionalized.

And for those who believe the media hype and avoid crack, there's always weed.

Amid this madness I wonder if even *we* are still the decent folk. As an eclectic artist I feel surrounded and suffocated by cookie-cut Negroes who can't comprehend a brother who doesn't conform and is not afraid to break from the herd. My ears are assaulted by cheesy synths, canned drums, and braggadocio. I hear the Mary Jane Girls' sex and drugs anthem "All Night Long" oozing from practically every vehicle cruising in the midnight hours looking for a hit. It becomes a very black thing to be a crackhead. Every mention of the drug in society and on the media is a euphemism for the current state of Black America.

Everyone is tainted. It becomes an embarrassment to admit I am from Jamaica, Queens. It is humbling but no surprise when my older brothers start "entertaining" Queenie, the neighborhood crack whore.

QUEENIE IS THE FREE-SPIRITED MOTHER who set me up for my first carnal encounter with her oldest daughter, Jewel. She is also a longtime friend of Mom's. They met in the downtown clubs in the 1950s, selling each other bad smoke. In the '60s Queenie was a stripper/go-go dancer. This was her claim to fame and gives her something to brag about, which she does often. She believes she is some sort of celebrity and should be treated accordingly.

"The Queen has arrived, y'all. Bow down to the Queen, all hail the Queen, God save the Queen!" she announces when entering the scene. Years of drinking, drugging, chasing wealthy men, and raising three teenage daughters have left her physically ravaged and almost completely mad.

Audrey and Queenie were mainly get-high buddies who stayed in touch throughout the years, sharing a smoke while recounting Queenie's failed marriages and Audrey's attempts to create and maintain a healthy, stable home life for herself and her children. Through their thirty year acquaintance Mom has recognized a great deal of jealousy and backstabbing in her "friend." Queenie really hates Mom, who has survived the years with her shape and dignity intact. Queenie is envious of Mom's olive skin and "good" hair—hating her as many dark-skinned, nappy-haired women hate their fairer sisters.

Mom has severed ties with Queenie on numerous occasions. "That woman's a liar, a cheat, and can't be trusted," she rages. "She's no damn good!"

Loud and boisterous, Queenie is never outdone. I see her seducing both my brothers at one of the last of Mom and Dad's wild jazz house parties. Queenie finds her way into these soirees, trips a little, and then feels up all the men. She has conditioned all who come into her circle that her name is synonymous with "party." Of course, no one has any respect for her but somehow this is acceptable to her. In her dark mind she sees herself as "a star living in a world of extras."

Queenie is the same age as Mom but looks at least ten years older. The "good life," which she always claims to live, hasn't been very good to Queenie. She always has a decadent way about her, pointed tongue darting lewdly about a mouth spewing a hoary laugh. Her face and neck are slathered in heavy beige makeup to cover her chocolate brown complexion. Dirty, unruly hair hides beneath bad wigs pinned to audacious hats or sequined turbans, while she sports flashy, trashy leather and silver and gold brocaded clothing. She bathes herself in cheap perfume and glitter. You always know she's coming and where she's been when she's gone.

My brother Kal, older than me by three years, is now a military man. Being a mediocre student with a proclivity for mischief it was either the military, McDonald's, or jail. He's been coming back home every summer from his base in Florida. Queenie, after three failed attempts and countless affairs, is married again—this time to a well-off, retired dentist. She seduces my brother to gain the ultimate advantage against our mom. Queenie turns him out with all-hour sex-and-drug parties and midnight rides in limousines, which she rents with the dentist's money.

It takes but one ride for me to see the extent of the debauchery and decline of Queenie and my kin. Queenie is often high on liquor and crack and supplies my brothers and childhood friend Kubir Ali money with which they buy *more* crack. Once she gets them high she suggests a long drive where sloppy, unrepentant backseat sex ensues to the sounds of New Jack Swing and winds down to slow jams on the popular New York overnight black radio program *The Quiet Storm*. During the sojourn you're subject to Queenie's bizarre, inscrutable, drug-inspired be-bop-babble punctuated by her signature phrase, "Did I say that right?"

Though I avoid Queenie, I seek closeness with Kal. He is the most like Dad—aloof, pensive, and hard to know. I make concerted efforts to reconnect when Kal is home on leave in the fall of 1987. It is with Kal, while bereaved and vulnerable, that I smoke my first joint.

25

BELLA THE NURSE AND I PLAN a get-together away from the constant scrutiny we are under back on the locked ward. I leave on privileges first, at 6 PM, trek across the campus, and wait just outside the unmanned gates, which abut the neighboring township of Bellerose, Long Island. I am conspicuous as a black man loitering around the outskirts of this white middle-class neighborhood, and it is generally known that any darkies in these parts are from the hospital. I often find a bus stop to stand by or tree to lean on but I am also worried that evening staff might drive by and spot me. More than once I dive in the bushes until I see Bella's distinctive headlights drive up the street. She pulls up and explains that her husband has called the ward, will call again later, and we cannot be together.

On our next planned meeting we are both scared silly when, after a successful pickup, she believes her husband is following us a few vehicles behind.

"Are you sure it's him, Bella?"

"It look like his car. Ai! Now he's right behind us. Ai Dios!"

"Well, whadaya think? I mean, is he dangerous? Are we safe? Whadaya think he'll do?"

"He will kill us."

"What!"

"Oh yes, he will kill us," she says with a certainty that disturbs me.

Several blocks away from the hospital, Bella slows to a crawl, allowing me to jump and run. I feel as if I am trapped in one of those Spanish telenovelas. Her man also drives a white Bronco, made famous recently by another crazed, jealous husband.

We finally agree to meet for a drama-free evening, driving up to a nearby tree-lined lot that is always empty. This same lot is where Gaia and I often go for our backseat trysts. Bella is nervous and it shows as she is dripping with sweat. It is exciting to feel her hot body through her soaked blouse as we kiss, caress, and embrace each other. I notice the front and back windows begin to fog over. Bella gets so enrapt that she bites down hard upon my lips as she sucks and kisses them, soon licking and slobbering on my face. She feels and squeezes me through my jeans, her face a wet, heavy-lidded, trembling display of ecstasy. Bella undoes my jeans and withdraws me. "Ai Dios mio!" she exclaims, proceeding to perform oral sex. She does so gently at first, and then builds to sloppy abandon when I sneak my hand past the hem of her pantyhose and into her underwear.

As we sit wrapped around each other in her car's backseat, bathing in the afterglow, I try to get to know her better. "One of the Mahatas tells me you've had some kind of major surgery that changed your life. I don't mean to pry but, if you feel comfortable, could you tell me what happened?"

Bella is embarrassed at first then sheds an isolated tear, which drops from her chin onto my hand. With a brave face, she tells her story with dread and drama.

"It begin with fatigue. Breathless, losing weight, and feelings very depressed. I didn't know what was wrong and didn't bother to get help. Always too busy, with kids, and work. After many month I notice I am more and more tiredness, and even shrinking. Many, many days I spend at home because I am too tired to get out of bed and come to work. My job was in, how you say, jeopardy? It wasn't until I begin making plans for will that I was convince to visit a doctor. After many, many test it was discover that I have a block coronary artery. I would have die had I wait another month. Within the weekend of discover the problem and how it's severe, I have open heart surgery to remove the block."

Bella casts her eyes down. She unbuttons her blouse, not only to flash her nipples but to reveal a long, raised, pink surgical scar, about the width of my index finger, running down her porcelain chest.

"I thought when you suck me before you see me, my imperfection."

As she shows me her "imperfection" her face displays a fearful uncertainty. As if she is waiting for me to heave in disgust. She offers, in a pained quaver, "You see, I am not pretty as you say. It is ugly. *I* am ugly."

"No, Bella. What're you talking about? You're not ugly. This is just another part of you. If someone loves you they must love this, too. It doesn't change the person you are . . . and you are a beautiful person. A beautiful woman. Why can't you see yourself as I see you?"

"It is hard to be beautiful, feel the way you see me. My husband make me feel very bad. He beat me, abuse me. He has shame because he don't speak English, can only work as a laborer, and is embarrass that I make more than him. I try to learn English, learn more, better myself. He always criticize, say I'm ugly."

"To control you, Bella. But this ain't El Salvador, this is America! Don't fall for that shit. Tina Turner, baby. Tina fucking Turner."

"Do you know last night he even put Tabasco on his fingers when he eat the food that I cook for him. He no wash his hands. He have sex with me and put his fingers in my culo, and he laugh. He burn me down there and he laugh. To punish me."

"You don't deserve that, Bella. Nobody does. That sucks. I'll never hurt you."

"I know. You are good man. You are good to me. You love me, no?"

"Sure, Bella. Sure."

26

I T IS A COLD DECEMBER DAY. Two male staff escort me via state van to the supreme court in Kew Gardens, Queens. I have an application for escorted off-grounds privileges set to go before a judge. While I hope to have it granted and move along legally in the system, I feel nervous. No one must know that I've been venturing off hospital grounds, into the community without official state or court approval, to have sex with my social worker and nurse every day for the past year.

I have a good set of supporters with me. There's Gaia; Dr. Santi, my treating clinician; the head of the forensic committee, Dr. Follow; a court-appointed independent doctor who will speak up for me; and Barry Newfeld, my Mental Hygiene Legal Service attorney. Both the Queens district attorney and the state attorney general are here to block my furlough application and slap me with a two-year retention order. Barry is cautious throughout, intimidated by the very resistant, crusty Judge Brown.

The independent psychologist, who interviewed me in Gaia's office several months ago and picked up something fishy about our "possibly enmeshed therapeutic relationship," testifies as such, but is still recommending the furlough.

My sister Carol is here to glare, intimidate, and give testimony as to why I should never leave Creedmoor. Under oath she denies the ten-day trip I made to California nine months before the offense to stay with her and mind her children. Undaunted, Barry continues his questioning.

"Is it not true that on this trip, that you say never happened, your brother Issa, under a lot of stress, confessed his addiction to marijuana to you, and begged you for help?"

"No, that is not true. I don't know why my half-brother would make up such a thing. He must be crazy."

Carol never speaks my name, referring to me only as her "half-brother," a distinction that our family never made in all our years together.

"I am afraid of my half-brother. My children are afraid of him." I glance back at my nieces, now tragedy-stained teens and surly young adults scowling at me from seats in the rear of the courtroom. "I don't know him. And after what happened I don't want to know him."

I understand how she feels, and my guilt and remorse intensifies. I am suddenly filled with shame and sadness. However, I believe were she to get involved in my case she'd know me better, realizing there is nothing to be afraid of and that I need my family's guidance and help.

But she is now consumed with grief and greed, fuming over insurance money payouts that Lauren's son Jason received, and estate proceeds, which she has been trying to wrestle into her grip for years now. With me out of the way, locked up in the crazy house, there's one less sibling she has to work on swindling.

Carol ends her testimony reinforcing her fear by recounting an isolated trip I made home last year. Escorted by Gaia, I acquired a locksmith to break a lock Carol had installed on my upstairs bedroom's door, recovering whatever was left of my belongings. Carol wasn't home at the time but Lauren and Bichi hosted the haunted homecoming. I felt very much like a thief under pressure, grabbing up distant memories from another person's life, mostly old toys and an armful of warped LPs. Gaia officiated over the whole affair and claimed under oath to have gotten clearance from the forensic committee. This turns out to be untrue, or at least a little fuzzy to the memory of Dr. Follow.

When testimony is done, Judge Brown finds my case credible: I am not dangerous and am deserving of further progress and community reintegration. While I do receive another two-year retention, the judge grants me escorted furloughs for one-to-one day trips into the community but "only with male staff and *under no circumstances* with his social worker Gaia Sapros." It could have been worse. While still installed as my therapist, the independent doctor's testimony and the judge's ruling suggest that she may be overstepping her boundaries. If they only knew.

27

CREEDMOOR'S MAHATA WORKFORCE is overwhelmingly female, and thus not allowed to escort me out on my newly acquired privileges. I try getting the males to take me out, but the treatment team denies me repeatedly. Gaia relays their rationale: "They say we don't have male staff available for recreational escort, that they can't afford the overtime pay. I also know they prefer whatever male staff we do have to be on the wards, to maintain a strong, dominant presence. It's bull, and they'd never admit to it, but in the end it's not fair to you, and that's what makes me angry. They sent you out two-to-one male when you didn't have anything because we got letters, outside interest, and they wanted to save face. Now that you've earned it, they get cheap, pinch pennies, and cry about overtime. Why do you think I started taking you out in the first place? I knew you'd have a hard time getting off the ward."

Gaia and I still slip away for trysts off the grounds, but not as often. I begin to appreciate the delicacy of my situation. "I'm getting closer to discharge," I say, "and I guess I don't want to fuck this up."

"But what about me? What about us?" she rages behind her closed office door.

"The order forbids you by name to take me out. By *name*! If we get caught there'll be no excuses. No way out."

Still, Gaia persists, wanting to keep the juices flowing. Spoiled by the intense intimacy that we achieved in anonymous motel rooms, she offers time and again to meet me for afternoon delights or evening rendezvous. But I always give her a story: "It doesn't feel right . . ." "It's contempt of court . . ." "Gotta play it safe . . ."

Being confined to this facility where Gaia has to come daily to see me, there is nothing I can say or do to influence her other life, yet I have watched my role grow from patient, to friend, to companion, to lover, and now savior. I cannot deny that the overwhelming reason I continue to hang in there is the consistent, extremely willing sex Gaia and I have. She's introduced the monkey-style position into our repertoire and loves deep throating after removing her dentures, but can I save her from her wasteland of a marriage in exchange?

After a time Gaia informs me that her forty-year-old unmarried daughter knows of our affair. Sheryl Sapros, ill with multiple sclerosis and dependent under her mother's care, cries, "Ma, you're not going to leave me, are you?"

"No, honey. You're coming with us."

If I am to run off with Gaia, as she often entertains, I know now her sick daughter will be in tow. And with her I'm sure will come the suspicions of me, a twenty-something-year-old mental patient with no money romancing her mother, a sixty-something financially secure state-employed social worker. Many nights I sit up thinking about Gaia's middle-aged son finding out about us and wanting my blood. And I think of Gaia's husband and see myself in his place, fearing that behind these adulterous acts karmic chickens will come home to roost for me some twenty or thirty years down the line.

Behind her locked office door I often voice these feelings I am having, but Gaia takes this to be my setup for a dump off. She begins to cry, collapsing before me in a weeping mass that is heartbreaking. "You're not going to leave me, are you?" she sobs. Maybe the smart move is to bow out upon Gaia's declaration, "Just tell me now so I can spend the next week crying my eyes out." This refers to a planned weeklong vacation that we would spend together, mostly fucking in motel rooms. I don't follow my gut.

"I don't wanna leave you, Gaia. I love you." And I do. But I also feel by this time, two years into our relationship, that it is over and I'm just going through the motions.

I am eager and compelled to continue my affair with Bella, though. Our time together has more raw sexual potency. When I do acquiesce to Gaia's repeated pleas to get together, I attempt the same unbridled freakiness that I have with Bella, but it is not the same, nor should it be. Gaia is older, softer, and requires more patience and tenderness. She knows she's losing me.

"There's nothing wrong with a quickie," she begs. I tighten her up in her office and she appears grateful for it. When pressed for time we do it in the backseat of her car in the hospital parking lot at the side of the building. This is something even Bella won't do.

Though not without their issues, Gaia and Bella are the closest I've come to dating outside the realm of what Creedmoor has to offer me. And even then our community are allowed no more than swapping snacks and cigarettes for hot promises, although more can and does transpire, often in the bushes or the bathroom stalls. Not for me, though. The socials that the hospital organizes are awkward and more than a little scary for me. I never go. The females are unpredictable and often violent, breaking out into ugly scratch-fights. I realize that nymphomania is indeed a mental disorder, and a simple suggestively arched eyebrow can elicit mad passionate sex from most of the women here. I just don't relish the scorching diseases that may accompany it.

Even though I am violating the rules and the women are breaking the law, I'd rather engage with staff than the patients. I see it as validation for being "normal." Because I have no family support I have to rely on Gaia and Bella and whatever they see in me to survive. Without them I'd be wearing Velcro sneakers and state-issued clothing—famously bereft of style and an immediate tip off that you are a nut, a retard, or a con.

"I want you to be happy," Gaia says. "In love, preferably with me, out of Creedmoor, and living a normal life that you can't in here. Don't forget about your goals. We talked about them, remember? Don't forget about what you want, what you can achieve. The sky's the limit for you."

Gaia makes me feel worthwhile and appreciated, impossible things to come by in this hospital. While I know our union is wrong, I try to convince myself I'm being helped, getting the aid I anticipated upon accepting the insanity plea. Maybe the system does work, though it's considerably lopsided.

Gaia's been working for the state for thirty years, and recently received an employee recognition award, but she tells me, "They're pressuring me to retire. The state says they need to save money. They're always crying broke. They want to get rid of me so they don't have to pay my full pension. I've got the time and the age and they're trying to push me out the door so they can hire someone younger for half what they're paying me. They'll have no experience and so the state can push them around and turn them into good state workers, lazy and incompetent. Well, my work's not done yet. I'm not leaving till you are out of here. I'll shut the light off when I go."

GAIA GETS WIND OF A PRESTIGIOUS outsider art exhibition to be held at the legislative office building in Albany, New York, and encourages me to apply. She and I try to get Creedmoor's Department of Rehab to pay for frames to adorn the three of my paintings that are accepted in the exhibit. Rehab refuses to relinquish budget monies for individual patient endeavors, in keeping with their policy that all art-related funds get allocated to the Living Museum. Gaia is pissed but not surprised.

"Damn it, I'll pay for them!" she screams, cursing the hospital. "But you're coming with me. I don't know what you're looking for. You'll have to pick them out. We can go to the art shop just down the block." We rush out during her lunch hour, desperate to get the work in the show. The trip takes fifteen minutes.

Several days later, with three of my best pieces framed and on their way up to the governor's office, I am summoned back to the building from my job across the campus at the activity center to meet with Unit Chief Stan Markum, who resembles a polar bear if mated with Jimmy Durante. He sits before me in a small room, cradling a piece of Post-it paper and a Paxil promotional pen. "Enya Face reports to me that on Monday she saw you driven off-grounds in a car by the social worker, Gaia Sapros. Is this true?"

"Uh, Monday? Uh . . . Well, yeah, we did go off-grounds. It was to the art store up the block. We needed frames. We asked Rehab and . . ."

Markum waves me off. This was too much information—useless information. He has what he needs to file his report. He has his confession. "You do know that you and the social worker are in defiance of a judge's order, right? You were granted escorted furloughs but only with male staff. And specifically not with her. You do know that, don't you?"

"Yeah, I know."

Content that he has what he came for, the unit chief settles into his seat, cocks his head, then says, through a scary smirk, "Ya know, you rub some people here the wrong way."

Locked away in this small conference room as he says this, it smells of "I'll deny every word if repeated." It also stinks of "don't forget you're a patient," that timeworn put-down disguised as clinical advice for "realistic" goals. And that ultimately reeks of "don't forget you're a nigger." And the mentally ill are just another form of nigger. The real tragedy is if you happen to be both.

Sitting as this man reads me the riot act I start to feel very small and alone. When his name came up during our game of If They Saw, Gaia mentioned Chief Markum's distaste for me. "Stan doesn't like you, Issa. He doesn't like or understand you, as a so-called mental patient, in his charge, who doesn't conform and refuses to be labeled as such. And he's jealous, because you're a patient in his care with true talent. Something he lacks in all areas." Now, I finally see him and it frightens me.

I am allowed to go back outside to my Rehab PEP job. But I can't paint. Not today. I am racking my brain for ways out if the hospital starts to close in. I even contemplate running, but for only a brief moment. I know it would be a poorly planned escape and would put me in deeper trouble than I already am. Maybe things will be okay.

After all, they let me back out after the interrogation. How foolish is that?

28

1987. It begins as a small nodule on Dad's lower gum, which he shows me on an afternoon just before he rides off to work. "No biggie," I tell him. "It looks like a canker sore." The real problem occurs when Dad collapses while performing on the Manor bandstand. Diagnosing it as cancer in March, the doctor says to Dad, "You can live six months or six years depending on your outlook." Then the cancer grows aggressive and attacks his lungs.

Upon learning that Dad's ill, his mother makes the long trip up from Florida by train to be with him. Dad's love for jazz and the lifestyle created a wedge between him and his mother, Naomi. Fifteen years older and steeped in the church, she clings to her Southern Baptist roots as if to purge her of the shame and the impropriety of sexing young and not getting married. Her sister and father raised him, Dad believing well into his teens that his mother was his sister. All summer she nurses and mothers him, as she never could in his youth. When Dad's condition becomes terminal, Naomi encourages him to return with her to Tampa. Mom begs Dad to stay. Granny Naomi leaves without him, bitter, knowing she'll never see him again. Dad never makes it back home.

While cradling him in his end stages, picking him up to help him use the toilet, I find myself thinking back to a moment in my youth when Dad was about to leave for a gig and he called me over to give him a hug before he left. Already distant from him and detesting his cigarette smoke, which always whirled around him, I rejected the embrace, which hurt him. Dad tried to bully the hug from me but I stood firm, proclaiming, "If you keep smoking like you do you'll be dead before you're sixty!" This bit of fortune telling reverberates in my head the entire time Dad lies dying in his bedroom and, true to his doctor's "six months" determination and my teenage prediction, by September, at age fifty-five, he is gone.

Kal arrives home on bereavement leave just as Mom gets the call. Realizing Dad has passed before they could say their final goodbye, Kal cries, "He couldn't wait for me." Mom, Smiley, Kal, and I drive after midnight to the morgue of Brooklyn's Veteran's Administration Hospital to identify the body. We all weep at the sight of Dad's corpse. I cannot believe he is really gone. Dad was a musician who got in the business for an intense love of music and a stronger love of women. Mom confides in me later that Dad died with the clap.

The following night Smiley is out with Queenie and the local get-high boys, chasing a crack high to numb the pain of losing our father. Kal, Kubir, and I are home, in my upstairs bedroom, reminiscing. It is here that Kubir offers up a thick marijuana joint. I have never smoked pot before, but in honor of Dad's love of the weed I figure a small toke will be just fine.

As I smoke the joint, imitating the hissy draw that I've heard every day of my life from my immediate family, my mind expands and my perceptions alter. Not only do my thoughts unfold, but my body appears to enlarge as well. I begin laughing uncontrollably, hunched over, careful of bumping my head on the ceiling of my room, which is now getting smaller, making me feel like a giant in a doll's house. My bedroom is no longer my own, with the once familiar autographed poster of troubled pop icon Brian Wilson scowling down from the paneled wall, or the framed autographs I had collected from minor left-of-the-dial pop singers, or the canvases of some of my recent paintings. It turns dark and I feel as if I am in a Turkish opium den, where the only light to be seen is the blue strobe of a thirteen-inch television flickering in the corner and the orange firefly glow of the joint, moving from Kubir's mouth to Kal's to my own.

After the joint turns to a roach and another makes the rounds, I am totally stoned and out of contact with myself and everyone else in the room. I am alive but only in my head, my thoughts ping-ponging against the inside of my skull, then multifoliating, then disintegrating in a kind of time lapse. Captain Kirk on the TV is suddenly profound and the music that accompanies his fight sequence is akin to a Wagnerian musical drama. My inherent feelings of sadness and embarrassment melt away as I see my brother and Kubir eye each other as conspirators. They always saw me as uptight and enjoy watching me get loose. As Mom enters my room I want to embrace her, saying, "Now I know why you smoke! Now I *know!*"

She rushes in, ordering us to come downstairs. I fear for a moment that we are in trouble for smoking the joints or the loud laughing that accompanied it. However, outside we discover an old, rusted, and fading blue van idling, with two Iranian priests inside beckoning to us. Abdullah Ali, fellow jazz musician and Muslim brother of Dad's for more than thirty years, has summoned the two holy men. Abdullah is also Kubir's father. Mom, Kal, Kubir, and I pile in with them and we drive at high speed down Linden Boulevard to the local funeral parlor in St. Albans. As is customary in the Muslim religion, or so I am hastily told by Abdullah as the van accelerates, once a brother has passed he must be tended to by his family—prepared, blessed, and buried within twenty-four hours of his death. The van seems on the verge of collapse while speeding along the slick streets. It is windy and damp after a brief midnight shower. It is the perfect atmosphere to enter a funeral parlor in the middle of the night, if you're into that sort of thing.

The mortician, in his pajamas and robe, is in a foul mood, having been awakened to sponsor this strange, late hour religious ceremony. Stranger still is our inappropriate giggling as we're ushered down very narrow stairs to the basement of the establishment. Here I see Dad laid out on the mortician's gurney, his naked corpse ruined by the cruel disease. I'm no longer looking at him as I used to, as I knew him, sinewy and robust. Now, I see that he has shrunk, collapsed in on himself, ashy discolored skin clinging to a bony frame. Cancer has kicked his ass.

I am scared and run. Returning upstairs, to the warm, low-lit, carpeted parlor, to be with Mom.

"Oh son, you can't stay here. This is the women's place," she tells me, sitting serene and beautiful in an immaculate white gown. *My* place, as Dad's son, a Muslim, and a man, is in the cold, concrete bowels of this house of death, performing a foreign ceremony while speaking in an unlearned tongue.

The two Imams instruct us, after we clean our hands and feet, to wash Dad's corpse and "prepare him for his journey to the next spiritual plane." We all do as instructed. We bathe Dad's cold, almost stiff corpse as if he were still alive yet unable to do so himself, reminiscent of his condition while living during the last few months. The Imams watch, nod, and speak approvingly. Then we wrap Dad's body in white linen, his Islamic burial shroud, leaving only his face exposed. Lifting him gently, Dad is placed in a modest coffin, the Imams anointing the body with blessed Muslim oils. Prayers are then said in Arabic.

Throughout the ceremony I feel panic and fear rush over me in waves. If I were not so fucked up on the reefer I'm not sure if I could have gone through with it. The drug provides a detachment from my feelings of intense grief and fear. I believe the distance is necessary at this crucial time. I discover my way out.

I also don't want to embarrass my brother Kal, who attends to Dad's body and performs the ceremony like a brave soldier. I am so proud of him on this night, even though he is as high as I am, if not more so.

My family see my marijuana use as an achievement; "Did you know Issa is smoking now?" I hear them whisper. While they all know I am smoking I treat it like a dirty secret. I do not join them in the round table dining room discussions where they all roll and smoke and laugh. I am a pitiful joint roller. I cannot tell one grade of grass from another. Never taking advantage of the family's fantastic pot contacts, I cop from the obvious spots on the outskirts of Central Park and Washington Square, always getting beat. But I go where the smoke is, coat-tailing seasoned users, learning the ropes, mirroring and updating my mother's sordid premarital life, scoring for two-bit rock bands, becoming a sycophantic nickel and dime dealer and rock and roll turd.

Dad's death takes a terrible toll on Mom. She has lost her

companion, her lover, and the leader of the brood. She is very alone now in a house full of grown ne'er-do-well children and bills to pay. She puts up a brave face for all the vulturous acquaintances seeking to pry into her business in the guise of offering support. The local indigent elderly bachelors and widowers start appraising her figure and her assets. She starts to look afraid, which I'm not used to seeing in her. I notice she is smoking pot more frequently.

To cope with the grief behind the loss I begin to smoke more heavily too. Within two years it becomes an addiction. But, as always, I rationalize my usage by saying to myself, "Well, at least I'm not doing crack or some other shit."

29

HAUNTING THE ACTIVITY CENTER, I fear how my treatment team will handle my going off-grounds with Gaia. While surveying my murals and bullshitting with the bored rehab staff, I spot a dark, striking figure striding through the hall, disappearing into the library. Intrigued, I follow.

I have never in my carnal career made the first approach. Though I appear confident and sure, I am usually shy and feel awkward, day-dreaming of crushes. I always settle for those who make the first move, making it easier for me to accept that I am wanted while staying in my comfort zones.

As I enter the library, the figure, with long, silky, black hair bleeding into a secondhand cape, whips around to face me. It is a young woman, her face doe like, innocent and open, but evidence of anger and disappointment burn through her, permeating the pleasant façade, instilling within this attractive black-clad beauty an intensity that makes me want to know more.

"Do you work here?" she asks impatiently.

"Yeah, well, not here in the library, but . . . what do you need?"

"I just want to know how long I can keep a book if I take it out. Is there anybody who works here?"

"Uh, I don't think so. I guess you could just take what you want and bring it back when you're done. They'll be happy just to get it back. Not too many serious readers here."

She pauses for a moment then surprises me by saying, "You're cute."

"You're pretty cute too," I smile back.

After settling on Poe and Emily Dickenson, we exit the library, getting friendly, mutual attraction ice broken, drawing close as two wounded people trapped in Bedlam, neither so damaged that we cannot relate to each other.

"Call me Lily," she says when I ask her name. Tall, slender, and twenty years old, this lovely Goth ingénue is a bright girl with a penchant for quoting dark poetry. She starts a speedy ramble that I recognize all too well from smart people recently let loose from a psych ward.

"It's good to be off the ward. Ya know, as a modern hospital this place sucks, but the ruins porn of Creedmoor are amazing! I've been here for about two weeks. I always hang around here trying to get into their theater but it's always locked. I love the stage. I'm an actor. I prefer to be called an actor and not an actress. I think that gender distinction is insulting. I'm also an artist. I often draw tombstones and nooses hanging from tree branches. My parents can't handle my art so they committed me. The multiple suicide attempts didn't help either."

The eldest daughter of six, born to an alcoholic white trash dad and an abusive West Indian mom who refuses to admit she is black, Lily is plagued by delusions and a crippling depression, living in a dream world where she is a beloved movie actress. Lily spends much of her existence running from the hell of her ugly racist household. Fabulously attractive, she lives from one dreadful audition to the next, daydreaming of that one plum role that will bring her notoriety and enough money to escape. As she continues her rambling download, I finish my diagnosis while admiring her resilience.

Out in the courtyard with Lily for about an hour, we stare dreamily into each other's eyes. We make a good pair, dressed in austere black as we are, but her consorting with a darkie like me proves a bit provocative for some of the onlookers, including Enya Face, scowling down as always from her office above us.

I am summoned back to the ward by one of my least favorite Mahatas, Rufus, a big black Panamanian who is brutal and cruel to the other patients. He often looks at me disparagingly, maybe because he sees the truth of what he is in my eyes. Feeling that I won't be back to finish my current mural, I take my time giving my brushes one final, thorough clean. Rufus escorts me away from Lily, sitting out front of the activity center, across the grounds, and back into the building.

I am being transferred, going next door to 6-B, known as the worst ward in the hospital. I am given time to quickly pack my things and five minutes to say goodbye to Gaia, our exit conference. We sit across from each other, alone in her office with the door partly closed, and the tears start to flow. She then stands and pulls me to her bosom. Cradling my face, she cries, "I'm sorry . . . I'm sorry." It hurts to see her so broken. I am now crying just as hard and start comforting her. "It's OK," I say, "It's going to be OK."

But she knows better. She must know what they have in store for the both of us. I kind of expected this. I felt an end was near. It went too well for too long. We fucked in this office, all over the campus, and illegally gallivanted all over New York City like a boning Bonnie and Clyde, yet they nabbed us for a fifteen-minute trip to the frame shop just down the block.

I see in her face that she is crying for me. Not for her career, which after thirty years of exemplary service is in jeopardy. No, she is shedding fearful tears for me, and how I will be handled by the hospital, how she may have jeopardized my discharge, how she may have ruined my life. I don't like looking into such baleful eyes and seeing my life flash before them. Suddenly, I take more to comforting myself with my pitiful goodbye. I need to believe it . . . "It's OK. It's going to be OK."

30

JUNE 1989. With Dad gone, Mom divides her time between winters in New York and spring and summer up in Toronto. Mom is designing, constructing, and maintaining gardens for wealthy Canadian homeowners. She has parlayed a few chance meetings and impressive floral arrangements into a modestly successful freelance garden and landscaping business. It employs her fine artistic skills and green thumb, keeping her busy and putting some Canadian coin in her pocket.

When Mom's not here the house feels empty. Without her we're all lost. I grocery shop for myself and my teenage nephew, but it's mostly breakfast cereal and TV dinners. Smiley and Kal prove to be unreliable, treating the family home like a crack house.

Queenie and her exploits are the talk of the neighborhood. That my older brothers are tied up in the talk is a huge embarrassment. My shame is tempered, realizing that most of the neighborhood chatter emanates from envious cretins who wish to join the party. My brothers were her favorite party boys, if only to spite Audrey.

The amazing thing about Kal is he grew into a strapping young man due to the strenuous military training. You'd never suspect he is a drug fiend when he comes home. Only his faraway eyes betray him.

Smiley is even deeper in his crack addiction, neglecting his cleanliness. There is an overall dinginess to him. His hair is unkempt, his teeth dull. Noticeable also are his eyes. Once light brown and seductive, now the faint glimmer of humanity has been replaced with a hard, arrogant depravity. He was born for this time in his life, becoming an addict in full. Now he schemes, manipulates, steals, and overindulges, content in knowing that while some poor, desperate, skeletal woman is fellating him as he beams up, the same scene is playing out in almost every other house on the block, in the neighborhood, in the city.

Kubir makes no pretense about his allegiance to crack. Regardless of his gifts as a talented horn player, he is also a desperate drug addict. He resembles a predatory rat in his dirty hoodie, with black shifty eyes, an ashy beige face, and a twitching rodent's overbite, complete with chintzy, whisker-like moustache. Although always small, lately he takes to looking like a poster child for the Crack Smokers of America. He is around more frequently now trying to get his high on; otherwise he's sure to pursue his jones elsewhere in South Jamaica.

With Mom away her two eldest sons disrespect the home, inviting Queenie and other depraved trolls inside for crack parties and sex on the living room couch. Hearing and smelling these activities from my upstairs bedroom sickens me. I had forbidden them from smoking crack in the living room several times before, but I hold no clout. Smiley moves the smoking from his basement apartment to wherever he pleases. When they aren't violating the house, Queenie and the boys are again on the road and "on a mission."

"The mission" eventually makes its way from South Jamaica to midtown Manhattan, driving right up to the door of my job as assistant manager at a Sam Goody's music store. Queenie and Smiley are wrapped around each other in drug-induced slumber, farting and snoring loudly in the back seat of Kal's shiny new candy-apple red Camaro Iroc-Z. It's impressive, even if it is considered a Guido-mobile.

"Nice ride," I say, settling in the passenger seat.

"Queenie bought it for me. Don't tell Mom," Kal smiles from behind the wheel with a mix of glee and embarrassment.

"Whatever," I shrug.

As soon as I sit on the plush burgundy interior Kal reveals a small homemade ceramic marijuana pipe, stuffing it with a generous helping of pot. Driving through the city he holds the pipe in his mouth, igniting with a lighter in his free hand. Inhaling deeply, Kal passes the pipe over to me, instructing with a deadpan, "Careful now, there's something in there."

After a hard day's work I am hungry for a pot high, yearning for the weed. I take the pipe in my mouth, flick the lighter as Kal had done, and in moments the euphoria fills my head. As we drive over the Fifty-Ninth Street Bridge and onward down the long strip of Queens Boulevard, Kal and I trade blows on the pipe. We smoke non-stop, replenishing with more pot. Suddenly, I hear a loud sizzling in my head, which becomes deafening. Whatever is in this pipe bowl is frying my brain. My vision grows cloudy and then almost completely dark. The high-pitched noise continues for a full five minutes. I am very frightened but show no troubling signs to my brother. I want him to think I can handle it.

Although I hate what drugs, South Jamaica, and Queenie are doing to him, I want desperately to impress my brother Kal, who since joining the air force is now the pride of the family. I want to belong. I am not a refined pot smoker but I indulge if it will connect me with him, or anybody, who knows me well. I do not know myself, and what little I thought I knew is growing increasingly vague.

QUEENIE'S HUSBAND EBENEZER JONES wises up and cuts off her privilege to use his credit cards. She can no longer traipse around South Jamaica with drug-induced drivers and party boys, squandering Jones's money on booze, crack, limousines, and much younger men. I occasionally see her skulk down the boulevard, bundled up tight in fancy rags in the heat of summer, chasing the rock. It is sad and pitiful witnessing the total financial, moral, and spiritual decline of a middle-aged mother of three. But she is one of a million such tragedies, and I am relieved as she sneaks a menacing glance while walking past the house, continuing on her corrupt quest for the seven-minute solution.

MOM PULLS INTO THE DRIVEWAY in her old blue '76 Camaro. It's good to see her return, as if she knows of the chaos invading her home. She is the avenger, the rectifier, or so I hope. I feel obligated to tell Mom of the behavior of her two eldest sons. I am a child again, tattling for brownie points, and a pat on the head. I want so much to be the good son.

"Oh father! Oh father!" she cries out. Mom always resorts to that pleading exclamation when the news is bad. I am never sure if she is beseeching Arthur Phipps, God, or perhaps both when she needs the strength. Mom is tired after the long drive, and maybe it isn't such a good idea to tell her about the mayhem so soon. It is sobering realizing she is not the super woman I grew up idolizing but rather a widowed grandmother who isn't getting any younger.

"Oh, Iss, this is not good. I can't go back to Toronto, not with all this nonsense going on here. I just knew something wasn't right. I could feel it. It was in the air, in the *stars!* I'm going to have to stay back for a little while, suspend the business up north, till I can make things right again. I worked too hard, Dad and Gramps worked too hard, to have this foolishness go on. But listen, Iss. I'll need your help paying the bills and minding the upkeep of the house. Can you do that, son?"

"Sure, Ma. No problem."

The end run of this coming of age rite occurs when Mom attaches me as a cardholder on her American Express account. At last I am a member, acquiring status and much-needed credit. I ignorantly think it can't get any better than this.

31

I TRANSFER MY BELONGINGS TO THE WARD across the hall, 6–B, ward of no return. I've heard that all patients deemed incorrigible are transferred here to rot. It is easy to disappear into the walls of this ward, surrounded by these forgotten men, all thought to be too much trouble or difficult to control. The hospital knows my family would rather I spend the rest of my life inside. That'll make it easier for Creedmoor to ignore, abuse, and lose me, one of many dirty grey smudges in an imprisoned pattern on their warped wallpaper.

As I put my things away in my new bedroom, situated closest to the nurse's station so I can be closely monitored, Unit Chief Stan Markum enters the ward, stands in my open doorway, and offers a curt orientation.

"An Albany investigative team is coming down to question Gaia about possible improprieties. You got your exit conference, right?"

"Yeah."

"OK, good. You and Gaia Sapros will have no further contact. Understand? It's over."

Gaia still sneaks in the occasional care package (home cooked food and pastries, but it's not the same). Various secretarial staff, some who are fiercely loyal to her, drop the packages off, saying, "I shouldn't be doing this, but you know who it's from," before cracking a sad smile.

After a few days, Chief Markum again storms down the long corridor, this time asking me to stand outside my doorway, in what becomes an uneasy reprise of the periodic random shakedowns I had to endure in my brief stay on Rikers Island. He surveys the representational oil paintings that I again display on the walls of my bedroom, including a prominent painting featuring him, naked in a cluster-fuck of strangling administrative figureheads. And, like the Gestapo, demarcating "degenerate art" from the benign, he confiscates several pieces of interest from my room. With the offending works tucked under each arm he declares, "I want to show them to the administration. They may offer hints of pathology," before trooping back down the hallway. My pleading, "Can I get you to sign a release or something?" is met with a smirk and a closed door.

I discover shade from the scorching heat via the ward staff. The young black Mahatas, all survivors of the streets who know me by reputation ("smart artist," "cool guy," "dude who don't belong here"), rally to my aid and my plight as a young black brother caught up in the system, maybe seeing themselves in a similarly tight and untenable position on the American landscape. They become my eyes and ears, filtering information from their staff meetings with administration.

"They said you can't be trusted, man. They callin' you a manipulator and a job threat. We were told to stay away from you but to also listen carefully to everything out of your mouth. The verdict is in, bro. You is the devil." They laugh and dap, amused by the hospital's histrionics while also cluing me in on the joke. Somehow it isn't funny.

I feel more and more paranoid. I am told by Chief Markum, "Don't isolate yourself. It will be better for you if you continue to interact with the staff." I don't know whom to trust. I am scared and none of the professional staff seem to care. Gaia's departure has left me adrift, bleeding in shark-infested waters. She surreptitiously calls the ward payphone, often to keep my spirits up, but I am sinking. This may be what they want, the orders they've been told to follow. In this place of very clearly defined hierarchal roles I have crossed ranks and, in their minds, usurped power. I imagine that the professionals, when faced with one of their own that doesn't act according to code, fulfilling the taboo that is their wildest dream or nightmare, are titillated, shocked, and enraged. In another closed-door session, Chief Markum says, "Me and the administration want to see if you'll break."

I never thought they were in the business of knocking patients over, nullifying what they supposedly stand for: care and treatment. I never thought I'd be chosen. Perhaps he feels I put too much negative light on his unit. Maybe he's embarrassed. Maybe it's personal.

Primed and poked, I am passed to Dr. Anil Ramma, the chief psychiatrist. I never liked this man, and I don't believe he cares much for me. He seems to walk around with blithe disgust toward the patients under his care, a thick black downturned moustache accentuating his disdain. He appears to enjoy having somewhere to go where he can be better than the people around him, where he is in charge, where he is crucial to our freedom, and he doesn't think us worthy of what he has and prefers keeping the status quo.

Ramma, head of a strong and scornful Hindu professional clique, calls me into the chart room to tell me what the administration expects from me. "We want to put you through a battery of psychological tests. This testing is for the purpose of determining a new diagnosis."

"Oh, come on, doctor. That new diagnosis will clear Creedmoor of all responsibility for whatever they think happened between Gaia and me. And what about my paintings? You're using them for this new diagnosis too. I feel like I'm being railroaded."

"Do you really think that?"

"Yes. I have genuine distrust of the treatment team and the administration," I declare.

"And I have genuine distrust of you!" Dr. Ramma smiles, as if amused by my moxie. "I'll sleep well knowing you are in here. It doesn't bother me. But this is what *we* want. It's up to you what you want to do."

"Well, I don't feel comfortable, on this ward, with your tests, with this whole situation. I'm gonna let MHLS know about all of this."

"Don't underestimate us, Issa. We have methods of dealing with every eventuality. You are an enigma. Our not knowing how to deal with you isn't good for us . . . and it will not be good for you." He smiles again.

The Mahatas find it ridiculous and sad that I have been slapped with a profile as a seducer. They start calling me "Casanova" and

"MacGyver," but still feed me choice bits of confidential information along with their encouragement. They offer their honest, insider's belief that I am being screwed. Most staff is supportive but only from a distance. More like whispers behind pillars so as not to be seen conferring with the enemy. It is here that I see clearer the complexity of their role. At first I was angry about being here, looking at the employees with a jaundiced eye, casting aspersions on the entire hospital ward staff for the transgressions of a few. Now, when I really need them, the Mahatas keep watchful, compassionate eyes on me. Sidling up when I seem unsteady to tell me, "Keep your head up and your hat on. Try not to crack, brother."

My Mental Hygiene Legal Service attorney Barry Newfeld, so far never an aggressive don't-worry-I'll-get-you-out-of-here type of guy, doesn't seem to recognize what I describe over the phone to him as the hospital's breaking techniques. Maybe he wouldn't admit to it if he did. Even though MHLS is an outside agency, Barry developed a reputation with the other insanity plea patients as a "good state worker," one who goes along to get along, agreeing with whatever the hospital doles out for us because he lunches and laughs with members of the hospital. He tries to pacify me by feeding me his favorite line: "It may look bad right now, Issa, but don't worry. It's all good time."

"Funny, Barry, but I didn't think I was doing time. If I wanted to do time I would have gone to prison." Five years into this I discover that, in a way, I have.

32

ISOLATED AND DESPERATE FOR ANY KIND OF SUPPORT, I continue to take Bella's calls from 6-A's nursing station. Now that we're separated, the phone contact is safer but not wise, for soon she wants more.

When one of the ward nurses goes to lunch the nurse from the adjacent ward is required to cover. This means dropping off the ward keys to the remaining nurse in case of emergency. Thus I begin to see Bella enter the ward and strut down the long 6-B hallway like it's a fashion runway, dropping off her keys with my ward's nurse, the stern Mrs. George.

It's common within the Indian community for the married women to adopt as their surname the Christian first name of their husband. As a result there is a proliferation of Indian nurses at Creedmoor named Mrs. George, Mrs. John, Mrs. Paul. I'm on the lookout for Mrs. Ringo.

When not threatening the patients with a needle in their ass when they act out, 6-B's Mrs. George often engages her pets in a seduction of heavily mascaraed sidelong glances worthy of vintage Bollywood.

"Do you like this? No. You don't like this. Do you?" she teases, while loosening her bun and then slowly brushing her long black hair, or readjusting the scarves of her sari. One or two of the thirstier patients frequent her nurse's station but I stay away, not really interested and already in a mess of trouble.

Hearing Bella's heels clack on the hard marble floor announcing her approach I hide in my room, but she taps on my door with her keys, begging me to come out and meet with her. It doesn't matter to her that following the Gaia scandal I am now being watched for any and all inappropriate behavior. She has to have her man. I emerge, like a Broadway star coming out to meet a Stage-Door Jenny, and escort her back down the hall and off to her lunch, "Alone," she bemoans.

"What do you have that make me want you so? And how can you cheat on me with that old woman? Tell the true. Why? I love you. I kill you. I love you . . . I kill you!"

33

THE WOMEN IN MY LIFE are causing me to spin slowly out of control, what with the clandestine phone romance of Bella, daily calls from Gaia, and weekly visits from Lily, who was recently discharged and has become my very visible main squeeze. Slapped down to nothing and watched closely on the ward, the only relative freedom I have is in the visitor's room. There, Lily and I are completely alone with no observation, thanks to a three-inch square of construction paper I strategically place over the window on the door whenever we're in there, something I learned from Gaia. Although our incarcerated courtship is slow it is a beautiful romance.

Lily and I make great use of the visitor's room's privacy but Mitch, a top dog on the ward, often interrupts us, creeping in drunk and slurring, "I'll give you three hundred dollars to sit here and watch you two do it." I am stunned and Lily is mortified. We decline. When he leaves, Lily jokes, "I'm worth much more than that."

Mitch's drunken conscience gets the better of him as he peeks in ten minutes later, offering one hundred dollars to apologize. *That* I almost take.

I try to be discreet by keeping the women from finding out about each other, but it is pointless. They all know. Bella looks wounded when Lily visits, knowing that I have found another to take her place. Lily asks why the night nurse and I act so strange together the few times Bella lets her on or off the ward. And Gaia sounds pained when she learns I can't take her calls because I am off the ward in the visitor's room.

"Who is it? Who's visiting you?" Gaia demands. "It's not that damned nurse De LaPuta, is it?"

"Of course not. And what makes you think I'd have anything to do with her?"

"Issa, there are no secrets in Creedmoor!"

"What have you heard?"

"Stop playing games! She wants you! She may have already had you," Gaia bellows, "but watch out!" I begin to bluster in feigned disbelief but Gaia won't be shaken. "I can't tell you what to do. I know how you are. *You* know how you are. Just watch out because you're the one who'll get hurt if you get involved with *that* one. She's a Spaniard! They're born to seduce. That's all they know how to do."

"We just talk from time to time at night on the phone. Besides, she's married with a few kids."

"I know but that doesn't stop some people." The irony of Gaia saying this surprises me. "Don't let her get her hooks into you, is all I'm saying. Watch out for that honey-dripping tongue! You're going to do what you feel, I can't stop you, nor do I want to, but just be smart. She'll be the first to talk. She'll be the first to point fingers and she'll be the one who'll say, 'He did it, I didn't do anything!' And I don't want you to get hurt anymore. The last thing you need is something like that one to mess you up, so be smart!"

LILY IS QUITE BEAUTIFUL. She is also terribly wounded. She has a long history of abuse and traumatization. I care about her and want to help keep her out of the hospital, so I do something that is daring and foolish, if well-intended. I suggest a free therapy session for Lily with Gaia in her Forest Hills office. That office and her severance package from Creedmoor are keeping Gaia afloat. In phone conversations with Gaia I tell her how bad I feel about her dismissal.

"Don't let it bother you," she soothes. "I just hope you can keep it together and keep fighting to get out. It's going to be rough. It was always difficult, but now . . . after what happened . . . *I'm* sorry."

Lily keeps her appointment and spends the entire session telling Gaia about her love for me and the exciting sex we have in the visitor's room, blowing the lid off our romance. Gaia gives Lily the best advice she can muster, "Leave him immediately!"

Lily senses something's awry. She terminates the session and confronts me about this odd therapist during our next visit.

"We were involved," I confess. "Intimately. She used to work here. She used to be my social worker. And my therapist. And we got caught and she was let go, and that's why I'm on restriction. But I won't see her anymore, Lil. I can't, obviously."

BUT MY AFFAIR WITH BELLA jumps into full swing again, except for the sex. Her hungry looks while dropping off the keys are desperate and obvious, barely hidden from the staff. When she calls my ward payphone from the phone in her nurse's station next door on 6-A, the more astute patients who answer announce, "Hey, Iss, it's the nurse," or "Bella wants to talk to you," before handing me the receiver. Her voice and ways are unmistakable.

"Is there anything that you want to eat that I can pick up for you?" she asks. Seeing as Creedmoor's cuisine is bad and steadily getting worse I accept her offers. I eat very well but I am surprised and uncomfortable with the twenty- and then fifty-dollar bills she leaves at the bottom of the bags. As much as I don't want to take money from her, which I equate to taking food out of her children's mouths, she doesn't take no for an answer. It keeps me in pizza, deli sandwiches, Chinese food, and quarters for the phone, but ultimately I feel like a whore.

Bella calls one evening and asks, "Do you play any instruments?"

"Well, I know a few guitar chords but I'm not very good."

"But would you play one if you had?"

"What, a guitar?"

"Yes."

"Sure. I've got nothing else to do. And I'm afraid if I start painting they'll confiscate my work again."

"OK. Then watch for the mail. You will get a present . . . from me. Tell them it is from a friend. And like Antonio Banderas in this new film, what is it—*Desperado?*—I will want to hear you play some beautiful music for me."

"Yeah? Over the phone? *That's* romantic," I toss sarcastically.

"It is a start."

Within a week I receive a brand-new shiny black Fender acoustic/electric guitar, just like Banderas's, except *my* gig bag isn't equipped with artillery to help me break out of Creedmoor. I also acquire a boss *Complete Beatles* songbook, which I barter from an inpatient acid-casualty who actually believes he *is* John Lennon, for my coveted snake-skin boots. It is time, much like the Quarrymen did at the turn of the '60s, to ditch the cowboy gear and go mod.

The guitar is a beauty. Whiling away the many long hours and days and weeks and months restricted to the ward, I am rarely seen without it. I wrestle song after rackety song out of the sleek instrument, exploiting the few chords I know and banging out others that aren't too hard to wrap my fingers around. After gleaning the Holy Grail, as I see it (early Beatles, early Dylan, early Costello, and the basics of '50s rhythm and blues and rock and roll), I eventually start churning out my own work. I walk around, like a wandering troubadour, playing these original songs to the chagrin of just about everyone on the ward, some of whom call out requests for "Stairway to Heaven" and other classic schlock.

I've found another outlet that is less liable than painting to be confiscated and used against me. The song is mine to perform, given to the air, and then gone. It is creativity that is safe from Creedmoor's clutches.

ADDICTED TO OUR PHONE SEX and late night serenades, Bella is becoming a problem. More and more eyes seem to be on me and I don't want her nightly key-drop visits to arouse any more suspicion than they already have. It is hard to break off our relationship, especially after all she has done for me.

"What do you want for Christmas, mi amor?" she asks, as I escort her down the hallway of the ward, strolling like troubled lovers on the beach.

"A brand new start."

"You can't mean that. I thought you love me."

"Look, Bella, we can't go on this way. It's wrong. It's adultery."

She stands in red-faced shame, as if I had just screamed "WHORE!" to echo down the corridor. "No! No! How can you say that? I love you. I love you! Do you love me? Do you? Por favor, mi amor," she whispers, pleading for me to reconsider. Begging for another chance. This hushed desperation softens my resolve.

"OK, OK. I'm sorry. I'll think about it." She slips a fifty-dollar bill into my palm as insurance.

ALTHOUGH I SEX IT UP WITH LILY on a regular basis (prompting Mitch to say, "Damn, man, you got pussy on call!") I still find the time and desire to pleasure Bella aurally. During the long cold winter evenings Bella and I are both bored and horny. Following a particularly raunchy bout of phone sex she devises a scheme to meet again, alone in the ward's visitor's room.

At 10 PM, well past evening visiting hour, Bella calls and tells me to meet her by the door to the visitor's room that leads onto the ward. This door is at the far end of the long hallway and away from many eyes on the ward that most likely won't be looking. The only Mahata visible is Jinn, an absent-minded Indian schlub who is sitting down the hall, leaning back in his chair, reading *People* magazine, and picking his nose. I walk from my bedroom up the hallway, glancing back at Jinn, loitering by the visitor's room door as instructed. Bella enters the visitor's room through the door outside the ward, and then opens the door inside my ward, allowing me to slip in.

Once inside we keep the light off, which heightens the excitement. The only illumination comes from the harsh fluorescent lights of the ward shining in through the square porthole in the door of the visitor's room. Bella steps back against the wall, eyes to the ceiling, clutching her keys close to her chest, breathing rapidly, almost hyperventilating.

"Are you OK?"

"Mi corazon . . . mi corazon . . . un momento por favor. Let me catch my breath . . . mi amor."

We embrace, and she kisses me, breathing heavily, while her frenetic tongue dances in and around my mouth like a freshly caught fish on a hook. It had been more than a year since we were together this way. I break from our kissing to help regulate her breathing. She struggles to speak.

"I miss you so much. You make me feel love again, worthwhile, sexy. Please, mi amor, make love to me." We undo each other's clothing and ravish each other hungrily.

I HEAR A KEY WORKING ITS WAY into the outer door's lock, pull my clothes on, and bolt through the other door leading onto the ward. Running down the hall to my room I see Indian Jinn, smiling.

"Push push! Eh, Issa? Good stuff? Push push? Ha ha!"

He must've spotted me and alerted Mrs. George, now checking the visitor's room to see what is going on. Inside she finds Bella, face flushed, makeup smeared, and clothes in disarray.

It doesn't take long before another investigation is called. As an "administrative decision" I am removed from the ward and sent to Creedmoor's Secure Care Unit. If 6-B is Stalag 17, Secure is the hospital's Siberia.

As I exit the ward in a perp walk filled with shame and dread, the patients huddle at the front door, faces pressed pig-nosed against the window, crowing, "Was it good? Was it good?" "Get it, brother! Get it!" "Yeah, dog!"

The Secure Care Unit holds a concentration of no more than ten patients deemed the sickest, most dangerous, or most unpredictable. There you endure microscopic observation and intensive pharmacology, designed to get you medicated, stabilized, and back on your ward within thirty days. I am held there for three months. Though already stable on 15 milligrams of Stelazine, the administration takes no chances and doesn't know what else to do with me but up my meds another

15 milligrams and keep me on high guard. I am put on one-to-one male staff observation in Secure, which is very rare, reserved only for homicidal drug dealers. Bella, like Gaia a year previous, is quickly and quietly dismissed, asked to retire as a state employee.

When I return to 6-B the treatment team and all of Creedmoor are polarized. Employees believe either that Bella, like Gaia, should have known better, blatantly broke the rules, and got what she deserved, or that I am a crafty scumbag who preys on people's vulnerabilities and got their colleagues and friends fired.

SIMILAR TO THE FREQUENT CALLS I receive from Gaia, a year after her exit Bella calls me on the ward payphone. Now working in private home care out on Central Islip, Long Island, near where she lives, I am happy that she has bounced back. Bella still has very strong feelings for me and I have a fondness for her, but it is clear that with me incarcerated indefinitely, locked down harder and under greater scrutiny than when she was here, there is no way of our carrying on.

"I love you like no other, mi amor. I will always love you. Remember me," Bella cries through the line. She leaves me with a hundred-dollar bill as a mailed farewell, in a Valentine's card stuffed with colorful confetti Xs and Os, which tumble out like tears.

34

I TAKE INDEPENDENCE DAY WEEKEND, 1989, off from work. Even with Mom around, and Lauren's eldest son, Jason, staying with us, I feel lonely. My constant pot smoking has made me flaky lately and I wind up alienating people and isolating myself. I am not a social smoker. Sitting in the sun in my backyard, watching Mom buzz around the rear deck door leading into the house like a queen bee contemplating her hive, I envy her. She multitasks with a joint between her lips, cheerily pruning plants and feeding the cat, while I am burnt out and lethargic from last night's high, yet still voraciously hungry to smoke again. Alone. In the dark.

"Iss, would you like some barbeque?" Mom asks, stoking the coals in the hibachi grill.

"I dunno, Ma."

"You don't know? What's the matter, son? You seem sad."

"I am . . . a little. And I'm bored . . . and, I dunno, I just don't feel like doing anything. But I feel like . . . like I can't sit still. And I feel like I don't have any friends. Not any real friends anyway."

"Don't you have friends at the record store?"

"Not really."

"Well, what happened to that girl you were seeing? The chunky one with the pretty face? Charlotte?"

"Scarlett, Ma."

"Yeah, her. I liked her. Where's she been?"

"Uh, we broke up months ago."

"Oh, sorry, son. That might have been a bad move. She was nice."

"Yeah . . . well . . ."

"Why don't you call Kubir? Invite him over," Mom suggests. "He's fun. And he's like family. You two always got along, didn't you? I like smoking with him and he's always down for a free meal. Call him up. We'll have a barbeque. It's settled. I'll start cooking."

Kubir brings with him a fifth of scotch and a generous helping of Thai weed. He and I sit under the large, healthy pear tree that is the centerpiece of the backyard. While he rolls several bulging joints from a ten-dollar plastic mini-baggie, familiar to all smokers and created almost expressly for reefer, I laugh at his comic mugging as the squirrels bomb us from the tree limbs above. The family always knows when the pears are in season because the squirrels emerge from their winter home between the floors of our house, dine on the fruit, then drop the masticated remnants.

Kubir and I indulge in the weed, chasing it with scotch, and soon I am very, very stoned. But I begin to feel stranger than I ever have before. This feeling is not like the depression-tinged mellow highs I had experienced up till now. Like a switch being tripped in my head, I am now hyperaware, attributing a universal significance to everything, from the random to the deliberate, the benign and the provocative. The blade of grass dancing in the breeze against my feet, to the chirps of the sparrows in the pussy willow tree, to the smell of the sizzling burgers Mom flips on the hibachi. Everything seems to click into place. Nonsense becomes perfect sense and meaning becomes enlightenment. However, though this awakening is derived from the normally goofy and harmless high of marijuana, there is an undercurrent to this feeling that is foreign and hostile which begins to magnify exponentially, overriding my high, laying me low.

Waking from this momentary fugue state, I notice Kubir and Jason engaged in a pensive game of chess. Watching the silent strikes and counterstrikes, I wonder who has the best strategy, and the best defense? Where do I place my allegiance, and how do I project my personal values? Whom do I root for? The scrappy kid or the savvy champ? David or Goliath? The black guy or the white guy? Africa or the world? And are the denizens of the Dark Continent truly the underdog or the once and future kings?

I wonder if this centuries-old battle, this eternal quandary, will ever reconcile itself, or if we should concede and move on, or if it even needs to be won. And I wonder if there is a place, in this mental/racial metaphor, this internal dilemma, for my mother, my nephew, Kubir, and me. High yellow, redbone, "light-skinded" black people. All of us multihued, mulattoed, mixed-race mutts, ourselves engaged, ordained, born into a racial game of stark contrasts, dividing lines, and definitive winners and losers.

Vulnerable and scared, my face and body slacken. I feel powerless, sitting on the periphery of what I perceive to be a new plateau of race awareness, and a racially divine mind meld between Kubir, Jason, and Mom. And I believe my mind is open for all to read, as if my skull were transparent, my thoughts projected like a hologram above my head, available for all to access and enjoy yet elusive and confusing to me. As I sit here discovering this, while still watching the chess game, I feel Kubir's presence step into my mind. Studying his next move, Kubir communicates the sarcastic thought: *You're weak! You're all heart!*

Well, at least I have a heart, you evil worm! I shoot back, telepathically. After sending him this, Kubir seems to give it a long ponderous moment to sink in. Then, putting his opponent in check, he slowly brings his finger up to his ear, digs in and twists, as if adjusting the volume on a listening device. I reason that this is his way of communicating, *I can hear you.*

This is something that I have never experienced before, so alien to me yet also strangely relatable as a symptom of madness, an index of insanity. A loose thread revealing an opening seam, a crack in the window letting in a wicked wind, foreboding a cruel winter. I now know what all men fear. You *know* when you lose hold of your mind . . . you just know.

Kubir is burrowing into it, sifting through my thoughts, like an auditor or saboteur flipping though a haphazard file cabinet of crap, projecting caustic commentary on my most cherished ideas, the things that make me who I am. I feel paranoid, even amid my family.

Noticing I am on to him, Kubir breaks from the game. "Hey, Iss, can I use your phone?"

I decide to personally escort him from the backyard, up to the deck, and into the house and my bedroom. I feel a showdown is about to take place, but I'm a bit worried because: a) I know how slick he is, adept at getting out of sticky situations, and b) I am dealing with a man aligned with dark forces.

"Iss, you want a hotdog?" Mom interrupts, cutting between Kubir and I, allowing him some lead time. I am brought back to my youth, when she would quiet me by popping a raw frank in my mouth. While this used to comfort me, now I feel uneasy. How can she even think of such folly? How can she not know how evil Kubir has proven himself to be? She treats him like a son and assumes all is as it should be. As for me, I do not want this man, this evil presence, left alone in my room, poisoning this house.

Rushing upstairs to my front bedroom, I find Kubir languishing on the bed, cradling the telephone. As I stand there, waiting for him to notice my discomfort, hoping he'll get off the phone, I begin to believe he is not on the line with anyone. He is judging my reactions, creating conversation to suit the situation, like a blow-by-blow commentary of what I will do next.

"Is he asleep?"

"Let's wake him up."

"He's such a lazy fuck. He's gonna blow it."

"Nah, I don't think he knows. He's not smart enough."

"That's it! That's it!" I scream, "Hang up! Get off the phone! Get off the fucking phone!"

"What's the problem, Iss?" he asks, calm and knowing, putting down the receiver.

I am livid, yet I can't articulate what is irking me. Just then, like the first time I smoked with him nearly two years ago, my bedroom starts to look unfamiliar to me. The light changes. The room goes dim, then stark, as if it's a vast wasteland. It is a striking and inexplicable change from the sunlit room it was. The antique toys that I collect and display all around it start to mock me. I am very small and akin to these playthings, an insignificant, worn-out trifle, not knowing or comprehending the whole of the world and its dark secrets now slowly revealing themselves to me.

"It's really heavy, Iss. I'll tell you about it one day," Kubir says cryptically, disturbing my glimpse of oblivion.

"Get the hell out of this house!" I grumble. His eyes roam my bedroom, perhaps appraising it for final plunder as he often did in the clutches of crack addiction. He will not get that chance. Conflicted, coming to truths and becoming a man, I realize that this close tie must be severed. I've known Kubir all my life, but as I come to the epiphany of his mind-reading and the dark arts, I also know he is not good to have around.

Out on the front stoop, tearful and flush with emotion, I give Kubir a final embrace. He rejects this, shrugging me off and away from him. This is again a sign of my "weakness." I am indeed "all heart." As I watch him walk up the block toward the bus stop, I feel triumphant yet also cheap, unsure if I cleaned the house of evil or banished a lifelong friend.

Returning inside, standing in the living room, unsteady but attentive, I hear a heavy shuffling noise upstairs. Running to the front door I notice it is ajar. Could Kubir have snuck back into the house? Nervous and fearful, I run upstairs and into each room to ensure he is no longer here. Is he toying with me, reveling in his power, laughing at me in my fear?

In the rear bedroom, bending over a small battered couch sitting under a window overlooking the bus stop down the block, I gaze outside, searching for the warlock. Suddenly, I feel stimulation in my anus, the sensation of a small probe, perhaps a finger, sliding in and poking around. I then experience a hard ramming entry, as if I am being sodomized. Lying forward across the couch like a prone porn performer, breathing heavily, releasing a loud, post-penetration gasp it is clear—I have been fucked! The many years of Kubir's crack money borrowing and shystering have caught up with me.

I regain my composure and slowly tread downstairs, stopping at the kitchen dining table. Jason is sitting there enjoying one of Mom's spectacular hamburgers while she prepares a pitcher of her tasty homemade carrot juice. While he smacks with delight I am too shaken up to join him. Mom takes her favorite seat just away from the table, where she can view Linden Boulevard through the living room, the entire kitchen, and also peer down the hallway, into her rear bedroom and out onto the backyard.

"What's up, son?" she asks, noticing my distress. "You're not eating. Are you all right?"

"It's the drugs, Ma. It makes you read minds. It turns you into something evil! You must know this, don't you?"

"*Drugs?* I don't even know why you're taking *drugs.*"

Her emphasis of the word is humbling, as if she is mocking my estimation of marijuana as a harmful substance. And I don't have a valid reason for using. I guess I just finally fell in line. Distracted by a large fly buzzing outside the kitchen window, I believe this is Kubir in another form. "A shape-shifter," I exclaim, "Of *course*! Look at him!"

Mom and Jason follow the bug with narrowed eyes to inspect the insect but see only a common housefly. They do not see Kubir's human head on the bug's body, nor do I. However, this is just one aspect of the hellish abomination I believe Kubir to be. Ceasing to make sense after a while, I know by their faces that I am not believed and come off like a nut.

"Iss, I think you smoked too much," Mom confides. "It's OK, it happens. Just stay here, have something to eat. It's hot out. Stay inside and cool off. Don't go out and make a fool of yourself, son."

I believe I have come upon frightening revelations about a close family friend. And if he is a malevolent force then who else could be gotten to via marijuana? And isn't it fitting to have this awesome awakening on Independence Day? When else can I finally see behind the veil of the mind? When else can I declare my freedom from the trappings of believed reality, discovering that there may be something *else*, something bad going on?

Unsuccessful in my attempt at warning my family of the evil around them I retreat to my bedroom and konk out, the result of liquor, marijuana, and madness under the hot summer sun.

The next morning I wake up at 10 AM, groggy and two hours late for work. It is the beginning of a routine that I cannot break and that, over time, will intensify in its dereliction. I hit the phone, calling my branch to say I will be late for the manager's meeting being held there at noon. I then spend most of the morning working off my high, slowly, sluggishly readying myself for work. I dress very antiestablishment and chic in skintight trousers, Beatle boots, sleeveless Superman T-shirt with a bootlace tie, and vintage seersucker blazer. This is certain death when attending a manager's meeting but I've long since stopped caring what those uptight, white bread midwesterners who owned the company thought about my wardrobe.

Coming out of the subway in Manhattan, I walk downtown toward the store lost in thought, still reeling after yesterday's marijuana meltdown. In the crosswalk at Forty-Seventh Street on Third Avenue, an old white woman of about seventy is crossing in the opposite direction, walking uptown. This woman goes out of her way to bump into me.

"Watch it, nigger!" she barks in my ear. I freeze in my tracks. I have never in my twenty-four years heard this word directed at me by a white person. It is jarring, inevitable, and necessary in waking up as a black man in America. This is something that I thought I was immune to—or never really thought about. I'd encountered the subtle slights, hard looks asking *What are* you *doing here?* I'd seen the nervous eyes, stiffened backs, and clutched handbags, not to mention being hawked and dogged in department stores by sales help and security guards. But this comment is different. This is the ultimate slur, the height of racial disrespect.

I turn slowly, looking with incredulity at the back of the woman's head, a small tangle of silver wisps, as she continues walking away. Standing in the crosswalk, my mind is racing, searching for understanding; perhaps she saw "passive negro" in my face and demeanor and decided to pounce. As outraged as I am, I realize how volatile it will be if I pursue her down the street and smack her upside the head like I want to. Surely, all of Third Avenue would run to the defense of a hobbling old biddy being beat upon by an angry young "nigger."

Storming the tail end of the manager's meeting, I fly into a tirade about the old woman's comment and anything else that pisses me off. I am paranoid, confused, and in a state of nervous exhaustion. All I can think about is hostile race relations in the city, crack taking over the suburbs, and how or if I can survive in this new world of marijuana-induced mind reading. As the awkward meeting ends I pull aside my store manager.

"Yeah, uh, Herm? Look, could you talk to the regional manager about maybe having me relocated to a Goody's outlet in California? Oakland? I just can't stay in New York anymore." I decide right there to move out west to stay with my sister Carol. I have, with that old racist woman's help, become more conscious of my race. On the way home I stop at a barbershop to cut off my chemically treated pompadour and shoulder-length locks.

35

W HILE I WAS COOLING MY HEELS for months in the Secure Care Unit,
all of the old buildings save the Living Museum were being decom-
missioned and sold to outside agencies. Decades-old wards and units
have become mentally ill chemical abuse residences, halfway houses,
and treatment centers for the developmentally disabled. Patients and
staff working and residing in the satellite structures across the campus
are systematically moved to Building 40.

Over several years 40 was renovated, first one side of the building,
then the other. Now that it's finished, cleaner, and fawned over by
the administration like a coveted pre-owned Mercedes, instead of the
retooled hooptie that it really is, Creedmoor almost functions like a
real hospital. The rampant sexing among coworkers is not that easy
to accomplish and sex between staff and patients is now impossible. I
overhear the Mahatas' discomfort with the new close quarters and many
patients don't care for it either. I'm sure if I were here for a short stay
I wouldn't mind it all that much. But as I've been here a while, and
will be here for a longer while, I can't help but be skeptical of the new
Creedmoor. You can spend a lot of money putting an expensive suit
and fancy shoes on a bum, but at his core he's still a bum.

This hospital's administration has always been top-down Caucasian
with a sprinkling of minorities who know their place and guard it
fiercely. Through the years I have heard talk of diversity, and I have seen
plenty of Asians and especially women advance in Creedmoor. However, the complete lack of African American psychiatrists in a facility
with a predominantly African American population is jarring. The black
patients feel culturally misunderstood and perpetually misdiagnosed.

There are a couple of token Haitians but they don't count. They're all light skinned and privileged and would probably come to blows if you called them black. The Indian contingent is equally distant from their darkness.

I have observed therapists go from white, aging Freud clones with ponytails and graying beards to nubile young white women with smart suits and tight butts. This may be due to the popularity of climb-inside-the-mind-of-a-killer forensic programs that have polluted the media over the years, beginning with *Silence of the Lambs*. Young girls must be glued to the set broadcasting *CSI* and other such creepy crap. I grew up with girls yearning to be Wonder Women, even Bionic Women; now we have to contend with Forensic Women. While one would hope that these ambitious young doctors would bring with them a compassionate and caring approach, I've found only the status quo, institutional incompetence, and overcompensation.

Sex is nonexistent in Creedmoor now thanks to new security cameras posted virtually everywhere, including in the corner ceiling of the visitor's rooms, feeding to monitors sitting behind the main nursing station for every Mahata to see.

"Show some restraint when in the new visitor's situation," Dr. Ramma suggests in my first treatment team meeting following the Bella scandal.

I hope Lily can keep it cool, which is hard for her. When she comes on it's hard for me as well. She's a gorgeous woman and any man would have difficulty keeping his hands off of her hot, wanting body.

Lily's visits used to relieve the tension of this hospitalization. They were like conjugal visits. The sex was great wherever we had it, whenever we had the chance, but ultimately it was cheap. We proclaimed our strong undying love but we were never alone long enough in a proper spot to make love. The best we did was have sex. Often we were just fucking, catching quickies here and there. Perhaps they're called quickies because it's the quickest way to lose a loved one if this is the only intercourse you and your partner engage in.

"Oh, baby, it's OK. We'll be all right. I love you. I'll never leave you,"

Lily promises. "Actually, I have to confess something. I have a fear that you will leave me." Hearing her say this is comforting but sad. By all laws of reason a young, beautiful girl like her shouldn't waste her life waiting indefinitely for some guy in the nut house. I find myself wondering not what makes me so special but instead what's wrong with her.

This poor girl is deep in love and has grabbed on for the long haul and I live it just day to day, letting fear overwhelm the beauty of what Lily is giving me every minute. I feel guilty for stringing this lovely angel along. Not that I lie to keep her, but I feel like she has manufactured her own lies and I feed into them. I am wracked with anxiety, waiting for the day when she'll say, "I have had enough." I've already endured several rounds of, "What am I doing with my life?"

As MY TREATMENT TEAM INDICATED, I have been re-diagnosed. No longer suffering from Drug Induced Psychosis, now I have a Psychotic Disorder, NOS (or Not Otherwise Specified, according to the psychiatrist's bible, the *Diagnostic Statistical Manual of Mental Disorders*). My new diagnosis NOS means that they don't know what is wrong with me . . . but there's definitely something wrong with me. I believe it is a convenient catchall.

It will be tough getting out of this hospital now. Everybody here knows my name, which isn't good when you're trying to exit quietly back into the community, especially after the terrible act that brought me here. I am considered "high profile," and not well liked to boot. The female Mahatas gossip and laugh about my predicament.

"I don't see it, I just don't see it," one of the sassier around-the-way girls says in her appraisal of me.

"Oh, I see it," another says, "and Issa may be fine, but he won't get me!" They treat me like some sort of sexual bogeyman.

My new ward therapist, Drew Chafe, a milquetoast Mr. Rogers type who sympathizes with me but also goes along with the flow, often validates my suspicions with his insider's insights. "Don't tell anybody I said this, keep this between you and me," he intimates, "but I believe that the administration, which you know is mostly women, have deep, subconscious, counter-transferential issues with you, in reaction to the offense you committed, most of them being mothers, having mothers, and then augmented, and for some really blown out of the frame, by the two female staff being fired following their romantic involvement with you."

Realizing how bleak it looks for me getting unbiased treatment in this hospital, Drew puts his finger up to his lips to shush me then pulls me close. Looking over both shoulders, like a henpecked husband accustomed to being listened in on and fearful of reprisals, he says, "If things don't lighten up for you in six months I suggest you get a private attorney and sue your way out."

The female administration, speaking through Chief Psychiatrist Dr. Ramma, like a vexed ventriloquist vomiting invectives through her dummy, believes that I am "manipulative, intimidating, have no insight into past behavior, display inappropriate behavior regarding staff and authority, and inappropriate behavior regarding women." They have now revised and formulated a treatment plan that will address these issues. This same treatment plan is purposely vague and nebulous regarding actual attainable treatment goals. Maybe that's because they know I can and will give them whatever they ask to achieve discharge. They are simply covering their asses, everyone signing off on means of treatment and feeling secure, while I languish in limbo.

36

ALWAYS GIVE RESPECT AND RECEIVE RESPECT and I gain rewards. It is the best the staff can do considering I've been locked up for many years. Some feel sorry for me losing my mind, my mom, and my family, then being stuck in the system and still not broken. Being assigned "the sick room," one of two single bedrooms where the physically infirm reside, was my consolation prize for surviving as long and as well as I have. However, after a good five-year run in "the sick room," it was inevitable that a sicker patient would come along and need it. My room goes to Stevens, a mellow dude who landed in a wheelchair after a drug-fueled shootout with NYPD. Because of the esteem they have for me, the staff does some clever rearranging and assigns me to the other available single room on the ward.

Getting adjusted to my new room takes work. It's much larger than the one I had for years, which is a plus, but I immediately miss my personal toilet, which was an impressive feature of the other sick room. It's a real drag having to rely on the ward bathrooms, which are often locked (to prevent unauthorized smoking after the hospital recently went smoke-free), and an unholy mess when they are open. Urine, feces, sputum, semen, and occasionally blood adorn the walls, floor, seats, and basins, all in a cornucopia of dank, standing water, with soggy paper towels and toilet tissue festooned about the place. Gnats dance around the drains. You have to assume the prowess of a circus acrobat or contortionist to navigate a safe and sanitary position above the bowl to do your business, wash your hands, and get out unsoiled. It is just what you'd imagine (and more) from a restroom in a madhouse.

Not only do I miss taking a clean, quiet, civilized dump, but I also utilized the private bathroom as a place where I could use my newly acquired cell phone without worrying about talking too loud and being detected. Lily snuck it to me, mainly because she is dissatisfied with never being able to reach me on the ward payphone. For that we must thank Pablo.

He, with his Mohican haircut and Hitler moustache, is a formerly twenty-years homeless man who was hospitalized in Creedmoor for defecating in a mailbox. A refugee from Cuba, Pablo's major delusion involves talking to Ronald Reagan and Fidel Castro on the telephone, acting as interpreter to keep world peace.

"Hola, Fidel? Listen, I no think you have to worry. Ronnie is a good guy."

"Sí. Sí, I know that he has the bomb."

"What's that, Ronnie?"

"Ai sí, I trust you but Fidel doesn't trust you."

"Qué?"

"You don't trust Fidel?"

"Put JFK on the line."

"Yeah, I'll hold."

Using no coins or calling cards, he simply swaggers up to the phone and punches in at least thirty numbers of indefinite combinations. Sometimes I think he's composing music with the dial tones. I'll walk by, waiting for my turn on the phone, while he is engaged in what appears to be a spirited and relevant bilingual conversation, only to hear the loud intermittent buzz that indicates a receiver is off the hook . . . and it *is* . . . and Pablo is still talk, talk, talking away. What makes it worse is that Pablo is too used to living and surviving on the street, so he will stand up for himself, get belligerent, and even come to blows if you balk at his phony phone calls. I find myself having to bribe him with chocolates to get him off the phone, but he always comes back, lips smeared with fudge, barking in his heavily accented, heavily medicated, slurred and broken English, "I need to talk to the president and save the World Trade Center."

The treatment team is aware that this is a major problem; calls can't come in and Pablo is terrorizing all who want to call out. The team has given up counseling him. He is unreachable by therapy or medication. The other thirty patients' rights are being violated, but the team simply says, "You have to remember where you are."

So I happily accepted Lily's gift of the cell phone. I am violating the rules of inpatients in the hospital, which determined with the ascendancy of the device that cell phones were forbidden because they could be used to compromise patient confidentiality. I believe the administrators are more afraid of the possibility of unprofessionalism in this place being broadcast to someone who might take exception and cause a little grief. I just want to call my people when I want, have them call me when convenient, and keep in touch with my lawyer without having to kiss Pablo's butt to do so.

I can understand the telephone becoming an instrument ripe with delusional and psychotic attachment. Here is this cheap, easily operated invention where you listen and talk to disembodied voices. They can be living or dead, real or imagined. If there are voices already in your head they can talk to the ones on the phone. In Pablo's case he has a three-way calling plan. Sometimes the front desk gets a call in from a relative complaining that the phone has been busy all day and they need to speak with their loved one. Then the staff is obligated to get Pablo off the phone. Thing of it is . . . it's a relative calling for Pablo.

The treatment teams of the past were much more proactive. With the threat of two hours in a straitjacket or a needle in your ass, it was much easier to maintain order. True, this uneasy reality created a situation where you were frightened into compliance; however, it also kept the monsters at bay, the bullies in check, and off-the-chain psychotics like Pablo off the phone. Nowadays, instead of the old, cold "Quiet Room," with nothing more than a bare, pissy mattress on the floor in the corner, they tout the "Time Out Room," with its comfy chairs, soothing piped-in music, and sunset murals as the more civilized way to subdue, decreasing mobilization codes, meds over objection, and restraint.

THE TICS AND TELLS OF MENTAL ILLNESS often out the sufferer. Due to my absolute lack of symptoms and an outgoing personality, the ravages of my disease aren't as apparent as in most of the hospital population. Often, when I'm not on the ward, staff who don't know me assume I am a colleague or a family member visiting a sick relative. This camouflage is helpful for attracting many women looking for a good time in the nut house, but inevitably the truth, and my locked down legal status, prevents these dalliances from being more than stolen kisses, hot quickies, and empty promises.

There are two clear earmarks of being a mental patient. One is having rotten teeth. Although there is great hygienic neglect in this community, the dental rot is mainly due to the medications and how the body reacts to them. Other side effects include annoying but relatively minor afflictions such as blurred vision, dry mouth, and increased thirst and appetite; the very serious and irreversible horror of tardive dyskinesia, a nervous system disorder characterized by permanent involuntary facial tics and body movements; nerve damage; organ failure; and death.

It must be said that most of these negative reactions are related to the older medications, engineered many decades ago, that tranquilized the patient, subduing the delusions and hallucinations while spreading out into other parts of the brain and nervous system, causing havoc on areas that didn't need to be disturbed. In recent years, newer psychotropic drugs have targeted specific areas of the brain, arresting the damage with reduced side effects and bringing hope to sufferers who were previously untouched by earlier drugs or the therapy that was administered. The down side of this is that after five or so years of consistent intake of these "wonder drugs," without the proper education of the patient about these medications and their relationship to diet, there is a likelihood of development of additional maladies such as diabetes and, strangely enough, Obsessive Compulsive Disorder. So it's pretty much a case of sticking with the devil you know rather than the devil you don't.

My teeth have always been a weak point for me—they're crooked, spaced, and have a slight patina. I haven't had the opportunity to have them fixed, as I would have liked. The dentists here at Creedmoor seem to get a bonus for each tooth pulled for all the aggressive yanking they propose whenever they look into your mouth. Knowing how bad the dental rot is in these hospitals I don't envy the dentists one bit. At the very least I have taken to a twice-daily regimen of attentive brushing and flossing, the latter being done on the sly because floss is classified as contraband and thus not allowed. It is sad that something so essential to good dental health is suspect and banned, probably to prevent someone from hanging themselves, or someone else, from their molars. Lily is even more vigilant than I am about her dental hygiene, due to a slight bout of gum disease brought on by her meds a while back. She always slips me a box of floss when I am running low. So in the fight against poor dentistry and drug-induced decay I am doing the best I can.

The other sure sign of being a Creedmoorian is your bad haircut. You have only two choices: let it grow wild or take your chances with an institution barber. Either choice is a bad decision.

Of course, you'll look mad and unkempt if your hair goes unattended, which is troublesome if you are a person of color with kinky hair. However, in my many years inside I can count on one hand the number of decent cuts I've received. It was bad at first, in the early 1990s when I was still playing out the '80s, asking for high-top fades and walking away looking like a devotee of Kid 'N Play or Bello Nock the circus clown. I felt that as an artist I could carry this embarrassment off, and maybe I did for a while, but ultimately I was unhappy and felt stupid. The only alternative to a custom cut is the baldy. You see a lot of these in the nut house. If you are trying to come off looking healthy and nonpsychotic the baldy does not help. It was inevitable that I would inquire about the process and practicality of getting dreadlocks done, seeing the style more and more on the young black Mahatas.

It took two attempts to get it right. The first lady I visited, on a secret trip into the community with Gaia, did a cock-up job and charged me fifty bucks only to have me walk away looking like Farina from the Little Rascals, with nappy knots wrapped in rubber bands. The second time, I snuck out under the auspices of attending off-ward programming and went alone, serviced by a gay guy working out of a nice little shop on Jamaica Avenue. He blended fake hair into mine, twisting it into a stylish dreadlock Moe Howard mop top. Yes, I had a weave.

I like how my real hair eventually grows in, giving me a Beatle-'do that is immortalized on my driver's ID, after another unauthorized jaunt allowed me to reactivate my license. This trip gave me a greater sense of accomplishment and self-worth. You'll never know how having a decent wallet with proper ID and active credit cards elevates your self-esteem until you find yourself with nothing but loose change, an expired condom, and a whole lot of lint in your pocket.

The dreads were a good look, giving me a hip, youthful, sexy vibe. However, I cut them off myself following my last restriction. Knowing a court date was inevitable, I did not wish to turn off the judge by sauntering in all Rasta'd out, especially with the heavy marijuana component to my case. I'm sure my dreads would be way down my back by now, but the pragmatist within me would probably still want to be shorn and clean for any future court appearances.

So, for the last few years I've had to rely on the tonsorial expertise of a succession of Delilahs and Sweeny Todds. I find myself contemplating my last cut by the new barber here. The job was done by a very pleasant young sister who is attractive . . . if you don't notice her cockeyes, which apparently doesn't help her perform an even cut. Still, she was so nice, and her barber chat was so uplifting, that I walked away thanking her for her time and talent then adjourned to my room to select a brim from my collection of hats to hide the dreadful 'do.

As bad as our new sight-challenged barber may be, she cannot compare in ineptitude to the one who occasionally subs for her. The Reverend, as he prefers to be called, is a doddering senior who only gives old-fashioned haircuts. When I suggest a faded short back and sides, perhaps the only look that compliments my angular features, the Reverend nixes that request and starts picking my hair blowout style. He ends up giving me, and all else, cuts that he probably calls "the Shaft," "the Superfly," or, if it is a baldy, "the Isaac Hayes." If that isn't enough he begins each session, just after wrapping me in the smock and paper clipping the toilet tissue around my neck, with the enigmatic loaded question, "Do you believe in Jesus?"

After seeing the hatchet jobs given to the preceding nonbelievers I always settle in and answer, "Hallelujah!" in the hopes of coming away with something not too devastating. Even with my feigned zealotry I am usually not so lucky.

LILY AND GAIA HAVE WORDS and then a meeting of the minds. They see I am in a very bad position and could benefit from their united kindness. Gaia prepares care packages of several days' worth of home-cooked food stored in Tupperware, pastries, and cans of Arizona Iced Tea. Lily drops them off during midweek visits. "She and I have become good friends," Gaia says, "something we both need. I've got an adopted daughter now, and she has a surrogate mom."

When not doting on me they go for long drives, take in a movie, or go shopping. I'm happy for them and pleased I was able to bring them together. They are the crux of a strong outside network that I am building for myself, however illegitimate it may be.

37

WHILE I'M HOUSED AT RIKERS waiting for my final court appearance and sentencing, Mike O'Connor, my court-appointed lawyer, has arranged a deal with the district attorney's office. Based on what the DA calls my "credible remorse," the accidental nature of the crime, psychiatric circumstances, and various tests and corroborating reports from two psychiatrists, I am allowed to enter a plea of Not Responsible by Reason of Mental Disease or Defect.

On the phone during my slot time the day before my court date O'Connor says, "OK, to be clear, it's the insanity plea. And it's an indeterminate commitment. The initial charge of second degree murder carried a sentence of twenty-five to life. If you take this deal and make the plea you will not go to prison. It's not a conviction: it's an acquittal. And you won't have a record. You'll go to a hospital. You will get the help that you need, and it's a better deal than going to prison. If you don't accept the plea of not responsible, the DA is offering a plea of manslaughter. Now just know that if you take that manslaughter plea it will be a conviction. And you will go to a penitentiary upstate. The sentencing is for five to fifteen years, with one year deducted for time served. And the DA says if you accept the manslaughter plea bargain you may only end up doing four years, if you get paroled the first time up. But it's still a conviction. It's still prison."

"Maybe that's where I belong. I feel guilty, Mike. And I hate myself. My family hates me."

"Look, as much as you hate yourself for what you did, I know, based on all the evidence and my sense of you, that you didn't mean to do it, that it was an accident, that you were not in your right mind, and that you are not a criminal. So take the plea. Take the hospital."

"OK, Mike, OK."

I go to court in a fine pair of khaki slacks, a smart blue button-down shirt, and a pair of tennis shoes that Clu gave me especially for this day. Common in quality western footwear, metal shanks were seen in the soles of my boots during an X-ray and the fine cowboy boots that I was arrested in a year ago were confiscated and now held in property. In the Rikers bullpen I found a discarded, dirty leather bomber jacket and donned it to protect me from the cold. I am uncomfortable with the manacles I wear and the insistent feeling of tiny legs crawling on my body. One particularly astute suspect I am shackled to in the criminal conga line suggests, "Yo, CO, make sure those irons are on tight. Homeboy looks bugged out."

I daydream the whole bus ride from Rikers Island to the Kew Gardens, Queens, Supreme Criminal Courthouse. Passing through familiar streets, I recall long drives and happier times when my late father confided in me during boyhood errands to visit his girlfriends.

"Before I met your mother, son, I met this other lady. Janice. We got married just after I moved up here. But she couldn't have children. All I wanted was a decent woman and three boys. When this didn't happen after five years of foolishness, arguing, and cheating, we separated. I couldn't pay alimony, got arrested, and went to jail. There is no sadder, discouraging experience than looking out onto the streets from that caged bus going from the detention center to court." I find out just what my father meant by that.

In the dark, dirty, crowded bullpen in the bowels of the court building, I meet with Mike O'Connor. He quickly runs through the finer points of accepting the plea. "So you're positive you want to accept? I mean, we've got to be on the same page here. 'Cuz once we get in there before the judge there's no taking it back, OK?"

"OK, yeah. I understand."

O'Connor leans forward, pushing his meaty pink face between the bars, and asks, "Do you trust me?"

"Huh?"

"Do you trust me?"

Looking at him, Mike O'Connor resembles a shaved mole in an expensive suit, but otherwise he appears honest. "Yeah, I trust you."

"Good," he says, punctuating with a rap on his briefcase. "'Cuz I got you a good deal. The Queens DA doesn't agree to this plea too often anymore. And if you stay on your meds and stay out of trouble you should be all right."

In the courtroom before the judge, I am asked to plead. Recount my version of events and admit my culpability. I mention the voices, the possession, and the threat to the black race, realizing as this slips from my lips that I am now more than anything an embarrassment to the black race. I start to ramble, intimating invasions of aliens and the presence of vampires. The court officer flanking my right brings his fingers up to broach a slight and comical cross while whispering, "Nanu Nanu." This amuses his colleague. What the judge has to hear is my confession, my admission of guilt.

Judge Leahy, an ancient, white-haired Caucasian, peers over his bifocals and waves me off, indicating he's heard enough. I find myself trailing off to a squeak, uttering, "I didn't mean to hurt her."

The judge hands down his compliance with the not responsible plea and orders me into the care of the Office of Mental Health and Hygiene. I am to be sent back to Rikers until the transfer to a hospital goes through. It is finally here. What I asked for: "The Hospital."

Now that it is imminent I wonder what I've gotten myself into. I remember my short stay at Kings County Hospital in Brooklyn. Yes, the food was good but I was surrounded by very sick, filthy, and often dangerous people. Now I don't look forward to going to this "Hospital." But I do want to get out of Rikers.

Back in the bullpen after my appearance, O'Connor informs me, "As a formality you will be committed to Mid-Hudson Psychiatric Center."

The other detainees, who make no pretense of eavesdropping, laugh and say, "Aw shit, you's lucky, bro. You goin' to Club Med. I want that dude as *my* lawyer!"

"After that, if you're doing well, they'll send you to a less secure civil hospital. Probably Creedmoor," O'Connor says. "You shouldn't have to spend more than a couple of years in a hospital."

All of us insanity plea patients across the country meet the same legal definition of insanity: that at the time of the commission of the crime, we did not appreciate the nature or quality of wrongfulness of the acts.

There was tremendous public outcry when John Hinckley Jr., driven by an obsessional fixation on actress Jodie Foster, was found not guilty by reason of insanity in 1982 for the attempted assassination of President Ronald Reagan. Though he now goes out on furloughs he still resides in a mental hospital in Washington, DC. Reagan called for total abolition of the insanity defense but was talked down by his administration after intense lobbying by various professional organizations and trade associations. Idaho, Kansas, Montana, and Utah abolished the defense completely.

Lorena Bobbitt famously severed her husband's penis after enduring years of rapes and physical and emotional abuse. She was found not guilty by reason of temporary insanity and spent five weeks in a Virginia state mental hospital. Texas mother Andrea Yates drowned her five children and was initially convicted, but her conviction was overturned in retrial in favor of an insanity plea in 2006.

There are plenty of people out there who are delusional and others who hear voices. These people do not meet the legal criteria for hospitalization: being a danger to self or others. Fewer still commit crimes while impaired, thus having to consider the option of an insanity defense. Now, joining this exclusive club, I recall Groucho Marx's famous quote, "I don't want to belong to any club that will accept people like me as a member."

I AM TRANSFERRED from the Mental Observation Unit and housed in a dark, dank unit in Rikers for inmates who are sentenced or have copped a plea and are now ready to move on upstate to officially do their time. Jake, a small, older, slick pimp who likes to watch me in the communal shower was recently convicted and sentenced to ten years for beating one of his hos.

"Sharday had to learn the hard way," he jokes, without shame. "She was rippin' me off and, well, there you go. I know it ain't cool to hit a woman, but you don't fuck with a man's pocket!"

Since he'll be leaving soon he was nice enough to give me his Walkman, which gets me through some long cold nights. Although I never say who the victim was, when I tell him in confidence that I just received the insanity plea behind a homicide, he displays a wide, gilded, shark's toothed smile, saying, "Oh man, you just won the Oscar, baby." This makes me feel sick.

38

OCTOBER 1989. I quit my job. Between juggling mounting mana-
gerial duties and grandiose dreams of art stardom, constantly high
on marijuana, something has to give. Knowing I can now sleep late, I
continue my romance with reefer. Seeking release, avoiding my mother,
and ignoring my nephew, I light up. I am liberated as my troubles and
mind fly to some distant place. Grabbing my Walkman, I fish for a favorite tape, insert it, and am again in a blissful musical state of nonreality.

Although Mom is in the rear, downstairs bedroom, and if awake
would surely hear the noise, I am not deterred. Nor do I have a care
for my teenage nephew Jason, studying in his room amid my madness.
I run in the back once more to take another long drag and then dance
deliriously into the hall and front bedroom like a whirling dervish,
freaking out for almost two hours. By 2 AM I am spent. Lying in bed,
chewing stale Entenmann's chocolate chip cookies, I tune into the TV
news. The top story is a major earthquake that has eaten up parts of
the Bay Area in San Francisco.

Rapt by dramatic footage in heavy rotation of cars disappearing
into gaping holes in highways, toppled buildings, and saucer-eyed,
traumatized residents searching for relatives and shelter, I think of my
sister Carol. She moved this past summer with her children out to
Oakland, neighboring the devastation. Carol crammed herself and her
four children in our rear upstairs bedroom for a spell earlier this year,
running from the spoils of her second marriage and an obsessive/
abusive ex-husband. She left New York for a new start and a better job
prospect in nursing, bravely going it alone with her kids in tow. Her
departure came earlier than expected. In doing so she stiffs me out of a

much-talked-about cross-country drive. "I don't want any more of this crack madness," she says, the evening before she leaves. "It's bumming my high."

I contemplate calling about her safety but overwhelming shame and embarrassment about my strange behavior when I visited her in July keep me from doing so. Instead I lie here, an exhausted, smoked-out mess, watching the flickering light as I doze off to the sound of Hendrix's "The Wind Cries Mary." While sleeping my answering machine records two desperate messages left by my sister urging me to get in touch with her. I don't return these calls.

When I wake again I am astonished to discover I've slept through a day set aside for job interviews and well into the next. Such negligence would never occur before but now it is routine. The reefer makes my dreaming feel like I'm dead . . . except I wake up, and I want to smoke again.

Stumbling out of bed, I peek in on my nephew, doing his homework in the room next to mine. "Hey, Jase. Wassup?"

Jason has a look on his face that chides, *You're in trouble*. I know he's right when I hear the door leading to the upstairs apartment creak open and Mom walk slowly up the stairs. I haven't been downstairs to see her for several days. I feel guilty and want to make up for it but there is no time for that now. Mom looks worried, tired, and small in her beige and white sequined caftan.

"Carol's all right," she says without being asked. "She and the kids were on the highway when the earthquake hit but they're all right."

"Were they scared?"

"Of course! Wouldn't *you* be?" Mom screams. "You should call her, let her know you were worried about her and the kids."

"I know, I know." I then confess receiving the two messages but Mom cuts me off. "You should call her, son. You see, I *knew* something like this would happen," she warns. "I know I'm not going out there now. Regardless of how good Carol makes it sound. Not even to visit, not to live with no earthquakes! I'm going to stay right here, where the ground is safe. The ground our house and yard is sitting on is sacred, boys."

Mom goes easily into this tale. It's one I've heard her tell many times since I was a child. As always it is stately and spooky, a real noble ghost story. Her voice gets hushed and all that is needed is a campfire and a flashlight underneath her chin.

"You know, more than one hundred years ago there used to be a stream running through what is now our backyard, and the Indians, in their travels, would bring their horses to the stream to drink. Since I've been here the neighbors would sometimes say they heard hoof steps, or even seen the ghosts of braves on horses slowly tracking through the park beyond the backyard. I've never seen them, but I feel them. Remember, we're protected! With the spirits of dead Indians around us there's nothing bad that can happen to us."

Escorting Mom downstairs, she sees that something is not right with me. With a little coaxing from her I finally come clean about my excessive pot use, repeated errors at work labeled as "incompetence," and what I saw as no other choice but to resign from my position as assistant manager at Sam Goody's.

"Oh no, Iss! Oh, I'm so sorry, son. And you were there for so long, doing so well. Well, don't worry. You'll find something better. I'm positive you will rebound in no time." I believe she is being positive to keep me from getting discouraged and lazy. I know she doesn't want another unemployed freeloading son under her roof.

I feel so relieved confessing my joblessness to Mom that I decide to confess my fears as well. Sitting in the jungle-decor living room, with Mom working on a colorful quilt, I drop a major bomb. "Ya know, Ma, I'm not feeling well but it's worse than you think."

I want to tell Mom that I doubt the reality of my surroundings, about the plots I believe to be going on, how the English language is being subverted, and about the seemingly millions of other things that I think are happening but probably aren't. I want to tell Mom that I think I am going insane.

"Ma, I think the problem is mental . . . I don't know what it is really but I've been real stressed lately and it may be affecting me mentally." I see in her face that I've told her something she doesn't want to hear.

"Oh no! Not mental! Please don't let it be mental!" she screams. She doesn't want to believe that her baby has more than just a scrape on his knee, something that will heal and go away. This is a typical reaction in most African American homes—denial of mental illness.

Suspicions of mental health professionals, and American health care in general, prevent many African Americans from accessing appropriate care due to prior experiences with culture biases, historical misdiagnoses, and inadequate treatment. Mental illness is frequently stigmatized and misunderstood in the African American community.

Most black families with a relative suffering from mental illness will stick them in a back room or the basement. They'll feed and clothe them and let them mumble and shout and smoke to their heart's content so long as they stay in the house and don't embarrass the rest of the family. With the advent of crack and superpowered marijuana, more and more blacks are flipping out, uncontrollably so, and the hitherto unspoken option of hospitalization is becoming a reality. I know nothing about hospitals and the elusive concept of seeking professional help. I hope Mom will know what to do.

"Do you want me to put some healing oil on your head?" she asks, getting up from her quilting, heading to her stash of cures. I hesitate. Mom grows insistent. "Come on, let me put some healing oil on your head. I'll rub it into your scalp and it will take the sickness away."

Mom believes in her herbs, ointments, and healing oils. She has always displayed shamanistic qualities from way back. At this point I would have let her rub fresh horseshit into my head if she said it would help. I am desperate for a cure for my odd thoughts and suspicions. If Mom thinks healing oil will alleviate my strange mental irregularities then I am with it.

I haven't been this close to Mom in a long while, too long. Here I lie, my head resting on a towel in her lap, as she massages the oil into my hair and scalp while soothing me with loving affirmations. The balm in its bottle resembles olive oil and it has a slightly mentholated scent to it. I expect it to tingle on my scalp as it did in my senses but

I do not get that. What I get is closeness with Mom at a time where I had felt alone with guilt and fear and self-doubt.

As the oil on my scalp softens and slackens my hair, so go the past few months of illness, bizarre behavior, and standoffishness. "I love you, Ma," I cry, with my head in Mom's lap and tears in my eyes.

"Oh, Iss, I know. I love you too. It's been painful for me, and lonely after Dad's death."

"I know, Ma. I'm sorry. For ignoring you, neglecting you."

"It's OK, son. It's been a bad time for all of us. But it'll pass."

I'm not the least bit ashamed or embarrassed to cry, or have Mom rub healing oil into my head. In fact, I want it. I want more than anything for her to understand my sickness and help me get better.

"I can take you to Sister Epiphany if you like, son. She can take just one look at you and tell if there's something wrong," Mom says as she worms the oil through my hair, deeper into my scalp.

Sister Epiphany is one of many faith healers Mom has befriended through her favorite herbs and powders store in Brooklyn. The two swap recipes, antidotes, and cures. I would have preferred a medical doctor but this suggestion is better than nothing. I agree to go and Mom says she will make an appointment for the coming week.

But we never go to see Sister Epiphany—or any other doctor, for that matter.

39

I CAN ONLY ATTEND THE LIVING MUSEUM during weekday mornings, from 9:30 till 11:30 AM. No longer doing figurative oil paintings—visceral images have been deemed "inappropriate" and grounds for censure and possible re-diagnosis—I move further away from standard painting to abstraction and conceptualism via monochromatic body prints.

The first morning is dedicated to canvas prep, the following morning a commitment to the painting of the body and the image press. I complete a series of large-scale life-sized paintings in which I abandon the traditional artist's tools and use my body as a brush. It's very liberating and cleansing . . . until the cleanup, that is. I am fortunate to have my studio in the very rear of the mammoth space where, when done, I walk nude, undetected, to a nearby lavatory with a slop sink big enough to stand in and wash the latex and acrylic paint off my body.

These black and white body prints, depicting the figure of a man trapped in various painful states of arrest, are all I can do artistically without scrutiny from those who are looking for excuses to keep me locked up. They are much more cathartic than my regular paintings. They are transformative. I call the series *Body and Soul*. I am making a personal statement about race polarization, the dissonance within myself as a product of a multiracial home, as well as providing commentary on life as a black man in a white American mental institution.

My body prints are eerily reminiscent of the 1970s work of black installation artist David Hammons, even though I had never heard of him before Dr. Marton pointed out the striking similarities. "Very good, Issa," the doctor enthuses, "this is like conceptual outsider art."

The outsider art boom is growing in the 1990s, and while even the

Living Museum trucks in this and I marketed myself for that genre in my initial artistic emergence, I don't feel my work truly fits that mold. My output is not obsessive, naïve, primitive, psychotic, or produced by an old, frail sharecropper, as is usually expected from the artists tagged with the label. Many outsider art collectors troll the nursing homes, mental hospitals, and dilapidated shacks of the rural south for next month's flavor, largely in the hopes that the artist has died without a will or surviving family member smart enough to muscle in on them and stop them from cashing in big time. While I am black and virtually self-taught I don't downplay my attendance at an art high school or my brief stints at the School of Visual Arts and the Art Students League. I am also a native New Yorker with a hint of savvy and a firm grasp on conceptual and political constructs, rendering the cliché of the sheltered daydreamer in a world of his own inapplicable and slightly offensive. Especially since this is the only way I am marketable in conjunction with my race, my psychiatric history, and following the narrow trail blazed by upmarket art star and fame casualty Jean-Michel Basquiat.

The Living Museum provides a vital outlet to express myself without limits or censorship, unlike when I'm painting on the ward, where confiscation and re-diagnosis is the ever-present reality. And staying close to Dr. Marton and the various volunteers and visitors allows me to keep current, informed, and relevant in my own work. It is by far the best thing for me, even though my treatment team wants to limit my time there. They say, "It feeds your narcissism."

I AM BEING FEATURED in an HBO-financed documentary feature film about the Living Museum by hot young filmmaker Jessica Yu. During a year's worth of initial filming the budget seems small, craft services consisting of deli sandwiches and Chinese takeout. However, midway through production, after Jessica wins an Academy Award for Best Documentary Short for her previous film, HBO showers the Living Museum project with money, comely interns, and sumptuous lunches that grow more opulent with each day's shooting.

It's strange to sit in my bedroom, on my ward in a mental hospital, and have Hollywood people film me. While I sit tapping on my laptop I hear them whisper about which shot will be best for whichever purpose, yet I am still essentially a prisoner—if not of the system then certainly of my own terrible misdeeds. I find myself having to act for them, like a successful artist, like a man at peace with himself. Neither feels quite right.

Will I be helping myself by participating in this project? Are there any significant gains in opening the family wound that is Issa Ibrahim for it to leak upon and stain the public? Will I forever be known as that crazy nigger who confesses his sins three times a week on HBO? Do I deserve any better? It has become clear to me how poorly regarded I am by the powers that be behind these gates, but will there be higher gates I'll have to scale to escape public opinion?

Aware that the film is nearing completion, I draft a letter to the film's legal department, requesting they omit any mention of my family or intimate details of my offense in my portion of the Living Museum documentary. Jessica honors my request and I feel safe again, secure that compromising information about my case won't be released to the public to be used against me. Like the schoolyard, some of Creedmoor's patients and staff can be cruel. While I firmly believe that full disclosure helps me heal and may help others, now is not the time.

BARRY NEWFELD PREPARES A CASE contesting the hospital's application to the courts for another two-year retention. The hospital fights it, their reasoning being that I still suffer from a mental illness that requires inpatient care. In my forensic committee meeting, they announce, "The old order is up in a month . . . and you're obviously not going to be discharged in a month so we go for two more years, yes?" It is a formality but one which they approach like a victory. Then they look at me collectively, with their cold, captor's eyes. I am nervous, helpless, and drained.

"How do you feel about that?" they ask. I hate that more than any of the standard devices they employ here because it does not matter what I, as a patient, really feel about any of the decisions they, as caregivers, make. If anything that question is merely a ploy to get the patient to open up, speak his or her mind, and show a "lack of insight" by disagreeing with what the caregivers believe is the best thing.

I have come to understand why the DA in my court case was so adamant and persuasive, according to my public defender Mike O'Connor, in trying to get me to plea to a reduced charge of manslaughter instead of the insanity plea back in 1991. It seems my plea is considered a defeat for the district attorney's office. A black mark on a long record of convictions that hints that a criminal is "getting away with it," in addition to a potential career embarrassment that they would have to explain to the public and their constituents were that prosecutor to entertain future political aspirations. But getting the insanity plea is by no means getting away with anything. Though you avoid prison, at least there you have a definite release date. Involuntary commitment to a psychiatric hospital behind the plea is a potential life sentence. I've seen aged, broken-down insanity plea patients die in here. Some committed violent crimes and were in remission from their illness for decades but never mastered the art of acquiescence and kissing ass. Others committed minor offenses but never got their mind right, became institutionalized, and got comfortable in captivity.

That said I consider myself very fortunate to have received the plea, as I am sure there are plenty of brothers in prison who got psychotic on drugs and committed a crime, some as serious as homicide, who are doing hard time bugged out in solitary confinement. "Not too many people get the plea in Queens County," Barry told me in one of our first meetings, "and beyond that definitely not many black defendants. You are a scintilla of a sliver of a slice of the whole pie that is the criminal justice system."

By law the courts require at least two psychiatrists to agree that the defendant was insane at the time of the offense and didn't know the difference between right and wrong. It will also take at least two psychiatrists to agree on a patient's improved mental health and absence of dangerous thoughts, impulses, or behaviors to persuade the courts that an insanity plea patient is ready to be released. The burden of proof is on the doctors and the patient to convince a judge or jury that he is no longer insane. Without the hospital's support, and with all the junk in my chart, I realize that my attempts at achieving discharge are Sisyphean. I struggle to get to the height where I can gaze at freedom, only to tumble back into darkness again and again.

40

I T'S FEBRUARY AGAIN AND I'M FEELING MISERABLE. I put up the front like I want help, which I do, but I'm jaded. I'm not really getting the best help in Creedmoor. The programming is atrocious. The groups, when they do run, are more like mandatory time wasters where they talk at you but avoid real contact. The professionals should teach by example but all they demonstrate is apathy and burnt-out indifference. And most of the Mahatas appear to be loafers, opportunists, and coldblooded gangsters on the sneak tip. I know the system is faulty, and at times detrimental to some trapped up in it, but I still naively believe it will work if you work with it. So far it isn't effective, and that's frightening.

Slapped with retention, I have no one to confide in. Feeling alone and afraid, I am quick to buy in to the naysaying of Angel and Yucifer. They are the mental health Mutt and Jeff. They say, "You'll never leave Creedmoor."

Yucifer is a towering, lop-gaited bear of a man who pled insanity after stabbing a diplomat on the steps of the UN. I know him vaguely through noncommittal nods we shared in Mid-Hudson, as I was escorted to art rehab and he was on his way to an upholstery workshop. He arrived at Creedmoor just months before me. He claims to associate with the devil, even introduces himself as such, while dropping Muslim doctrines in fluent Arabic. He is presumed menacing and induces great fear in the ward staff for his slow strolling, tongue rolling, and popped eyes, which protrude out of his black skin like lidded golf balls. Even with those off-putting physical tics, I know Yucifer as an extremely intelligent and sensitive guy. He's the Building 40 chess champ (staff included) and has a filibuster ability that would rival many in Washington. He also has a poly-substance addiction that would rival many others who are presently deceased. I have seen him down fifths of straight rum, joint after joint of marijuana, chase that with crack, and even shoot up heroin, all in one day.

Angel, his partner in crime, is five foot nothing with the pencil-thin moustache and dramatically bowed legs of a western desperado. He lived all his life in Spanish Harlem until his heroin addiction drove him to madness and mayhem, murdering his girlfriend and her mother some fifteen years ago. He possesses the most evil eyes I think I've ever seen, redder and deader than Christopher Lee's Dracula, thanks largely to the whiskey, weed, and horse he devours in a round robin of wanton abuse.

Like Bayou next door, they inspire fear, respect, and need in the other addicts on and off the ward. I'm surprised I fell in so quickly with them. I believe it was due in part to the lack of coherent conversation found on the ward. I'm not a bug out, and they determined I'm not a threat, thus I am all right. We were also all insanity plea patients. We confide in each other, we look out for each other. We pool our weekly eight dollar personal needs allowance to order in Chinese food, though they are always loaded, and I front them quarters for the phone, though they usually use it to call their connection.

Yucifer and Angel control an impenetrable drug operation from 6-B. It is invincible because the staff makes it possible to continue and flourish. Many Mahatas act as moles, lookouts, and even suppliers of the dope that the two patients sell. Some of the Mahatas conduct their own business as couriers and pushers to patients who can afford their inflated prices for speedy, reliable service and discretion. For thirty or forty bucks you can score a small bottle, or a dime bag of weed, or two fives of crack. The extra vig is the price of convenience and silence.

When out of depressed desperation I feel the itch to smoke again, Yucifer fronts me a joint gratis. While high I get loose and cocky, giving them the laugh of their lives when I tell them the amount of time I believe I'll spend in Creedmoor. With thirty years between them, my estimate of "two to three more years tops" is met first with incredulous stares, shaking heads, and then uproarious laughter.

"Drugs, a fatality, *and* gettin' caught fuckin' the staff? Yeah. Y'know, you may get out sooner than that," Angel crows before nodding out.

When given the cold facts from the other insanity plea patients as well as Barry Newfeld on New York State's excruciatingly slow handling of my type of pariah, I see no alternative but to give up hope and resort to the dope I used to use and used to be. The staff knows I am getting high. They just turn a blind eye (and stuffy nose), much like they do with Angel, Yucifer, and others who cop and use on the wards. So long as I don't do it right in front of them, show them a modicum of respect, and of course don't bug out, I am safe to do whatever I want.

41

SUBSPEAK. This is the emerging new language, introduced to me this summer and revving up these past three months, set to be the pre-eminent mode of speech just in time for 1990. It is spoken as often as contemporary English and it's something that I just cannot comprehend.

Subspeak is a concurrent conversation, a differentiation of what is said and what is meant, a means of using the subtle nuances of syntax in your speech to intimate more than the obvious, the art of entendre, ambiguous wordplay. If you master this, the entire lexicon is at your command. The simplest statements take on deeper meanings and the more adept you are, the more fun you can have. Someone well versed in the form can effortlessly communicate intense sexual desires to another party and receive indications likewise, and all within the context of something as mundane as ordering lunch.

On an autumn evening out in the city with acquaintance and Lower East Side celebrity Handsome Dick Manitoba, I discover my difficulty with language and comprehension becoming worse. I try to keep up with Manitoba's conversation but always lose my focus. He starts looking annoyed as he tries walking me through the basics of social bullshitting, only to have me drop off time and time again. It is sad to sit where I am, engaging Manitoba in topics worthwhile and interesting only to make an inexplicable left turn and watch his expression quickly change into one of boredom. Most interesting to talk about is Manitoba's five years of sobriety from heroin. He spares me the details of his infamous addiction, only to say, "I'm glad to be off the junk. My anniversary is coming up this Halloween."

"Ya know, I also wanna go straight," I confess. "I gotta stop smoking marijuana. I think it's really fucking with me."

"You just have to tell yourself you don't want to do it anymore. Pot, horse, no matter what it is. It helps when you see that you may self-destruct if you don't. Hopefully you won't go too far before you realize this."

The conversation slows to silence when left too long in my hands, littered with false starts and unpredictable fade-outs, like a bad concept album. My uneasiness in this Second Avenue pub makes me inadequate in areas where I don't have to be. To make matters worse I am being eyed by two young white women down the bar, trying to get my attention. They appear to be European.

"Go ahead, kid," Dick encourages upon seeing their interest, "make me proud."

Manitoba ducks away to talk with friends at a nearby table, leaving the women giggling and raising their eyebrows suggestively. I feel pressured to act on this; with Manitoba so close and knowing I am on the spot, I have to prove myself as a young black stud. After polite smiling back and forth, just to reassure my belief that they are indeed interested, I rise to the occasion. Using no pick-up lines or smooth dialogue, I am simply myself. Bad move, considering I am a graceless poser. I am greeted with giggles as I say hello.

"So, what would you ladies like?"

"Hot chocolate," they reply in unison, even though I notice they're nursing margaritas. This is a covert signal to me indicating what they want—a hot-blooded, black to the core, African American male. All that I have come to believe I am not. Stumbling and pausing a moment too long with a pale and nervous face following their very telling request, it is obvious to them that I am not the one for tonight. But how were they to know I was a dud? I certainly look the part of a hip, young, black cocksman, in my snakeskin boots, denim, and leather. But faced with subspoken signals and the *true* language of love I am inept. Manitoba sees the uncomfortable *"Get this jerk outta here"* looks on the young women's faces. They are politely tolerant but I can tell they hope for something, *anything*, better than this.

Subspeak is also a useful tool for an attack on another person's character or weaknesses. This is where it is most dangerous for me. I am not prepared to combat the barrage of seemingly harmless words and phrases tossed at me from all sides. This is the only way people can tell if you are truly in tune or not. Male or female, black or white, young or old—subspeak ability is the yardstick by which all people are measured, and I am not measuring up.

I am suffering a major breakdown. I am frozen with inertia, fueled by fear. Fear of riding the bus and train, feeling exposed and shunned as an antique in cool clothing. Fear of walking the city streets only to be scorned as a zombie, for surely I wore the scent of a jobless cretin like a foul stench. Though I try gaining employment as an artist doing paste up/mechanical work in various small design firms, after a while I resort to the old standby—record store employee, rack jobber, only in a different locale.

Most of my unhappiness at Sam Goody's involved their staunch, sticks-in-their-asses approach to selling records. I mean, fuck the tie, apron, and name tag that is a required part of the company's uniform. Give me print shirt, jeans, and blue suede shoes! Tower Records in the East Village seems like it would suit me just fine. Tower's people have the right look and attitude. Who cares if most of them don't know their assholes from the hole in the middle of a record. The fact that I do makes my prospects brighter, not to mention my closet full of clothes that identify me as a downtown dandy.

Unfortunately, Tower won't match my pay grade or honor my tenure as an assistant manager at Sam Goody's, meaning I will have to climb the ladder again. When I try to talk my way into an enviable position with the hiring managers, subspeak rears its ugly head.

"We got plenty of managers, assistants, and trainees in the pop and R&B departments. There's no way you're gonna muscle into that. Maybe you belong downstairs with the classical LPs. Whadaya think?"

In the new language, as it insinuates itself today, I am a classical LP, stale and old-fashioned. Not at all like modern pop, R&B, or even a new age CD, as one employee boasts of himself in a phone conversation that I overhear and am distracted by. Before embarrassing myself any further I bolt from Tower's hiring office, never to return.

My last few stops are the Lower Manhattan vinyl dungeons.

Assuming these obsolete hovels are run by aging hippies not so hung up on references, ties, name tags, looks, or attitude, I discover they are run by said hippies' sons, looking to turn a buck on a small but still profitable business.

While doing an obligatory trial run on the sales floor, one owner and his snarky staff field customers eager to use this future-is-now form of communication my way to everyone's amusement, everyone except me. The one LP that seems to be requested by every customer who approaches is Rodney Dangerfield's *I Don't Get No Respect*. It appears all of New York has come into the store to tell me about myself. I am wrong to think my years of experience in the industry and encyclopedic knowledge of music will put me a few notches above the common slug creeping in looking for a job. In the end, all that matters is how well you dodge subtle barbs while wrapping your tongue around key subspoken phrases.

What disturbs me most is the undercurrent of racial prejudice that I encounter in practically every job I interview for. It is often a disappointed or contemptuous look cast by the interviewer upon seeing I am black. On many occasions, in the middle of conversation, certain subtle slurs are introduced to throw me off guard. Out of nowhere "cotton" and "Tom" will cough out of the interviewer's mouth, as if to accentuate some crucial point. The point is driven home that I am a nigger looking for acceptance in the white man's world. What's worse, I am looked upon as a Tom. I never thought my articulation, congeniality, and can-do attitude in interviews equated to Uncle Tomming. Should I go into these interviews brooding and militant? As a result of these off-putting interviews I wind up feeling intimidated at job prospects conducted by Caucasians. I am disappointed, believing that the system has won its battle with another starry-eyed but ultimately unrealistic young black American man.

42

THE UPSTAIRS BEDROOMS AND KITCHENETTE AREA, which I use as my art studio, are littered with wrinkled clothes, scattered LPs out of their sleeves, stacks of cassette tapes, dirty dishes, art supplies, newspapers, magazines, and junk food wrappers, all lying atop untouched drawing paper and canvas. I used to get high and play music to work myself into a creative mood. I'd even concede that initially it was helpful. Now, though, the art has not only taken a back seat but has been kicked to the curb, abandoned in favor of the possessed music and dance marathons I hold with myself in the space where I am supposed to be hard at work on my true talent. I want so much to end this charade yet I am enslaved to the marijuana, the music, and the movement.

I don't last more than a half hour, puttering around debating with myself whether I should abstain or indulge, before I finally give in to the hallucinogenic allure. I roll a healthy joint and ignite it with both giddy excitement and self-loathing. Soon, I am in my other world again, the world where I am not too shy to sing and dance and cavort about.

Like a dirty secret, I wait until Mom and Jason are out of the house or asleep to turn off the lights, putting covers over the windows so even the streetlights can't shine in, and change into the evening's outfit. This could be striped 1963 Beach Boys touring shirts, shrink-wrap-tight leopard print jeans, Edwardian Beatle jackets, Princely nut-hugging G-strings, Nancy Sinatra–style go-go boots, or former girlfriends' panty hose and brassieres. My clothes closet looks less like a wardrobe and more like a costume shop.

Music complements the mind-blowing experience. Prince's music was always a favorite when I was getting high and fucking somebody, but I'm not fucking anymore. No, I am a solo sky pilot tonight, as I've been every night for months since breaking up with Scarlett. While lighting up I play some Cat Stevens, her favorite artist, and as the mellow folk cradles my high I reminisce.

A robust, caramel-colored sister with a classic face and quirky style that recalled 1940s Hollywood, Scarlett was a prize, a jewel that I threw away. She always kept her hair swept back in a severe bun, like a young countess showing off her smooth complexion, bedroom eyes, cute upturned nose, and thick sensuous lips framing her brilliant smile. Strong and stocky but in a sexy way, she had the typical black woman's body type: smallish breasts, high, round, protruding rear, and thick shapely legs. Full of charisma and personality, developed when she was a bright but overweight and acne-spattered teenager, Scarlett possessed a great sense of humor, reminiscent of her idol Lucille Ball. Mugging, quipping, and slipping into funny voices, she wasn't afraid to go all out to make me laugh.

We met in the mid '80s, through her repeated visits to Sam Goody's. She was looking for long-out-of-print John Lennon LPs. I was delighted to discover that she was a Beatles fan, making it easier for me to ask her out. On our first date I invited her to my house and showed her all the Paul-is-dead clues, playing vinyl backward and poring over the album covers. That she lived in Queens, further down Merrick Boulevard in the township of Laurelton, made us practically neighbors. This once tony upper middle class black haven was also starting to tarnish as crack made its way down Merrick, sold in the doorways and on corners from bustling Hillside Avenue, past Rosedale, and well into the all-white township of Nassau County. Scarlett and I were oblivious to crack but, after Dad died, she and I smoked pot constantly. I grew to know how Dad must've felt with Mom, finding a compatible mate that I could share my jones with.

The kiss of death on our five-year romance occurred ironically enough this past Valentine's Day, after I spent my last ten dollars not on a card or flowers but rather on a dime bag of weed. She refused to join me for a lover's day toke or the sloppy sex I hoped for after getting zooted. Days later we took a guilt trip to the jewelers in Green Acres Mall on Sunrise Highway in Valley Stream, where I put a down payment on an engagement ring. I was trying to buy some time but the clock had run out. Her being my age and holding down a lucrative administrative assistant's job with potential for growth, complete with a car and apartment, while I dicked around aimlessly getting high under my mother's roof was too much for my fragile ego to take. I thought I was doing her a favor by suggesting we split. I was embarrassed but recovered the down payment I put on her ring. That quickly went to the reefer man to celebrate my newfound freedom.

With a joint at my mouth, headphones on, and my Walkman slipped into my back pocket, I have no wires or coils, women or cares to hold me back as I dance the night away. Skipping tiptoed from the rear bedroom to the front bedroom I stop for a moment before the bathroom mirror. As is now a ritual, I inspect my face. The moment I spend transfixed before this mirror turns into several minutes, which elapse into an hour and then two. Staring, mugging, adjusting and re-adjusting for hours, I look at my face from every angle imaginable—extreme left, extreme right, worm's eye, bird's eye.

My left eye begins to wander ever so slightly of its own accord, as if controlled by another person inside of my body. Being right handed, my left side is weaker, but my left side is noticeably smaller too. First I think it's smaller because it is sickly, malnourished, even ignored. Then I believe it's smaller because it is the woman in me manifesting herself at last, making me a bizarre, inverted hermaphroditic creature.

Desperate to see just how tragic a specimen I am, I undo my pants and pull them down to my knees for a nude look at my feminine frame. Why, I even have the *hips* of a woman! As alarmed and ashamed as I am of my bizarre body, I also believe it is unique, an oddity that should be shared with the public. It is before my bathroom mirror that I decide to enter the field as a nude model, taking my exceptional physique to the masses, and making some much-needed cash. I will also finally try to give up reefer cold turkey.

For now I ride out my high staring at my body and face. My head

is too narrow, my eyes off center, my jawbone is receding and disconnected, my teeth are moving, one of my nostrils is small like a pinhole,
and the other gaping with wild hairs creeping out, encrusted with
boogers . . . My face is a horror show of malformed bits and pieces.

If these are the outward physical effects, what is going on inside?
Could the post-war propaganda equating pot smoking with male breast
enlargement be true, only now going horrifically haywire? How else
will my mind change in light of my discovery that there is a woman
trapped inside of me?

And another thing . . . What is her name?

43

MY SLEEP IS FITFUL. I feel middle-of-the-night frights snake their tentacles under my sheets to penetrate me and drink my essence, becoming stronger by devouring me. I've learned not to sleep so heavily. Soon, I don't sleep at all. I lie and listen to the whispers, the dark, mid-evening laughter. I hear the devil in all of them, laughing at me, mocking me, waiting for me to sleep. I am certain more than one of the thirty on the ward emits a gaseous sedative designed to lull enemies into a wide-eyed coma, where you see but cannot *see*. You cannot and will not see them approach and hook onto you with their many-armed apparatus, the tentacles with teeth at their ends, the teeth that puncture and suck. They are vampires, cannibals, and devils. I must watch out for them, for surely "sleeping" in their midst signifies my retreat and defeat.

I awake earlier than all and hit my station. I must remain in this "laundry room," which I've discovered is also my captain's quarters/ engine room. The dials and switches of the machines power and drive my ship. Not only captain and engineer, I am also maintenance supervisor. This is my job, washing and drying the crew's clothes, using my urine as detergent. Then I can rebuke and baptize them en masse.

It's working. I can see the offenders better. The ones that mean well glow with my urine and accept it, feel cleansed and as a result are less offensive, even benevolent. They've become helpful in spotting the others, those who feel uncomfortable in my pissed-on laundry, irritable and confrontational, squirming in the cleansed fabric. The more astute demons sense something's wrong with the clothing and refuse to let me dress them. They need not wear the anointed garments, for in refusing to comply they mark themselves.

I feel alone with these alien stowaways on this celestial voyage, traveling at mind-boggling speed in this Building 40–sized spaceship. I hole up in my quarters. They know I'm not to be fucked with. They peek in on me just to see how far I've come. Perhaps they wish to spy the blueprints and take snatches of information back to the others. A quick scornful side glance squashes all opportunities of them knowing the outcome before I do.

The dryer speaks. Its tumbling questions me when I question myself.

"Are you SURE? Are you SURE?"

"Are you CERtain? Are you CERtain?"

"I don't THINK so. I don't THINK so. I don't THINK so."

I soon ask the machine questions. Confer with it as if it were a two-hundred-pound Magic Eight Ball.

Stripping off my clothes, I work up a sweat doing nude calisthenics. Becoming winded and dizzy, I fall to my knees. Crawling to the laundry room window, watching the tree branches and their leaves, their movements silhouetted against the streetlights become a vision of my plight.

I see myself lighted only by a torch, like an Olympic runner at midnight. The torch illuminates three bat-winged demons following close behind and beside me. Taunting me, hoping I'll falter and drop. And what of Heaven? My destination, my home, is miles ahead of me. I am tired of running on this moon- and torch-lit desert road but I must continue. I must do well; make proud my God, my people, and myself. I dare not fail.

I decide to make a flag. I will use one of the bed sheets. Blood, sweat, toil, and tears, this will be my flag. It will be the flag of the workingman, the flag of honesty and pain. I piss upon the linen, creating a large, wet spot. I then prick my finger with a sharpened piece of contraband to draw blood. This produces a pale pink mixture with the urine. Nearing completion, I squat and extrude, making quite a statement upon my banner.

All that's left is the sweat. By now I'm drenched with it so I roll upon the expelled waste and blood, painting myself with the wet and muddied dung. Then I sprawl on the sheet. As I swirl and writhe, it becomes a large Rorschach blot of pain and determination. I move as if I am making angels in the snow, flip over and swim like bathing beauty Esther Williams, then imitate the circular sideways run popularized by Curly from the Three Stooges. Soon I am almost completely covered with my own waste . . . and it is good.

The dryer speaks.

"It's *IN* here. It's *IN* here."

"Keep *LOOK*ing. Keep *LOOK*ing."

"Be*HIND* you. Be*HIND* you. Be*HIND* you."

I vault from my crap-encrusted creation. Anchoring my weight, and soiling the eggshell white dryer as I heave it aside, I look for Evil. Will I find some small crouching troll who, when cornered, will strike with desperate ferocity, perhaps attempting to eat my face? Will I find a large black hole, the portal to Hell, where I will have to neutralize Cerberus, the three-headed devil dog standing guard, and all the many demons of Hades before arresting Satan himself? Will my super suit of shit, piss, and blood protect me from the icy flames of the demon inferno, or the countless lashes, gashes, and stings that I will surely suffer in my quest to subdue the Beast?

No. I am surprised to find a small white head. No body, no soul, just an old face, squashed and battered. Master of deception that he is, I am almost fooled into thinking it is a dashed and soggy cigarette butt that I hold between my soiled and bloody thumb and forefinger. Before I let his vast influence and trickery defeat my purpose, I toss him into the heart of my pennant, like a match onto a pool of gasoline, and it becomes a lake of fire. Like the rain, snow, sand, and sea, my blood, spit, shit, and piss will cauterize and sterilize this foul, insignificant, and pitiful demon. If this demon's severed human head is scaled down to a snubbed cigarette butt then I must be at least one hundred feet tall. Like the experience in my bedroom the very first time I got high, I must have grown as I smoked and performed my flag ritual, but this time my quarters and ship have grown with me.

I squish the devil head down into my sanctified waste then place it upon my tongue like a communion cracker, chew the obscene being and swallow quickly. Satan will not live like Jonah in this big fish but expire amidst my acids and bile. I will digest the demon and shit it out, buried in a crap casket, then deliver the demon spirit like a claim check to the Almighty.

The bastard robbed me, us, *all of us!* He took from us what was so precious and perverted it. Satan, he the whitest of the severed white heads, locked up all the brothers, destroying us with his medication, stealing our black masculinity, our ability to produce the strong, healthy seed necessary to further our cause and keep us alive. And it was only happiness we wanted. Life, liberty, and the pursuit of happiness, as was so diabolically lifted to become one of many hypocritical slogans for this land of bloodsuckers.

I am enraged. I must let the sleepers know what he has done to them! Standing above the banner, I flail and jerk angrily at my penis, dropping pearls of semen and tears in the center of my standard. Now my quest is complete; all that's left is to lament. On my knees I bawl like a baby. I fall further, crashing and splashing upon the messed and fetid sheet. I call to God, Jehovah, and Allah . . .

I call out for forgiveness for coming too late—so many have suffered, so many have died without mourning or glory, many more mired in mediocrity and half-realized meaning.

"Allah Akbar," I moan, the words filled with sadness.

Again, "Allah Akbar."

I twist upon the sheet, turning round and round, resembling a psychotic street dancer from the ghettos of my youth. I upend and stand on my head, repeating, "Allah Akbar."

I chant faster, my breathing becoming labored. The Islamic mantra takes on a strange rhythmic cadence. My praise of the Father, the Creator, mutates into a sorrowful damnation for the rape of my people. "Allah Akbar" becomes "All our egg power," shouted in a rapid-fire grievance and call to arms.

"A L L O U R E G G P O W E R ! A L L O U R E G G P O W E R ! ALLOUREGGPOWER!"

44

"**C**ODE GREEN ON WARD 6-B!" is called over the building's public address system, indicating a patient is out of control and all available staff must respond. I am subdued by six Mahatas, dragged out of the laundry room, and thrown into the Quiet Room. I show my defiance by sending a stream of urine under the door then drawing a star and crescent on the padded wall with my own feces. Brutally subdued with a knee on my neck, clothed in pajamas and wrapped in a straitjacket, I am transferred for one more go 'round in the Secure Care Unit. During this time I am visited by one of the hospital's psychiatrists and scare him with my version of the truth.

"Y'know, Dr. Soon, if Jesus were to come back they'd probably put him in a mental hospital."

The doctor looks up from his notes, startled, as if I'd just reached deep inside him and pinched his heart. While I believe I've finally found and touched that most elusive of all beasts, the God-fearing psychiatrist, this exchange does not prevent him from filing an application to have me medicated over objection.

I am held in secure for the entire spring until my appearance in Creedmoor's infamous on-campus court, where patients usually get the shaft. After several more weeks of psychosis, isolation, and legal stalling I go before a judge. It is encouraging to see Barry Newfeld fight like a bulldog for me but I very quickly lose my patient's right to refuse medication. I guess God wants it this way, or so I seem to pick up in my bathroom communication after the verdict. Though my radio to Heaven will be losing its signal, changing format from the Mod Gospel to some sickening type of Kenny G smooth-jazz slow-death, God's ambassador chimes in loud and strong one final time.

Issa-as-Jesus makes an appearance in the mirror of the courthouse restroom while I splash my face with cold water. It is both comforting and unsettling to finally see the man that I used to be and the man that I hoped to be, staring back at me. Not yet touched by the corrosive effects of whatever "wonder drug" will force him into retirement, he is poker faced and cool, displaying neither the triumph nor the weariness of ping-ponging through the centuries. Separated by the glass, standing kissable close, as if in an identical room on the other side yet also in another dimension, he offers consoling advice. "Don't fight it, kid. Take the shot. It's your best move."

The next day on secure, the treatment team summon me into the nurse's station. Realizing that I will be forcibly restrained and juiced up if I refuse, I go willingly. The team, all knotted brows and folded arms, is prepared for a fight but I take the shot like a champ. I am given an intramuscular shot in my buttocks containing 100 milligrams of Haldol Decanoate for three consecutive weeks. Then I will receive my monthly maintenance dose of 200 milligrams.

The day after the first injection my thinking is clear and I am no longer paranoid, delusional, or psychotic. It is miraculous and obvious to me that I need the meds to function properly. To explain and excuse my behavior during this relapse, I am re-diagnosed again, now becoming a full-blown sufferer of Schizophrenia, Paranoid Type.

Maybe my recurring delusions of omnipotence draw from my wishing for the power to erase a grave error, raise the dead, undo the tragedy of my mother's death. If I cannot bring her back then I might redeem myself by saving mankind. Unfortunately, these desires, dreams, and fantasies become distorted, married to an unspeakable guilt and remorse. These are burdens that I must learn to live with, if I am to live at all.

Self-pity and many years of this incarcerated nightmare have worn me down. I have to accept the truth about my addiction, my illness, and about myself, and I believe it is time to give in. I see now that what I've been doing for the last eight years isn't working for me. I've been blinded by pride and pussy, but neither will get me out of here.

Now, thinking back on when Chief Markum returned my confiscated paintings and sneered, "Your art's not going to get you out of here, you know," I am at a loss for what will.

Coming to Creedmoor, housed in newly minted treatment units such as Mentally Ill Chemical Abuse or its sister Chemically Addicted Mentally Ill, two delineations that seem more like diagnostic hairsplitting, mine was a rare but not unheard of occurrence. A caution made camp via the film *Reefer Madness* in the '40s, ridiculed as old fogey finger wagging in the '70s, and dismissed as utter bullshit by everyone from hip-hop devotees to hipster hydroponic hemp growers in the new millennium.

However benign and beloved marijuana is projected to be I cannot forget or deny the influx into the asylums in the early and mid 1990s of young men like me who ignored the crack pipe but got caught up in the web of weed psychosis. Though we gave testimony in various groups of the problems we had, it was in quieter moments, during lights out in the dorms, or sneaking a stogie in the bathrooms, that we shared our stories and I recognized myself in these men. All of us teary eyed, mystified, stupefied that our harmless romance became an obsession leading to madness, and, in my case, accidental death.

Named a Schedule 1 drug by President Richard Nixon in 1970, the majority of recreational pot, around 72 percent, was imported illegally from source countries, mostly in South America. Due to growing time, transportation, and distribution, the pot the average American consumer was getting was old and stale. The advent of homegrown hydroponic systems in the '80s signified a boom in fresher, higher quality connoisseur strains. These superpowered strains of cannabis complemented and competed with crack. This was not your father's marijuana.

With technology advancing, strains became more specialized, bred specifically for potency and targeting for medicinal effects. At best it hits harder, lasts longer, and takes you where you want to go. The ability to cultivate and specify your high is as sophisticated and focused as a sommelier enjoying fine wine. And at worst, according to twenty-year studies published by the National Addiction Center at King's

College, London, it is addictive, damaging to the brain, and linked to schizophrenia.

However, none of the research on cannabis and schizophrenia establishes a definitive causal link. Results of a Harvard University study suggest that having an increased familial morbid risk for schizophrenia may be the underlying basis for schizophrenia in cannabis users. It's not cannabis use by itself, but that cannabis consumption interacts with genetic susceptibility to schizophrenia.

As with alcohol, the vast majority of casual users come to no harm. But a small proportion of drinkers become dependent and develop alcoholism and various physical problems. And for cannabis, a small proportion go psychotic. The marijuana legalization efforts are in full swing because voters agree it isn't any worse than alcohol and that the war on drugs causes more social and personal damage than the drug itself.

Once stabilized on the new medication, I am sent back to 6-B with a keener sense of self. I know now that I can never smoke pot again. I don't believe with all it has taken from me (my mother, my family, my dignity, my freedom) that I will miss it.

45

THE CREEDMOOR CASEWORKERS, all burnt-out baby boomers, try mustering up some of the old fervor when dealing with the young, minority, mentally ill substance abusers of the 1990s, but the Kumbaya smacks of "come back later." The liberals get older and more frightened of a newer crop of patient bringing crack, hip-hop, and gangster culture with them. They watch as we drift through the system, recidivist and listless. The apathy grows contagious with neither side of that great dividing line of sanity knowing or caring about the other.

New York State's good-hearted but failed experiment at deinstitutionalization emptied out the asylums but most nonforensic patients were discharged to the streets without follow up or medication, creating an overflow of homeless mentally ill, schizophrenic squeegee-men, and paranoid, potentially dangerous panhandlers. For every "difficult discharge" stuck on a locked ward, there are four frisky singers in the subway crooning for a buck, or others locked in a Starbucks restroom bathing in the sink.

Following the change of administration in Albany in the mid '90s, with a pressured and nervous Republican governor, an uncompromising and reputedly racist Republican mayor of New York City, and the climate becoming unfriendly and intolerant of the mentally ill throughout the country, we find ourselves on serious lockdown in this and many other "less secure" psychiatric centers.

It's particularly tough for all psych patients following the tragic death of Kendra Webdale. She was an attractive young photographer and journalist pushed in front of an inbound subway train at the 23rd Street and Broadway station by my former Creedmoor admissions unit dorm mate and fellow schizophrenic Queens native Andrew Goldstein. But it is harder for the poor woman's family, agonizing over their loved one's senseless murder. They implement system change, follow-up care, and accountability to prevent mentally ill people from wandering out of hospitals unchecked and without sufficient meds in their system. With the similar subway push killing of grandmother and seamstress Soon Sin four years earlier at the hands of a homeless man with a profound psych history, and the renewed outrage over lax hospital security and policies spurring Assisted Outpatient Treatment, dubbed Kendra's Law, it seems I am on the vanguard of a new movement in psychiatric treatment with my medication over objection court order.

I MISS MY FAMILY. I wonder how they are doing. I used to write unanswered letters, begging for understanding and forgiveness. Now I just hope they'll forget. But knowing how precious Mom is—to me, to them, to the neighborhood—I know they will never forget, or forgive. Should they? Ever? I suppose I've given them a stronger reason to go on—namely, keeping me locked up.

My oldest brother Smiley places an unexpected call to the hospital. The call is transferred to my ward and I am summoned into the treatment room to speak with him. My treatment team feels it will be good for us to reconnect, at the very least via this phone call. As much as I want and need familial contact I am unsure if I want it from him.

I had put him out of the house in the fall of 1989, after decades of conflict within the family because of his criminality. His drugging and loafing had given birth to a creepy, thieving menace that no one wanted to live with.

Smiley stole from all of us; first Mom and Dad, then his siblings. There was a sad routine where after something went missing Mom would attempt to ameliorate the situation by asking, "Did you *see* him take it?" Without eyewitnesses, Smiley went unpunished and the family went away constipated with frustration and rage, knowing full well we were living with an inveterate thief. After Gramps's stroke left him speechless and bedridden, Smiley would creep into his room and steal what he could right in front of him, aware that the old man could never tell. When Granny Naomi came up from Florida Smiley got her too. No one in the family was spared. Once the bedroom doors were locked and there was nothing left at home to take, he ventured out onto the streets, where he promptly endured countless arrests, embarrassing Mom and the family. Still, like a good mother she defended, supported, and enabled him, but as a younger brother puzzled and pissed off by his aberrant and antisocial behavior I was not as tolerant.

I'd had enough of Smiley. It was up to me to impress upon Mom the fact that he had to go. Though Mom had had locks installed on the bedroom doors to keep him out whenever he was home, he'd taken to prying the hinges off with a screwdriver. He'd steal what he could and hock it for crack money. Mom cried bitter tears after Smiley pawned a precious pair of gold earrings in the shape of marijuana leaves that were a present from her oldest and dearest friend, Joan. They were a sentimental item sent from Seattle, where Joan moved to live out her last days while battling breast cancer.

After my checkbook went missing I went on a hunt, finding it stashed in his ill-kept apartment in the basement. This theft was the final straw. I gave my ultimatum and proceeded to put his things out on the side of the house, giving him a chance to salvage what he could before it went to the garbage man. Within a week the basement was cleared of my brother's belongings. He was too weak and strung out to make good on his threats of violence or retribution and finally disappeared into the darkness of crack-infested South Jamaica.

Finally the household was peaceful. Sure, Mom balked and whined about Smiley not having anywhere to stay, and what mother would want to see her child turned out on the street? But even she felt a sense of relief now that he was gone. I noticed the difference when she went to work leaving her bedroom door unlocked. That was unheard of when Smiley lived with us. After so many years not trusting her eldest son she may have been reluctant to trust any of us. I wanted so much to put her mind at ease, let her know that the worst was over.

Upon hearing Smiley's voice over the line I get nervous and scared. I try to play it off like I'm not. I never felt close to him so I am cool on the phone. He is also distant.

"Hey look, I want to schedule a visit," he says. "I just want some closure."

"Uh, yeah. I understand. That would be good. I'd like that too."

I tell the treatment team of his proposed visit. "But I'm also worried because he threatened to kill me in my last phone call I made to the house after I got arrested."

"That was ten years ago. Why hasn't he come to visit you all this time? Where's he been?"

"He just got released from prison after pleading guilty and doing time for a gun charge. It was brought down from attempted murder after he shot up the front of the family home. He got into an argument with my sister over his drug use and him wanting to move back in. He's addicted to crack. He's always been a problem. I feel embarrassed talking about this. Like my Mom and Dad were bad parents, didn't raise us right. What with his problems, and me ending up in here."

"Well, there *is* a lot of drama, Issa."

After thoughtful deliberation the treatment team leader says, "I don't think it would be a good idea to have him come up here and see you. Even though he would have to go through security downstairs, the hospital doesn't have the authority to physically search him, and it would set a bad precedent. And we don't know what he'd do, how he'd choose to hurt you. What if he tries to physically attack you in the visitor's room? It sounds like a messy and uncomfortable situation all around. No, Issa, unless you're dead set on seeing him again I'd suggest you keep him away. Stay safe."

"Yeah, I guess you're right." The treatment team doesn't follow up and Smiley never calls again.

The pain of my family's rejection and abandonment runs parallel with what I can only describe as a prolonged state of shock. It was enough just keeping my thoughts in order. Now that I am thinking clearly I just focus on the future, whatever future I can have with this

terrible stain on me, on my soul. I stay focused on surviving, on discharge. Since getting locked up I realize that there are only two directions I have to look at: the main door, beyond which is freedom, and
down the hall, where there is only death. I have to keep going just to
survive this indefinite hospitalization and my life as a criminally insane
drug addicted nigger, America's nightmare.

46

IN THE NEW MILLENNIUM the administration transfers me from 6-B, the Mentally Ill Chemical Abusers Unit, up to the tenth floor, Community Preparation Unit. The name sounds impressive, like they may want to give me a play, but I just move from one box to another. Unit Chief Markum and Dr. Ramma brief the CPU treatment team on my case. That can only indicate the worst.

When I sit with my new Korean treating psychiatrist, all she seems to talk about in her clipped and halting English is "your crime, your addiction to marijuana, your history of noncompliance, and how two female staff members lost their jobs because of you." After this demoralizing meeting I spend some time thinking about the past ten years and wonder, "What good have I done?"

As if wrestling with Mom's memory isn't daunting enough, now they want me to admit to all I've wrought as this "danger to women." Am I the piece of shit that everyone seems to think I am? This is what the CPU treatment team and the hospital administration want me to address. Dr. Chin makes it clear to me that "there will be absolutely no movement until you take responsibility for your actions."

Both Gaia and Bella were desperate housewives who saw an opportunity and seized it. Yes, I was getting fucked, but I was also agonizing over loving one or the other, or both, giving of my wounded and slowly reopening heart. After all the investigations are officially wrapped up an officer from hospital security says, "We've dealt with the two employees. We are not going to pursue it any further, and unless you can afford a legal team we suggest you don't take it any further." With Barry mum, no support, and my character killed, the hospital squashes any attempts of me filing criminal charges and now gets punitive, branding me with a damning profile.

While I was having a good time I didn't consider the fact that I was being taken advantage of. Sure, it felt like love, and everyone including my attorney is screaming, "Don't blame Gaia, don't blame Bella," but were this recast as poor blonde female seduced by a male employee, I'd probably be supported and discharged to prevent the scandal going viral or turning into a devastating lawsuit.

"I'M SORRY, Iss, but I've had enough."

Lily and I have spent the last five years pledging our love but it seems she can't go the distance. We've never dated. Whenever we were outside of Creedmoor's gates there was always an escort or two an arm's length away. That's no way to love and she's tired of living it. "She's not going anywhere," Gaia often said of Lily, recognizing her devotion and desperation. Well, now she's gone.

In her latest rehospitalization, thankfully not in Creedmoor, she calls from her ward payphone to announce, "I fell in love with another patient. We both have the same diagnosis and we're on the same medication. He isn't tied up in the system like you are and, well, I've just gotta move on."

I saw this coming from years ago but that doesn't mean it still doesn't hurt. Now, with Lily no longer a factor, I feel I can relax more and let this thing move at its own speed. For years, with Lily selling me a dream of her undying love, the picket fence, children, cats and rabbits, I found myself pushing the process and getting frustrated with the time that it was taking to get out. I wanted to fulfill the dream of a long happy life with her and didn't want to keep her waiting. Now she's gone and I don't feel that extra pressure. This is not to say that I am not eager to get out and on with my life. However, I feel more mature after losing her to the slow grind of the system.

47

It's Christmas Eve 1989. I am paranoid, edgy, and wracked with guilt. Within two months I've thrown my older brother Smiley and teenage nephew Jason out of the house. Though Smiley was a drain on us all, he is still her son and Mom is livid. Mom's most worried for Jason, now living with relatives, and she's pissed off at me. I try to relax but I can't. I try old soothers like listening to music but the effect is hollow. I have a yearning deep within me that I am afraid of. I want to smoke some grass.

I've been clean since the end of October but the stressors of leaving a job prematurely and not being able to find another decent one have torn me down. I hoped that after I gave up marijuana the strange thoughts would cease. There is still a part of me that knows the things I think are completely off the wall but I can't maintain and stabilize this part of my mind for more than two or three days at a time. I believe I have to self-medicate to cope. As embarrassing it is to admit it, I *need* the drug right now.

The problem isn't resisting the temptation, for I've already given in to that. What lies ahead is scratching up the cash to buy the evil weed. All that I have on hand is a mass transit token. I am thankful for that little bit. I use it to take a short bus ride to the local shopping district on Jamaica Avenue, finding the nearest cash machine. I don't linger in this busy buying center any longer than it takes to tap my low funds and quickly buy Mom a gift. I am back home in no time. Soon, I am on the phone to Dial-A-Dime, the neighborhood reefer delivery service.

Within fifteen minutes of impatient waiting, the weed-mobile pulls in front of my house. When I hear the car horn beckon, I have to perform the task of reefer retrieval. The Dial-A-Dime delivery thing has been in service for a couple of years now. They operate out of a legitimate neighborhood car service, hence the phone orders, stating your address and speedy delivery. All one has to do is go out to meet the deliverer, sit in the car for a moment (to make the transaction less obvious) and then return to your home. I have severe misgivings about parading my drug use before the neighbors because I believe *everyone* knows the weed-mobile. When people see that car pull up, hear the horn, and then watch it pull away without a passenger, it is sure as shit that one or more members of that particular house is smoking dope. During its operation, every member of the house, except my nephew, is seen at some time or another stepping into that sleek, silvery Town Car only to retreat gleefully moments later.

I know even before I light up that I won't get the high I am looking for. I am so disappointed in myself for breaking my sobriety and succumbing to the fog that I can't fully enjoy the act of rolling up, lighting up, and getting fucked up. I certainly do try, though.

Christmas day is cold and grey. Mom and I are together in the house but very much apart. We exchange gifts by leaving them at each other's bedroom door. She gives me the evil eye and cold shoulder. I give her tube socks and lunch meat.

I am busted and spiritually broken. I just don't care anymore. Mom appears to feel the same. I come downstairs and try mustering up pleasant conversation with Mom but there is none to be had. My efforts to console her ring false and empty, forced and guilt inspired. I am ashamed and it keeps me away all the more.

It feels as if a tornado has rushed through my life and upended all that wasn't already destroyed. Where do I begin? Or do I even have to? No, not now. I can just take a breather . . . relax . . . and smoke. In an ongoing pot-induced stupor, I smoke at all hours, taking brief respites to raid the fridge downstairs (while carefully avoiding Mom) and crashing when the lows are just too much.

Disillusioned by my poor joint rolling abilities, I secure one of Dad's vintage pipes. I discover that I get more out of smoking pot through a pipe than from a joint. It's much easier to stuff a heaping thumb and forefinger full of grass into a bowl than look for rolling papers. No more midnight's sojourns to nearby and not so nearby convenience stores, bodegas, and gas stations looking for *Big Bambu* or *E-Z Wider* to ensure I'd get my nightly blast. I also entertain the idea that I appear distinguished with a tasteful pipe in my mouth, regardless of what burns within.

48

THE LIVING MUSEUM FILM directed by the delightfully genuine Jessica Yu is a success and increases the program's profile and that of all the artists involved. With the help of some collectors who saw the documentary on HBO, and my work being featured in a group Living Museum show exhibited at the Queens Museum of Art in Flushing Meadows Corona Park, I am able to fortify my nest egg.

I flit around at the Queens Museum show opening reception, beaming, glad-handing, and even performing an acoustic coffee house set to polite applause, blissfully oblivious to the anger of my sister Carol. She discovered a painting of mine chosen to announce the show in *New York Newsday*. Having had no personal contact with me for over ten years, she went to the Queens Museum days before the opening, threatening to have my gun-nut brother Smiley come down there and shoot up the place if I weren't taken out of the show. Recognizing how unfair and inconvenient it would be to yank me out of the show at the last minute, the Queens Museum maintained me on the artist's roster while also remaining on heightened alert. I was not told of the threat till after the show by my escort Mr. Ding, like it was a choice bit of gossip.

I AM FORTUNATE TO BE ACCEPTED into numerous group art exhibitions in a newly burgeoning Williamsburg, Brooklyn, and wind up having an opening reception every couple of months that, surprisingly, I am allowed to attend, if only on two-to-one. I just ask my lawyer Barry to arrange a meeting with the forensic committee for review of whatever trip I am requesting. I also organize with Sherri Ferrone, one of Gaia's

Flushing Book Club girlfriends, to masquerade as my "art sponsor," thus getting me off the ward and giving me a warm home to go to on the holidays. It's a clever ruse that allows me to get out more and even see Gaia again.

The court-ordered escorted off-grounds privileges that I lost after the affair was revealed are indefinitely "on hold"; however, the Forensic Committee meets, and usually grants, permission for me to go out on these "special support network" excursions. It must be with two-to-one male staff, but once the escorting Mahatas get to the apartment and see Gaia there they lighten up and play along with the secrecy, everyone having a grand old time. Before her unceremonious departure she'd been at Creedmoor for thirty years and made a lot of friends, mostly with ward staff who knew that whatever went on between us didn't make us bad people, just people who made bad decisions. Away from the hospital, and on these holidays, I appreciate Gaia's kindness. It gives me hope for a better life if I ever do get out.

The Mahatas give me plenty of space and respect, but Mr. Ding can't resist displaying envy at what he calls my "macking the scene" and asserting control by pulling me aside and whispering, "If *I* ain't gettin' none, *you* ain't gettin' none!"

OVER TIME THE HOSPITAL HAS DESIGNATED all the single rooms not occupied by disabled patients as each ward's new time-out room. This means my new room is to be taken away from me. I am given a week-end to "pack yo shit" and move again, or rather squeeze, into a share further down the hall.

I fly into a mild panic, at a loss for whom to move in with, as com-patibility is crucial and I don't want to settle for just anyone. That's like mental patient Russian roulette, which can be disastrous. On the day of the move the staff allows me fifteen minutes to discreetly interview potential candidates, and I angle for the monstrous D.J. to be my next roommate. He is a slow-witted, deranged, hulking black male, but he's more of a gentle giant, although I know that jumps from one cliché to another. D.J. masturbates every night, sometimes twice a night, and he occasionally craps himself when he comes. He also serenades my anus when the lights go out, to the tune of "Copacabana." "His name is Issa . . . he has a butthole . . . made of diamond."

That said, he's the only patient I feel I can trust in here with my expensive computer equipment, TV, radio, guitar, art supplies, and my secret cell phone. I buy his silence and loyalty with peanut butter and jelly sandwiches and an endless supply of chocolates. This isn't the wisest approach, as he's stricken with a raging sweet tooth and diabetes, but seeing how badly he craves the sweet stuff I am confident he'll do anything to remain in this room and keep its secrets and treats flowing.

Coincidentally, D.J. was my first roommate when I was transferred from the sixth floor to 10-B a few years ago. Back then they told me I was advancing. This was the Community Preparation Unit, after all. Well, it was a year or two before that changed. I realized I'd made a lateral move when it became the Acute Stabilization Treatment Unit. I got a new doctor somewhere along the way, who once again rediagnosed me. Every new doctor feels a need to tinker with the formula, to feel like they've done something meaningful and they're making a difference.

My current clinician, Dr. Lautrec, is a matronly, late middle-aged Haitian woman who doesn't think ill of me but also doesn't speak up for me when it comes to discharge, intent on keeping the status quo. She is brought in mainly due to patient complaints of incompetence on her other wards. As this recently became the Spanish cluster ward, the administration reasoned that since her homeland shared an island with the Dominican Republic, her shaky Spanish qualifies her as an appropriate choice for a doctor here.

We patients are required to be out of our rooms during program time, 6:30 AM till 7:30 PM, but I hustle to get my door opened during the day, employing a mix of manipulation, commiseration, and puppy dog's eyes. I'm the only patient who gets to stay in their room. My less savvy, slightly psychotic roommate D.J. smiles at me through a crack in the door, displaying envy and resignation, saying, "Go on with your bad self!"

I hate to be out in the dayroom. I've spent too many years sitting in those uncomfortable chairs all day, overstimulated, watching bad TV while the radio blares, avoiding then becoming desensitized to the occasional violence that breaks out over a bogarted cigarette or cup of coffee. When not busying myself doing art I was like the other patients, sitting on the sill staring out the window at the cars passing and the fortunate patients not on restriction walking the grounds. I too have waited by the main door for a visit or just the hope of someone, *anyone*, coming on or off the ward to provide some kind of activity for my mind and "normal person diversion" from the ongoing unhealthy boredom and tense anxiety of this hospital. So I now value the quality time I can spend alone with my thoughts in the quiet of my room—relaxing, painting, singing albeit softly, hiding from the madness, mayhem, and Mahatas, many of whom know and allow me these extended periods to myself, peeking in to perform their occasional count, or calling me out for the change of shift.

LILY REENTERS MY ORBIT and I dedicate my time and talent to her. She is my muse, inspiring me, along with Mom's tragedy and my struggle to overcome it. As Lennon once quipped after his lost weekend away from Yoko, "The separation didn't work."

Too good of a girl to try a quickie in the visitor's room lavatory, especially with the surveillance cameras watching our every move, Lily will do no more than masturbate me in the window sill, and even then it's infrequent. She is banned from the Living Museum by no less than Director of Rehab Enya Face, who correctly assumes that we were having sex there. So now we plan days in advance for her to enter the grounds. She surreptitiously takes the long way around where, after cell phone coordination, I wait to sneak her in through a back door of the museum. There, in the Love Nest, a small converted closet deep in the bowels of the building where I put down foam bedding with blankets and towels for clean up, Lily and I finally make powerful love.

49

THE LAST TIME I SEE MY BROTHER KAL is in spring of 1990. The nightmare of intake at Rikers Island is now a memory. When I arrive at Kings County Hospital I am pleased to find out that the criminal/psych ward is housed in the G building. I believe this stands for God so I am sure I'll be in good hands. The sixth floor of the G building is a mini police precinct complete with its very own bullpen that I am placed in just before entering the ward. Based on bullpen authority, I am here to be evaluated by two doctors to see if I am competent to stand trial.

In this dreary pen I am visited by the ethereal presence of my personal angel Scarlett, same as I was just before leaving Jamaica, Queens, and intermittently ever since. I cock my head to listen for hints of The Great Plan, pearls of wisdom, or even sweet nothings, but I cannot hear her. Like a beautiful angelfish behind an impenetrable glass . . . I wonder if it is her or me in the tank? Her spirit waves and floats like a ghost, then with the blink of my eyes she is gone . . . never to return? With her essence goes the residue of my psychosis, the plots and schemes. I am not as paranoid as I was. My intense fear of the world subsides and I can once again sit in my skin.

I am somehow aware that Scarlett will never be with me again, that maybe she was never there. I am aware that I lost my mind and committed a terrible act. I am also more aware of my surroundings— this awful bullpen, the keys that continually jingle, and the door that is opened for me, letting me out of this miserable cage and onto a locked ward for insane criminals. I have a new life now, and a purpose. I have to own and understand fully what happened to me, how I could accidentally, inescapably, in the course of a botched "exorcism," take my mother's life.

Kings County Hospital's orderlies escort me off the ward after an hour-long orientation, past the cramped police station and elevators to a small visitors room where I see my brother Kal and Bichinado, my sister Lauren's boyfriend. I assume, much like with Dad's death two and a half years ago, Kal was summoned from his stationed base, this time overseas in Korea. And, similar to our father's passing, he was again cheated out of a final goodbye, not by cancer this time but by me. I feel embarrassed but my heart also races with happiness that he has come to see me in such dire straits as well as with fear that he will now kick my ass.

We sit amidst three other inmate/patients, Kal somber and compassionate and Bichi, acting true to his name, sarcastic and impatient.

"What happened, man?" Kal begs, disbelieving.

"Did *you* do it?" Bichi interrupts. "Cuz everyone thinks that scumbag Smiley did it. Not you. You know your brother Smiley shot up the house after your sisters asked him to leave? He comes back home and while everyone is grieving he was smoking that crack with Queenie and some other niggers. He had to go. I'm just supporting your sister, even though we're not married, but so what? I don't want my children or Lauren or me to get shot up by your crackhead brother . . ."

"OK, Bichi, OK. That's enough," Kal disarms with a take-charge calm that is an impressive indication of his military training and easygoing manner, pointing to his great potential if he himself were not a seasonal crackhead.

I am still unsteady, though my thoughts are in order and I can and do recount my last days with Mom. I try to explain the plots, the self-importance, how everything was loaded with meaning, even the names and destinations of the various causeways and bridges I traveled on my aborted journey to Canada.

"Like bridges to cross? Something you felt you had to do?" Kal asks, trying to understand.

"Yeah . . . I guess . . . like I was on a spiritual quest, a pilgrimage."

"Even though you were on the run," Bichi counters. I shoot him a nasty then mousey glance. My annoyance at Bichi's provocations melts to profound shame, guilt, and embarrassment.

With visitor's hour expired I embrace my brother and feel his strong love for me. Bichi says he'll keep in touch but I secretly hope he doesn't. While being escorted through the tight hallway, I turn and see Kal and Bichi waiting for the elevator. My brother glances back. Making one final connection, Kal punches his chest and throws his heart to me. I catch it and offer a rueful smile. I wonder if I've ripped it from him.

COME MOTHER'S DAY, twelve years past that brotherly meeting, and following many years of one-on-one analytic psychotherapy, I realize that when not in shock I've spent all this time punishing myself. Simultaneous illicit affairs, poisoned paintings, noncompliance, and reefer relapse have been subconscious attempts to undermine myself and whatever collateral I would consciously front toward appropriate behavior, healing, and discharge. My last therapist called it "self-sabotage." It was hard to hear him suggest this, and even more painful to finally admit it, but I have to take responsibility for all that I've wrought upon myself. I have to learn to forgive myself, live with myself, live.

Like a twelve-stepping alcoholic or addict I begin the long road of making amends. First to my family, via letters begging forgiveness, which as before go unanswered. Then I let go of the shame instilled by the women who worked here, whose lives like mine were destroyed.

I start writing down apologies to others and affirmations to and for myself. Acknowledging my failings of character, the reasons (but not excuses) for my behavior, and an understanding of my responsibility and deep wound regarding Mom, the intense hatred I feel toward myself as a result, and eventually forgiveness. And my strong resolve to carry on, survive it all, and thrive, if for no other reason than that old but totally true cliché—because she would have wanted me to.

50

I'VE BEEN STUCK WITH A HOST OF SUPERFICIAL THERAPISTS, most of whom play it safe, toeing an administrative party line. Those that don't retire leave me without exit conferences, which is unprofessional and injurious.

The hospital arranges an introduction to their highly touted new employee, Dr. Anne Maggoty. Barry says, "She's a well-known expert witness for the courts." I am wary at our first meeting when I notice her off-the-rack conservative polyester dress, dangling crucifix, and ugly plastic pumps, conjuring the image of a stern nun. She also has more than a touch of the mad scientist, with her hunched shoulders, graying straw-like hair, tight mouth, inquisitive nose, and crossed eyes.

This forensic psychiatrist meets with me weekly with the intention of filing a court report. I am as honest as I feel I can be while still a bit guarded. She notices my hesitance, which seems to excite her.

"I want to dig deeper," she says with piqued interest, "into your mind. Peel back the layers of the onion and see what's really there, because I don't believe you're being truthful with me. About the social worker, whom I believe you manipulated, about the nurse, whom I believe you seduced, or about your mother, who . . . well, we'll get to that. I want to begin an intensive weekly therapeutic relationship with you, for as long as it takes, to get to the truth. But I must warn you now, don't play chess with me. You'll lose."

I am scared and suspicious about entering into a therapeutic relationship with this doctor whom I don't like and who I believe doesn't like me. That she is also filing a report on me for the courts regarding my suitability for discharge I recognize as a conflict of interest. I run it by my lawyer.

"I hear ya, Issa," Barry says, "but it may be best to cooperate. Considering all that's happened in your case so far, compliance would fare better than resistance."

Dr. Maggoty seems to relish rattling me during the next ten months of intensive psychotherapy, like a blithely amused cat batting about a scared but determined rodent. "You're not as heinous as, let's say, a rapist of children but I do believe your offense is pretty bad," she springs on me after Easter, trying to pacify me but still passing judgment. "No one will tell you this, but for every offense an insanity plea patient commits there's a certain amount of time we want you to do," she tells me in a summer session, a blistering confirmation that the system is fixed. "I hope you enjoy your programming at the Living Museum because I can't see you going anywhere else for a long, long time. Not if I have anything to say about it," she leaves like a piece of coal in my Christmas stocking in our last session on the coldest of winter days.

Once this mouse is run down, rent, and gutted, Maggoty simply disappears, like the Cheshire cat, with a jagged, feral smile and a contemptuous glare, terminating the relationship without an exit conference. As hurtful as this experience is I look at it as business as usual here at Creedmoor.

With therapy discontinued and her forensic evaluation completed, she submits a forty-four-page report to the courts determining that I require continued hospitalization. Stating I suffer from "a dangerous psychiatric disorder with pervasive antisocial features" she throws away the key with her determination of me having "latent indications of a predator as evidenced by his dual seductions of female professional staff."

And I have been re-diagnosed again. To be consistent with Maggoty's report, I am labeled with Narcissistic Personality Disorder. While I fully know I am not a predatory sociopath I will admit that I have narcissistic traits, though not to the extent of a disorder. Narcissism, when tempered, is an essential component of a healthy ego. It fuels drive and ambition, giving one's life meaning and importance. As a disorder it impairs your ability to form normal relationships and alienates those who have close encounters with it. Though the *Diagnostic Statistical*

Manual of Mental Disorders in its third edition in 1980 officially recognized the disorder, there are descriptions of the syndrome going back to ancient Greece. It's named for the myth of Narcissus, the beautiful boy unable to love until spying his own reflection in a pond. He died by drowning, chasing himself into the deep.

The *DSM*, the psychiatrist's bible, was first introduced in 1952 to better treat post–World War II soldiers and "schizophrenic" housewives, attempting to take the focus away from institutionalization. It was 130 pages long and had a total of 106 disorders. The manual went through several editions with revisions over forty plus years, the most significant being the declassification of homosexuality as a disorder in a 1974 addendum. The current standard multiaxial system was instituted in the *DSM-III* in 1980. And included in that criteria for the first time was Narcissistic Personality Disorder, one of less than a dozen personality disorders, commonly considered failures of character development. The *DSM-5*, issued in 2013, contains a whopping 297 disorders.

My new diagnosis of Narcissistic Personality Disorder is problematic but not unexpected. It is conveniently slapped on me by hospital administration wishing to put the onus on me for the Gaia and Bella affairs. I also believe I would've wound up with that diagnosis eventually because I am an artist. That someone should think that what he says or does should be communicated to as large an audience as he can reach must strike many mental health professionals as grandiose and self-aggrandizing, regardless of whether the patient has the talent to back it up.

To be a creative artist in this mental hospital has its perks, as evidenced by the amazing Living Museum rehab program. However, there are drastic drawbacks. Heaven forbid an institutionalized artist makes the mistakes I made of flaunting my talent, exhibiting the confidence that comes with years of practice and praise, making a bit of money from it, and then reaping the rewards of an artist's charm and charisma by stepping over social and ethical boundaries. Like the Mafiosi whose wives my Dad crooned to, the well-connected dons embodied by Creedmoor's administration are not amused.

I learn all this information and more listening from Gaia over the phone. She's acquired it from Creedmoor's secretarial pool digging in my chart. Her friends here didn't like how she was handled by OMH in her final days as a state employee. Inpatients aren't allowed access to their charts, perhaps because the hospital believes the crafty ones would then anticipate the doctor's next move. It is imperative that order and control are maintained and the patients know their place.

After numerous therapeutic dump-offs, I opt to go it alone. But I am informed by the administration that regardless who I get next I must continue to participate in therapy. Barry recognizes what he sees as "a pretty devilish Catch-22. I know you've been hurt, and I can understand if you just don't want to open yourself up to be hurt again, Issa. But if you don't consent they'll label you 'evasive,' 'recalcitrant,' and even 'manipulative,' and that's not good for you. I'll write the memo if you want, saying whatever you want to say that'll express your reluctance or unwillingness to undergo therapy. But I gotta tell ya, Issa, they've pretty much got you where they want you."

51

THROUGH AGGRESSIVE CELL PHONE NETWORKING and snail mail correspondence I am fortunate to have developed a modest clientele that stretches all the way to Europe. I save all the funds that I earn from my sold artwork, sitting on a nest egg that allows me to replenish my art supplies, fund a portable recording setup, and plan for the future.

I have been contemplating taking my songwriting and recording more seriously. A musician, volunteer, and good friend from the Living Museum lets me borrow his four-track cassette recorder to play around with. Though recording devices are forbidden in the hospital, I sneak the four-track onto the ward and proceed to demo some of my more fully realized songs. Since then I've had the bug. I want to do this, but better. Already equipped with the guitar that Bella gave me, I use a couple thousand dollars of my recent artistic windfall to purchase a good microphone, studio-quality headphones, jacks galore, and a pretty advanced drum machine with bass capability. I finally smuggle in a sixteen-track digital recorder with internal CD burner. I am *not* fucking around.

Since I started writing songs proper I have been haunted by the idea of creating an album. As I've spent almost a third of my life institutionalized, not knowing if I would return to civilization, the time finally came when I had to ask myself, "If not now, when?" I compose, arrange, perform, and produce the entire project, recording in my bedroom/studio that is room 10-61. It is mainly a means of distracting myself from the standstill that my case is at.

I release the CD *Zombie Savant* in August of 2004, using Creedmoor's post office to mass mail countless hard copies to any and every contact I'd made as an artist over the years. I feel validated and proud when I am invited to produce music showcases at Bellevue's Alcohol Treatment Clinic and a Greenpoint, Brooklyn, art gallery in the fall. I had been declassified and brought down from two-to-one to only one male escort a year ago, which makes it easier to attend these and other openings.

The CD features the song "Hot for Charlotte." It could function as an ode to Charlotte Spritzer, Creedmoor's director, and Charlottes the world over, even if it is totally invented. It is not mean-spirited or lecherous, as the title may imply, but rather a loving homage, chronicling the three key phases of womanhood—ingénue, mover and shaker, and lady on the decline, underscored by the subject's enduring desirability.

My sending the CD as interior mail to this soon-to-retire CEO is a monumentally stupid move. Dr. Maggoty, recently appointed head of the Forensic Bureau, gets ahold of the story and doesn't let go, turning it into a scandal. However, I have my doubts whether she or anyone else even listened to the song. Weeks before the scandal broke, my treatment team had finally recommended me for Level 4, unescorted off-ground privileges. Unfortunately Maggoty states, in her denial to my privilege application, "the patient is sexualizing his relationship with the CEO and intent on humiliating women in authority."

While it was a foolish thing to go public within Creedmoor with the song, I did not intend to insult Ms. Spritzer. Sending Ms. Spritzer a copy, regardless of how I couched it in the accompanying letter, perhaps assumed an inappropriate familiarity. But knowing she is moving on and I am left in limbo, I want her to know me, to hear me, if only as I scream from the vacuum of my room, on a ward, in a building, in her hospital, one of almost five hundred scared, desperate cases. While I backpedal and gulp for air as the tide of diagnostic opinion threatens to pull me under, recognizing that I may be in over my head, I still believe the song is benign. I discover holding a mirror up to naked emperors can be a dangerous thing.

While this was rotten timing, what follows months later just stinks. I had been granted permission by the hospital over the years to attend many cultural events. They had all gone without incident. I enjoyed going with various friends in my support system to several venues ranging from my own art exhibitions to the local cinema to Carnegie Hall.

Having saved money to buy three tickets, purchased in June, I ask permission to attend a concert by Paul McCartney at Madison Square Garden on September 30, 2005, at 8 PM. I was hoping to take Lily in addition to the one-to-one escort who would be required to be with me as per my reinstated Level 2 escorted off-grounds privilege. Though I have remained symptom- and incident-free for many years I am denied the pass.

As an insanity plea patient with fifteen years behind me and an indefinite stay before me, the opportunity to see a live performance by a living legend whom I've admired since childhood and who is a major influence on me as a musician was one that was too good to let go by. Nor do I know if or when I will have this opportunity again. The people in my support system, knowing me well, felt it would be good for me. This was not an attempt to bypass protocol or proper channels, as my lawyer Barry informs me is the hospital's impression.

I write an internal memo imploring Clinical Director Dr. Bert Ferber for help, in hope that he can perhaps look into the situation.

"Unfortunately," he writes back, "the facility does not have infinite resources and must choose some subset of various potential occasions for which a one-to-one escort could be provided to you for the purpose of activities of various types in the community. Therefore I am declining to intervene with the resource allocation decision made by your treatment team."

I receive treatment team excuses ranging from "no staff available" to "no money for overtime and transport" to that old standby "it's not therapeutic," which could mean anything. Either way, it sounds like a lot of bullshit. The hospital slaps me down and rubs my face in it for the "Hot for Charlotte" affair, as if losing the furlough privilege application wasn't enough. Paul's music is the soundtrack to my life and being denied this opportunity to finally see and hear him sing live simply breaks my heart. I give the three tickets to Lily. She takes her sisters. They have a great time. I hate my life.

It is now that I lose all faith in the hospital's ability to conduct my case without grudges or bias. Yes, I was wrong to send that song with the questionable title to the CEO, but the ensuing tit for tat, bureaucratic bullying, and brinksmanship that I find myself embroiled in is draining and toxic.

I ask Barry to petition the court on my behalf and summon an independent forensic psychiatrist to review my case. My request is granted and Barry tells me I will get the same doctor whose favorable report got me out of Mid-Hudson Psychiatric Center in 1992.

52

I SEE MY SISTER LAUREN AGAIN on an Easter Sunday visit in 1992. She, her boyfriend Bichi, and their two small boys are escorted through the gates, three rows deep with razor-wire, leading onto Mid-Hudson's Building 81 yard. This honor ward, set in a smallish structure apart from the other buildings in the facility, is exclusively for the "higher functioning" insanity plea patients, most all of whom are white, middle class, middle-aged men. When Lauren and my eyes meet we both break out in tears. She runs to give me a long, warm hug. Gone forever is the lean hippie-chick I remember from my youth, replaced by an older, heavier mother of four. She is no longer flighty and mercurial, now somewhat bitter and sad. Unlike Carol's sole visit to Rikers, which was fraught with blame, I feel Lauren's love and concern for me. She sits and listens patiently to my telling of what happened to me and Mom with her still beautiful face open and kind, just as she did when I was a small child telling her tales of fantasy and imagination.

"Oh Issa, I feel so bad. It's just terrible. I'm so sorry. You know, I remember Mom smoking reefer when she was pregnant with you."

"Really?"

"Yeah. Maybe that has something to do with it. You think?"

"I dunno, Lauren. I dunno."

While her kids jump about and play with the ax murderers and serial rapists, Lauren and I sit outside on a worn and chipped-paint picnic bench and catch up. As she and Carol are locked in a heated battle over Mom's estate it becomes clear why her boyfriend Bichi is trying so hard to be nice to me though he hates me for what I did. He is angling for whatever monies Lauren can get from me in the estate settlement. I am not expecting Lauren to reenter my life, and she can make no promises, but it feels good for the both of us to reconnect today, as family should. I often took her to task for dumping her eldest son, Jason, off with us, where I pretty much had to help raise him. But I will always love her, knowing she is the best big sister I could have had.

During Tuesday night's group therapy session in 81's basement, I process the family visit. We patients are encouraged to tackle our issues, heal ourselves, as well as divulge and deal with the crimes that brought us here. While I am shamed by my act, and use these and other opportunities to heal, I encounter interference by other patients in the group who are very verbal and frown on "mother killers." This derision coming from some patients who have dismembered victims and raped the remains, which they then take for a walk in a five gallon drum, is hypocritical in the extreme, but I am steadfast and treat it all as a learning, growing, and healing experience.

The only patient who offers something resembling support is my dorm mate Thomas, who upon finding out what I did says, "Ya did a good crime, Issa. A good crime." After hearing him creepily whisper this in the middle of the night, as if in the throes of some beatific dream, I request a room change and wind up in the back dorm with two guys who killed their wives and a kid who shot up his high school with a crossbow.

The insanity defense is rarely invoked and rarely successful, used by 1 percent of all felony cases and resulting in acquittal in only a quarter of these. On average, a defendant acquitted by reason of insanity and committed to a mental institution is confined for twice as long as a defendant found guilty and sent to prison. All of the guys in 81's honor ward have at least a decade in the system, and this is just their first step in the process.

A month after seeing Lauren, I am interviewed by Dr. Lawrence Seagull, am found no longer dangerous nor requiring this level of intensive treatment, and obtain my release from this facility for the criminally insane. I am now allowed to move on to a less-secure facility. It all goes by so quickly. Only housed in Mid-Hudson for fifteen months, I don't get to put down roots. I don't get too close to any of the other patients nor anyone working here besides Building 81 treatment aide Mr. Cavo who, noticing I was a reader, would pass along various novels by Stephen King and James Michener. His last words to me the night before my transfer, performing an evening head count while I am doing sit-ups in my dorm, are, "Good luck and don't come back," said with a stone face that suggests no books and possibly a beatdown were he to see me again as a patient in this facility.

53

MOM ALLOWS ME TO TAKE UP TO MY ROOM one of the many full-length mirrors she has on the first floor. Now I can stare at myself, really watch the changes, and live the ultimate horror show. I am smoking more than I ever have before. Modeling at the Art Students League, I often find myself cutting out between classes to nearby Central Park to smoke a joint, returning to work stoned, disconnected, and delusional.

Leaving for work every morning, I avoid Mom. She is dogged in her pursuit, wanting more than just my by-now-customary mumbled "Bye, Ma." She calls me over, saying with dread, "You've got the devil's eyes!"

I am frightened by Mom's proclamation as I was many years ago when she took me to see *The Exorcist*, only now *I* am the one possessed! I pull myself away from her and head for the city but all I can think about now are my "devil's eyes." During breaks I hole up in the Art Students League's bathroom and stare into their mirror. I discover that Mom is right! The intense darkness circling my eyes, the vault of my eyebrows, and the myriad of tortured emotions are proof. Am I possessed, fighting a losing battle with old Beelzebub himself? As if my life isn't already a mess.

I know I can find clues to my present condition in Mom's room. I take time off (my job as a nude model affords me such luxuries) and while Mom is at work I explore her living space.

I used to sleep in this very room years ago. Here, just down the hall from the kitchen, I would lie in bed till late hours, TV on but turned down, listening in the dark to my family laugh and entertain themselves and their close friends with marijuana-drenched anecdotes and tall tales.

I was breathing it all in, trying not to catch the contact high. Over the years we'd all switch rooms in the house, starting when my sisters got pregnant and moved out (and then back in after a divorce or two) and when Gramps died. For a while the moves were spurred by my wanting to escape the smell of their reefer, until I too succumbed.

I haven't often been in Mom's bedroom without her in here to distract me. What I take in adds fuel to my paranoiac fires. Daylight is not permitted in. The windows and sliding glass door that leads out to the backyard deck are ominously covered with heavy curtains. All is dark except for sparse light cast by candles that burn on either side of the room. As in the rest of the house, Mom's large mirrors add dimension. The walls of her room are adorned with photo collages of the family. The photos not framed and hanging on the wall have homes in the many, many family albums of her huge library.

Her library looks erudite and innocent enough, being filled with numerous titles. As I step closer, squinting in the half-light, I read the titles off the spines and fear begins to sweep over me. Amazed that I never noticed before, most of the books deal with the occult and witchcraft, magic of the white *and* black variety. There are curious names like Crowley and Lovecraft. Tomes about Salem and the tarot. Astrology, numerology, palmistry, herbals, art, horticulture. The latter few are understood to be longtime interests and hobbies of Mom's, *but the others . . .* ? And in such abundance!

What makes me think the occult may not be just a harmless side interest is the night table at the side of her bed, round with a mirrored tabletop spattered with dried candlewax from numerous burning tea lights. Resting on this night stand is a sheet of lined paper with a detailed chart of our family tree done in Mom's hand. On top of the family legend is a saucer full of crudely crafted, strangely colored beads resembling a bowl of spoiling berries. Placed atop the beads is a photograph. Unable to see clearly in the candlelight, I draw closer, terrified to find that it is a photo of me. On this occult altar is one of my favorite baby pictures and obviously Mom's as well, developed in sepia, capturing an infant Issa, bright eyed, beautiful, cherubic, and naive.

"Just how she'd like to keep me!" I say aloud.

Narrowing my eyes in the dim light, I notice a rip on the photo paper just above the child's left temple. I attribute this blemish to my recent mental problems. The defect wasn't always there, on the photo or in my head. I believe the imperfection ripped, as if by magic, from the surface of that photo into my mind. Now, with the thought of my beloved mother deliberately sabotaging my life through occult practices, I feel lost with not even a safe home to retreat to. The unrelenting subspeak that I encounter while out in the city seems tame compared to the possibility of living with a witch.

Not thinking about what Mom will do when she discovers it is missing, I snatch the photograph from the altar. While leaving I think, *Maybe she's a good witch and the altar is for good luck*. Then I take stock of all the horrible experiences I've had since last summer and my downward spiral since Dad's death. These remembrances squash any good witch/bad witch deliberations.

I have proof that Mom has been using sorcery to tamper with my life. In my hasty exit from the shadowy cove, I trip over Mom's cat, Budwiser. *Don't all witches have cats?* I deduce. The cat's name used to be just Bud, and he used to be mine. However, over time Mom got sweet on him. The name change, or enhancement, was Mom's doing after attributing many human and "intuitive" characteristics to the animal. I've grown to hate the cat and see him as the ultimate turncoat.

Panicky in my retreat, I become entangled in the beaded veil that functions as a doorway and get spooked by the curious religious objects and iconic photos placed (strategically?) all over Mom's room. Jesus, JFK, and John Lennon's eyes follow me out the room. Fighting my way out of the darkness and candle-cast shadows and into the sunlit hallway, my heart beats a quick rhythm. Although I am satisfied to have taken this trip into Mom's occult-inspired dwelling, I have the irrational yet insistent feeling that she will know I've been in there. If not by the missing photograph then certainly her damned cat Budwiser will tell her.

54

THIRTEEN YEARS AFTER his positive psychiatric evaluation contributed to my release from Mid-Hudson, Dr. Seagull and I meet for another interview and get reacquainted, hopefully so he will find me suitable for release. Following a long review of my three bulging charts, supporting documents brought up from medical records, and a thorough examination, the doctor opines, "Like fruit, you leave it too long it's gonna go bad. It's time for you to get out of this hospital."

Dr. Seagull returns after a year to conduct an addendum to his report and finds that I am still in good mental health and asserts, "Mr. Ibrahim has maximally benefitted from inpatient hospitalization. Any risk that he will pose when he is conditionally released will not be decreased with further involuntary confinement." Dr. Seagull will go full steam ahead recommending release.

Seagull refutes Dr. Maggoty's lengthy report and her stringent assessment of me as a predatory sociopath. "What is she, trying to exercise some kind of mind control? I don't buy it, and you shouldn't either." He gets thoughtful, then asks, "What do you think? Should you still be here? Do you want to stay here?"

I make an attempt to appear humble and patient, trying to conceal my excitement in the face of this momentary vindication by saying, "Well, I know it takes time. A lot of really bad stuff has happened, my Mom, and the social worker and the nurse. Then smoking again and bugging out. And what about my family . . . ?"

"Come on, man!" Seagull encourages me with bluster. "Whadaya wanna stay in here forever? Strike while the iron is hot!" This is a very good thing to hear from a forensic psychiatrist who is usually called in by the courts to testify *against* slugs like me trying to squirm out of shit holes like this.

ONCE A NEW YORK CITY HORROR STORY, the infamous "Wild Man of 96th Street," who used to rant and rage dangerously on the Upper West Side of Manhattan, is now housed in Creedmoor. Larry Hogue works at the overpriced and chintzy deli on the second floor of Creedmoor's main building, and he's a decent and respectable gentleman, when not psychotic on crack. He has seen me come and go and asks, "What level you got, Level 3?"

"Yeah," I respond.

"Man, I wish I had Level 3."

I don't bother to tell him I've had those grounds privileges, and only that, for nearly ten years. Nor do I say, "Shit, man, you'll probably get out of here before I do."

Turns out, the Wild Man is indeed released to a residence on the grounds a few months later. It irks me but not too much. I am used to it, patients coming after me and leaving before me. I just focus on my case and hope for the best.

With the secret aid of a few good friends in my support system, and several thousand dollars from sold artwork, I finally bury Gaia's dinosaur Toshiba PC and buy myself a new Apple MacBook. Even more exciting, I have also signed up via auto-pay on my credit card to a wireless broadband access account. So now I am connected to the Internet. Much like my cell phone, access to the Internet is considered a dangerous thing in this hospital and thus forbidden. These pieces of contraband are essential for researching my case and contacting outside resources. I guard them and myself diligently.

Of course I do on the computer what everybody else does first. I look up old flames. I am pleased to discover a few have done quite well, including Clu, who was promoted to model's registrar at the Art Students League, and Bella, who assists military medical personnel. It's a job she acquired presumably through her oldest son, who is now in the

Marines. So it seems there is a way to bounce back from a demoralizing dismissal from Creedmoor.

AFTER AN UNSUCCESSFUL ATTEMPT in asking the court to appoint another independent psychiatrist I hire Dr. Allen Richman. I will need at least two doctors testifying on my behalf to impress the courts, and I want to bolster my case. Dr. Richman is a quiet, kind, and competent older gentleman who interviewed me in 1997. He was recommending discharge back then but in truth I wasn't ready: I still had one last full-blown psychotic breakdown in me. I believe now, a decade later, is my time.

Dr. Richman's fee is a reasonable $1,500: $800 given up front for the examination and the remaining $700 for testimony in court. I've been saving for several years and was expecting to pay a great deal more and thus I am hesitant. However, my support system suggests I spend whatever money I can afford toward getting a good doctor to counter the hospital's reluctance and Dr. Maggoty's attack. "You can't put a price on freedom," everyone seems to say.

Dr. Richman is impressed and satisfied that I am suitable for conditional release. Now I have two forensic psychiatrists who believe I am dischargeable and they are willing to testify to that effect, in addition to the Living Museum's Dr. Marton, who says, "Make sure I am subpoenaed. The hospital won't allow me to go voluntarily. Once there, against my will, as if, I will say whatever it takes to get you out."

THE HOSPITAL HAS GOTTEN WIND of my intention to fight it out in court. To avoid possibly losing the case, and in an effort to hold on to me, they have decided to recommend me again for Level 4. The catch is that I must consent to a battery of psychological tests officiated by Dr. Corby Edwards. He's a former therapist of mine from my days on 6-B, notorious for spending entire sessions not letting me get a word in edgewise. I'm sure Edwards used to be a decent psychologist once upon a time but, like all one-time worthwhile Creedmoor employees, he probably questions why he's still here and now just rides it out for the paycheck and benefits.

Edwards, bearded, bald, and pony-tailed, is an aging hippie who acts as a laugh track in case conferences of the utmost importance. He snickers shamelessly behind every desperate question I ask, as if I am a fool for trying to comprehend and clarify my options, viewing my fight for life and understanding of this very perilous situation with unbridled amusement. I suppose I am assumed recalcitrant and combative for questioning the professionals, or maybe he has passed his own judgment on me and sees my desperation as a guilty man trying to buy some time. He comes off, true to the opinion of other patients in similar straits who've dealt with him, as "just another sadistic cracker" laughing at my misfortunes.

We run through the tests quickly. The Minnesota Multiphasic Personality Inventory, Rorschach, Wechsler Adult Intelligence Survey, the whole nine. I have no fear of negative results because I believe that I am healthy and the testing is all subjective bullshit conducted, compiled, scored, and disseminated by an excessively eccentric employee who is himself but a minor meltdown away from his own bed in Creedmoor. I do not care one bit what the Forensic Bureau will do with his results or my case. I have my will and my strategy and both are strong.

Dr. Edwards's psychological evaluation is favorable but falls short of the discharge mark, staying on message with Maggoty and the hospital. The doctor claims to have uncovered "significant elements of rage" and "pervasive evidence of the patient faking good."

Barry is disturbed by this but says he's seen it before. "Basically they're gonna say you're unpredictable. A ticking time bomb. It's not good but I'll do all I can to minimize it when we get before the judge."

"Barry, it's crap."

"I know, Issa. I know."

55

THE MAHATAS HAVE A COMPLEX ROLE here in Creedmoor, from spiritual supporters to demonic tormentors. Similar to the COs of the penitentiaries, the Mahatas have access to all our personal information. And though you hope they will be discreet and professional, some do let their biases get the better of them.

During the overnight shift, while I am in my bedroom painting, the Mahatas sleep. Those that do not, or cannot, pass the time reading the patient charts. By and large they are ignorant to literature besides the money-drugs-and-pussy Blaxploitation books that have grown in popularity lately. At least they're reading. But they can find any number of compelling true crime or personal and family dramas contained within the bulging, blue plastic folders in the chart room. From childhood history to police report, autopsy to diagnosis, and in years of progress notes, our lives provide plenty of juicy meat for these beasts to chew on from midnight to six.

One early morning, as I shuffle from my bedroom to the dayroom where we sit for a spell before breakfast is called, an unfamiliar overnight staff calls out to me, "Yo man! That's fucked up what you did."

"Shit happens," I mumble back, too tired and defensive to engage or explain.

Some Mahatas pick the cooler, cogent patients to be their pets. Someone that they can joke with, boast to, and who they hope will have their back if one of the other patients decides to go ape shit. While I recognize Mr. Ding grooming me for this role, I resist, keeping my distance, never volunteering too much or laughing too loud at his crude or corny jokes. I avoid becoming his sycophant because he has a more than willing one in Mitch.

Tall, black-skinned, and weedy with a Fu Manchu moustache, Mitch has been in captivity for nearly forty years. Like many insanity plea patients he overindulges in liquor, drugs, usury, and sex whenever he can get it, and, like this population, he always gets caught. This leads to multiple restrictions and eventually decades of being locked up. He's never really lived outside. Considering how institutionalized Mitch is he functions quite well. Some people won't be stopped. He reads the paper, watches the evening news, and plays a wicked game of chess. He deserves a lot of credit for surviving in this place.

I get all this and more information not only from observation, but also from Mr. Ding. "Yeah, that Mitch is a bad dude," he whispers. "He killed a kid during a fight at thirteen while housed in a juvenile detention center. Fucked up, right? I mean, I've known him for years, and I'll give him my keys to let the other patients in their rooms, same as I do with you. But *really* trust him? Can't say that I do. He's a lifer. He'll never get out of here."

When I see Mr. Ding laugh and joke and commiserate with Mitch I figure he's also pulling him close and whispering, "Yeah, that Issa is a bad dude . . ."

Thanks to Mr. Ding and the other Mahatas who have taken a shine to me I have gleaned the personal histories and—most interesting to these gossipmongers—the crimes committed while sick that brought some of these insanity plea patients into the hospital. And while the other patients also eventually find out about each other, many minimize their own offense by decrying someone else's.

The most vocal and ugly of this type is Bernie from Astoria. He's verbally attacked many, including me, when his insecurity kicks in. Though never to his face, I end up calling him Speed Racer. Not only because he ran over and killed his Chinese landlady with his classic muscle car but also because he now fuels his diatribes against his peers with cocaine smuggled in by his brother during visiting time.

As in prison, the most hated are the child molesters and sex offenders. Mr. Ding tells me we have two here on the ward. There's Danny, a slight, messy, former accountant who stays to himself except when broadcasting odd sexual non sequiturs: "Three holes gets you bingo!" "If I only had a spoon!" "Everything below the waist is just a fetish!"

Then there's Billy. He's about fifty but has the body and demeanor of a teenager. With his tight crew cut, creased jeans, and pin neat bed making skills, Billy is called on by the staff to make the beds of the more disorganized patients who just can't get it together. Billy is also up early to take the main chair in front of the TV in the dayroom. There he sits and pinches his penis through his pants while watching *Sesame Street*. As the playful opening theme chimes and Billy pinches away I just look at him and Danny and the others in my midst and say to myself, *"I gotta get out of here."*

Perhaps the most tragic and sad are the patients who have lost hope and given up. Or those who just keep coming back. I find a friend in Jordan, a very intelligent and quirky escapee from the Hasidim. If someone were to call central casting for Shylock, Jordan would certainly fit the bill.

Jordan is fighting his umpteenth hospitalization. "And I think I'll win," he says with a charming optimism. "I've got my own lawyer, my niece and her children, my rabbi, letters from former mayor David Dinkins, who's a very sweet man, by the way. Oh, and an autographed eight-by-ten of Roger Grimsby from Eyewitness News."

"Isn't he dead?"

"Is he? Oh . . . well, I guess I can't use that."

Jordan appreciates the fact that I'm smart, an artist, and somewhat cultured. Of course I get wary when during a visit from Lily I see him swapping spit with his visitor, a burly, disheveled, sickly Hispanic man.

"Sorry you had to see that," he says when we're back on the ward. "That was Edison. We're just friends. You and I can be friends too."

"Uh, well yeah. We can talk and stuff but I gotta tell ya Jordan, I don't swing that way."

"Hmmm," he muses. "S'shame."

Jordan mounts his case in Creedmoor's kangaroo court. Dressed in an impeccable blue pinstripe suit and wearing his yarmulke for good measure, he has his dream team, family, letters of recommendation, even Roger Grimsby, and wins his discharge. Unfortunately, I see him escorted by hospital security back to the ward by the end of the week.

"Me and Edison celebrated my release, and, well, I guess you could say we *over*-celebrated. We drank a lot. I drank a lot. He was smoking that stuff, crack? And then he gave me some, and then we got some more and, it's very addictive you know. And before you know it I'm in the emergency room at St. Vincent's. They check my records, they see I'm from Creedmoor, and it was like, uh oh. I guess I shouldn't have smoked the crack, huh?"

"Nah, Jordan, I don't think so."

When Jordan realizes he isn't going to get any from me regardless of how friendly we are, he successfully puts the moves on Ernesto. With his broad shoulders, muscular frame, and impressive Romanesque profile I have taken to calling Ernesto the Gladiator. He is a sexual animal, fucking any patient who will take him. Jordan is in heaven.

Ernesto speaks absolutely no English and trying to communicate with him is often like trying to talk to the Hulk, full of emphatic eye movements and hand gestures, frustrated grunts, and garbled approximations of what could be English words. I really like the Gladiator. He has a very beautiful mother and sister who come to visit him regularly and are clearly suffering with him in his journey. The male Mahata staff are intimidated by Ernesto's size and not being able to communicate with him and talk him down whenever he becomes agitated, which is often. He makes several trips to the Secure Care Unit for fighting.

Then, in a bull session, Mr. Ding tells me, "Oh, did you hear what happened? Ernesto got involved in a fight with staff in secure. He had to be subdued, and then just died." I believe they killed the Gladiator.

OVER THE YEARS I'VE SEEN many heartbreaking family tragedies. The unconditional love. The obligation. The guilt trip. But the most painful family dynamics derive from sharing the ward with Vinnie, a chronically ill fellow patient, and witnessing his abuse of his doting elderly mother and somber younger brothers.

Vinnie rages, schemes, and overemotes like a rabid hedgehog, salt-and-pepper mullet framing wild, dark-rimmed eyes, a beak of a nose, and an under-bite of protruding, wickedly rotten teeth. He is intense and angry that his family has committed him.

"Ma! Ma! Look, you gotta get me outta here, Ma!"

"Look, you cocksucker motherfucker . . ."

"Ma! You cocksucker, get me outta here!"

"Fuck you, Ma!"

When not terrorizing his family on the ward payphone, Vinnie stalks the halls, trying each bedroom door to see if he can get in and sleep. "Why does Issa get to stay in his room? Who the fuck is he?" He constantly complains to staff, "Why can't I stay in my room?"

I invite Vinnie into my room occasionally because, while crude and generally nasty, he can be quite amusing and even charming in his own way. We have good times listening to my radio, talking music, and discussing Mafia films. And he develops a crush when spying several photos on my room's bulletin board.

"Who's that?"

"My girlfriend."

"You got a girlfriend?"

"Yeah."

"Big fuckin' man. Look at you, with a girlfriend. So what's her name?"

"Lily."

"Lily? Wow. That's a nice name. Is she white? Cuz she looks white."

"She's mixed."

"Oh. Mixed, huh? What is that, like black and white?"

"Yeah."

"But she looks white. Issa likes that white meat, huh? Huh? No, but she's very pretty. Can I borrow that picture?"

"No, Vinnie."

I have numerous falling outs with Vinnie. He just can't help himself. Once, jealous and angry that he couldn't get into his room, he tries my bedroom door while I am out on my morning privileges at the Living

Museum. Vinnie gets inside. When I return to the ward and my room I discover my guitar out of its case, the neck slathered with almond butter. The empty jar is sitting lidless on my dresser.

Exiting my room, I find the culprit, Vinnie, standing down the hall, stubby fingers and unshaven mouth smeared with almond butter. As I approach him he looks at me with shame, anger, and defiance. "Fuck you and your peanut butter!" He screams, "You nigger cocksucker! Fuck you and your peanut butter!"

I banish Vinnie from my room and my good graces many times but after a while he always comes back. "I'm sorry," he says sheepishly. "I'm a sick man. You know that, don't you? I'm a sick man."

"It's OK, Vinnie."

Always in trouble with the staff, Vinnie gets away with his shenanigans because of his involved family. Lily and I are often in the visitor's room, making out to tunes on my radio, when Vinnie's family arrives. I, like most of the other patients, don't get family visits, so it hurts to see and hear Vinnie curse and scream at his family during visiting hour. Vinnie is one of those strange but all too familiar cases where I'm unsure if he's spiteful, combative, and nasty because of his illness or because he's just a jerk.

Like many patients I've known in this journey, Vinnie gets discharged before I do. It's understandable. Though chronically ill he doesn't have charges or an offense. He's loud and destructive but really all bluster and basically harmless. But I hear him in one of his rants mercilessly expose and disparage Speed Racer as "an evil, murderous old Chinese-lady-killing cocksucker!" I am glad that Vinnie does not know what brought me here, even if he would return later, saying, "I'm sorry. I'm a sick man. You know that, don't you? I'm a sick man."

56

VERY LOW ON RATIONS back at the house, I am reluctant to eat any more of the food Mom has downstairs. It's both not wanting to sponge off what she works for and being distrustful of ingesting something she prepared for fear of turning into a toad or something. As a result my food intake over several months dwindles and I begin losing weight.

I hardly notice my eating habits drop off because there are far too many other things I have to worry about—like where my next high is coming from. However, I can't ignore the grumbles in my stomach and decide to venture to the neighborhood supermarket up my block. Apprehensive on my walk over, and suspicious of my neighbors as they hustle and rush from buses and shops into their homes, I quicken my pace to avoid contact with these once-friendly-but-now-questionable acquaintances.

On the way I am assaulted by subspeak, hostile gestures, and outright insults as I pass pedestrians on the street—"Nigger!" "Faggot!" "Dummy!" I don't dare stop to question or challenge these affronts to my race, manhood, and intellect. I just focus my eyes on the pavement and focus my mind on the reefer I will smoke when I get back home.

The threatening feeling of being exposed in the street becomes a concentrated fear in the supermarket. I believe everyone in this store can read my thoughts, as if I were on a certain frequency that they can tune into like a radio. Upon discovering this overwhelming network of information and communication, my first instinct is to turn from inside the market's doorway and run out into the open air and safe thinking again. But I am fixed to this one spot, immobile and horrified.

Standing bolt upright in that same spot for many long minutes, I realize if I don't do something I will arouse more suspicion than warranted, and Heaven knows what they'll do then! I walk slowly and deliberately, as if suffering a stroke and being rehabbed, past the bank of checkout stations that fester with nosey mind benders. Believing they are already channeling in to my station, I try to put a lock on my thoughts and feelings, especially the fear, as I pad to the nearest aisle.

Once in the aisle, hidden from most of the patrons and market help, I am tempted to exhale deeply and hug the wall of foodstuffs as if hiding behind a war-torn barricade. This cannot be done, as other shoppers emerge from down the aisle. I remind myself, *Watch your thoughts*, while trying to appear like them—just an evening shopper. Or was *this* even so?

Grabbing a gallon of milk, my mind screams, *No! No! No! It's white! White! You can't buy that.* Milk, as white as white can be, *must* have a Caucasoid, and ultimately evil, connotation, accounting for my assimilation into the Caucasian culture and neglecting my African American heritage. I was such an avid milk drinker since childhood, from breakfast cereal to Nestlé's Quik, that the evil "white menace" infiltrated and conquered my inner black self through constant ingestion of the liquid. I was whitewashed from the inside out. I am angry and in shock. I run down the mental list of items I want to buy and find they all have a negative connection, by color or name, as in what its name resembles, as the many brands bounce about my brain like a child's jumble puzzle revealing itself to be the Enigma code. And if a certain item is neutral my mind rejects it because of its placement on the shelves next to a more offensive or obviously disturbing item, like guilt by association.

I could spend all evening going over the items and through the aisles, spotting the edible offenders, intricately deciphering and exposing (within my mind, for remembrance sake) the deceptive products that I have bought on numerous occasions in the past, fooled by their innocuous packaging. Uncle Ben, Aunt Jemima, and the Cream of Wheat cook all laugh at me from the shelves. These new rules of shopping and, even further, healthy, "authentic" eating and living, are enlightening but in a frightening way.

What drives me out is the arrival of some of the men from the local fire station, garbed in heavy boots and jackets, some wearing helmets. Their presence is a terrible assault on my already traumatic shopping experience. I see their jobs as bogus. Yes, they are firefighters, but in a deeper subspeak sense. Their duty is to extinguish the fire and ire that burn within all black people for past and present injustices. Of course, the firemen that I see within the market are all white. Of course, they have come for me.

I panic, wondering, *Who told?* Perhaps young blacks who wake up to social and economic inequality start to emit a glow, and depending on how aware, or "dangerous," these blacks get, the "firefighters" are summoned to put 'em out. I've never seen myself as a truly aware young black man, but maybe they see (or are told) that I am a potential big burner, perhaps a troublemaker, maybe even a three-alarm martyr-type when fully awakened. I flee the market with nothing in hand.

Just when I am beginning to come to some degree of awareness as a black American man I discover that I must temper my thoughts and feelings. I am forced to keep all of my impulses suppressed. I have to make sure that my head is clear of incriminating evidence. When in the presence of people indoors I make conscious efforts to play brain dead. Although I have no exact idea what the "firemen" would do to me by way of extinguishing the fires of "militancy" beginning to burn inside me, I fear it is horrible, irreversible, and complete. After all, this network has its shit together.

57

A FRIENDLY AND HELPFUL Living Museum volunteer and I secretly put together and unveil a starter website for myself, showcasing my artwork and including links to my buddies the Spongetones, pop rock purveyors from North Carolina. My decadelong correspondence with these indie rock and roll gentlemen, via letters to their fan club, develops into mutual admiration after I start sending them prints of some of my artwork. The vague promise of "maybe putting your work on one of our releases" eventually yields one of my custom paintings on the label and inlay of their CD *Too Clever by Half*.

Less than a year later, after mailing off several photo-ready acrylic paintings for possible merchandise work, they decide on my quickly scribbled impromptu Christmas card band caricature for the cover of the new Spongetones CD *Scrambled Eggs*. Scribble, scramble, I get it. I am proud and grateful, fulfilling a dream born from tracing Beatles album covers as a child.

So now my work can be found on CDs, T-shirts, mugs, mouse pads, and even baby bibs, all of which will be entered into evidence at my hearing, bolstering my credibility as a talented and employable artist. My work is even being shown in successful Living Museum offshoot exhibitions in South Korea, the Netherlands, Austria, and Istanbul, some sponsored by pharmaceutical companies impressed with Creedmoor's rehab department and what they see as the results of effective treatment. It's bittersweet reaping the rewards of positive artistic achievement while locked up, creating constantly to take my mind off the many failed attempts at unescorted furloughs.

Though my case is stagnant, I lobby hard for and am granted an escorted pass to celebrate my birthday at swank Manhattan nightclub the Cutting Room. Escorted by one-to-one male Mahata staff, I am joined by two close friends and Lily. The biggest thrill of all is taking in a live show by acclaimed producer and recording artist Don Dixon. Playing guitar in his trio is Jamie Hoover of the Spongetones. It is like a dream to finally meet Jamie, after years of loving his music and our spirited correspondence, listen to some fantastic live sounds, and get a birthday shout-out from Dixon and the band from the stage. It is a magical night that couldn't have been better. While nursing a glass of white wine graciously ordered by the sloshed Mr. Ding, surrounded by friends, with a beautiful woman wrapped around me, digging the show, I almost forget I am a mental patient embroiled in a death match for my freedom. This special evening lets me know what I am fighting for.

Mr. Ding plays the role of reluctant overseer to an "unpredictable" charge, and "unofficial permanent escort" for the benefit of the treatment team concerned about my off-grounds passes. "Trust me, it's the only way you'd get to go out," he tells me. He's probably right.

He guarantees them no bullshit from me, and a firm grip on the proceedings, while gleefully getting overtime for duty spent off the ward and away from the hospital. Stone-faced and shoulder-to-shoulder when exiting the building, he lightens up and spreads out once our state van pulls away from the main gates. Lighting up a cigarette, flipping on New York black music staple WBLS, crooning out of tune to Luther, he settles in for a day of dereliction. Whether I'm meeting with Gaia, Lily, or other friends in my support system, going to an art opening, the cinema, shopping mall, or restaurant, Mr. Ding hangs back, always giving the proper amount of respectful privacy. I never quite forget he's there though, especially when he balks at my movie choices, always angling for a dumbed down action flick, eating up time trying on numerous ugly 8-ball jackets in the fitting rooms, and disappearing to the restaurant restroom when it's time to pay the check.

AFTER TWO AND A HALF YEARS waging my personal and costly war against Creedmoor's Bureau of Forensic Services, they step up to the bargaining table. Following Dr. Edwards's multiple testing evaluations, which were favorable though skewed on the side of retention, the bureau has decided to greenlight their recommendation to Albany for my unescorted off-ground privileges.

One of the more benign faces in the meeting to discuss this privilege possibility, besides Barry Newfeld, is Dr. Dina D'Amato. She is an ambitious young psychologist who has been acting as my therapist for the last year or so. She replaced Dr. Patricia Crapella, whom I've known since she was a young starry-eyed St. John's University extern from my days on 6-B in the '90s. The ineffectual Dr. Crapella moved up to become the right hand of Maggoty in forensics. Crapella gave glowing references to me when it became clear that D'Amato would take over for her as my therapist, and her recommendation came as no surprise as both are Long Island heavy metal headbangers. D'Amato appears to be even more so, with the requisite skinny body and long, teased, bleach-blonde hair. Somehow I can't respect a doctor who still listens to heavy metal. While she has a pleasant disposition D'Amato comes off like another team player and our sessions, much like those with Crapella, are meandering and empty. I figure she'll go far in this organization.

Dr. Maggoty officiates the meeting like she is doing me a favor and like she cares. But I feel that I am a very minor player in a major league chess game, where the hospital is threatened and puts forth their queen. Before proceeding, Maggoty asks, "I just want to know one thing before we begin, Mr. Ibrahim. Are you independently wealthy?"

"Huh?"

"I said, are you independently wealthy?"

Most patients don't and/or can't scrape up enough cash to hire independent doctors to counter her determinations, and the fact that I successfully did surprises and annoys her. While I revel in her ire, I feign discomfort and stutter back, "Uh, no. Uh, I saved a little money from sales of my artwork, but no, I don't have any money."

Trying to display fairness but looking more like a snake coughing up a leprous mouse, Maggoty levels her determination to allow the

Level 4 but "only if we go slow." Her quoting this time-tested stopping method, minted during the civil rights era to push back anxious, expectant, and uppity Negroes, eager for equality and fomenting for freedom, hits me in the gut. It seems she's become my Governors Faubus *and* Wallace in cheap polyester dresses. She closes with the cold proclamation, "I am allowing you to go to school and to work and *that's it!*"

Now, maybe I should look at the brighter side of that edict, as Barry suggests upon leaving the meeting. She's putting a bounty of time on the table for a school and work program, but an insanity plea patient, after many years climbing the privilege ladder, only gets a couple of hours a week to start and has to wait six months or longer for an increase. I'm unhappy being forced, as I see it, to go to school or work, tackling these stressful activities without a healthy amount of down time or decent leisure privileges. Nor do I relish the thought of having to study in the toxic and turbulent environs of a psych ward. It all sounds like a recipe for my next relapse. But I act sufficiently humble and walk out of the meeting with the attitude of, "If that's all you're offering, I'll take it," knowing full well in my heart that I will fight them tooth and nail for my freedom.

Many months of delays and adjournments have me now looking for something, anything. Upon hearing that my application for Level 4 is coming down from Albany, Barry has been in talks with the DA. That office has tentatively agreed to the privilege with a retention order bargain, keeping me in the hospital for ten months, if I drop the case. That sure beats the usual two years. I could do ten months on my head. And then if need be (and I'm pretty sure the hospital will push me to it) I will mount the case for discharge all over again—asking the court for an independent, hiring my own, asking my friends for letters of support, asking Dr. Marton to testify on my behalf (knowing that Creedmoor may punish him)—and just dig in for a fight. The upside to this will be that I will not feel as vulnerable as I do now without the Level 4: I can then show I can function on the outside, coming and going on time, responsibly and safely within the same society that the State of New York has kept me from.

Most of my supporters tell me to stay strong and fight, take the case as far as it can go. Others suggest waiting for the furlough. I keep my strategy, and determination, locked up tight for fear of ridicule and also because I don't know if I will win the case. The professional staff are treating my fight for freedom like a game of chicken, some keeping mum, others smiling smugly, convinced that I am a fool with too much money. All waiting to see who will blink.

It feels like I have no one in this place offering me support, because what I am doing is rarely attempted. The ward staff tries to pry me for information, but I continue to play it cool and aloof. Dissatisfied with my poker face, Mr. Ding, accustomed to institutional justice, sneers, "Careful how you spend your money, bro. It don't matter how many lawyers or doctors you pay for. The hospital always wins."

58

COLLECTING CLUES LIKE A DESPERATE MAN gathers food for his bomb shelter on the eve of destruction, I imagine every minute spent tonight is bringing the world I know closer to a horrible end, and an even more terrifying beginning for others similarly unprepared. Unity is the key to the whole process, a strong bonding of a mass of people, hell, the whole planet—even if it is at the hands, or claws, or tentacles of aliens. That the earth finally comes together to think and feel as one is a beautiful thing—and here I am left out.

It's been weeks of insomnia, fasting, and filth. With the very last of my money buying a dime of smoke, I've become almost skeletal, parading to and from my modeling job in the middle of winter in nothing more than a leather motorcycle jacket, sneakers, and a pair of black bike messenger tights. I notice and become startled by the brand name emblazoned on my thigh: Adidas. This innocuous logo brands me as a relic, a New World nonconformist. More than advertising the company's name I am exposing myself for what I truly am: *a did as*. I "did as" before: before the inception and worldwide acceptance of subspeak, before the imminent takeover by aliens, before our emerging into this strange new world. I am unwilling and unable to conform. In the evolving climate of this new earth, being *a did as* is a dangerous thing to be.

Nervously pacing, waiting for The Change, rubbing *Adidas* away with a thick black Sharpie, I don't expect what happens to me. Stepping out of my front bedroom I catch a rush. My eyebrows join my hairline. My eyes widen almost to the point of popping out. Standing rigid, feet apart, arms at my side, resembling a goggle-eyed gunfighter just about to draw, I get zapped!

My mind is suddenly flooded with *loud sound*—voices, like someone turning on a radio to maximum volume while it is between stations
and then whizzing the dial back and forth. I hear bits and pieces. Tastes
of things ominous and foreboding and then other words and phrases
interfere, overriding the previous proclamations. I stand still, hunched
with a contorted, concentrating face, trying to decipher at least one of
the myriad messages I am receiving.

I hear a voice. It is in my own voice, yet it isn't me. Not the "me"
I'd come to know. It is me "as if." As if I am "changed." Smarter, wiser,
better than I think myself to be. When I speak I hear other voices
clarifying the message.

"*You and others in your generation got gypped! Jerked! Burned! Fucked!*"

"What? What do you mean?" I beg myself for more.

"*You mid-sixties kids were cheated out of becoming the greatest this planet
had to offer in terms of outright genius. You are the Alpha and Omega. Here
comes the download.*"

As I hear this, into my mind flash millions of split-second images
of world events, American history, and, most important, *African* American history. I start to focus while reviewing millisecond clips of civil
rights struggles, multiple lynchings, a burning bus in Anniston, Alabama,
four dead girls in Birmingham, Bloody Sunday on the Edmund Pettis
Bridge, Malcolm, me as a baby, Watts, Dr. King. The images and messages continue but I fix on one in particular, which becomes superim-
posed over all and starts to slowly enlarge as the others race. It is the
damaged image of me as a toddler amidst all of those African American
achievers and milestones.

"Me? Could I have made a difference?"

"*You still can!*"

I look around the kitchenette and see nothing out of the ordinary
but seem to hear *everything*. I am hearing things that I don't want to hear
and learning things I don't want to know. The images continue their
pitch within my head as I now watch the 1980s take shape—economic
collapse, AIDS, crack, the war on drugs, and my failure to realize my
potential.

"Your place in history," a voice corrects. *"Your destiny!"*

"My destiny," I repeat, softly at first and then loud, with fury. Soon the messages become more obtuse.

" . . . They discovered a cure for AIDS, we can fuck all we want . . ."

" . . . In two days we'll all be dead . . ."

" . . . Beware the Antichrist, you have to kill him . . ."

"What? Wait a minute, wait a minute! I don't want to kill anybody!" But the messages continue and I realize I unknowingly bought into something that is turning remarkably dark.

"Why two days? What's going to happen? I don't want to kill anybody . . . I can't! Why?" I ask again and again, but the messages turn to riddles, except for one stunning declaration.

"The only one who can kill the Antichrist is Christ himself . . . and that's YOU!"

"Jesus? Me?" Suddenly I understand what they are saying. The fact that my name means Jesus in Arabic slaps me in the face. This Change is awakening to the Second Coming.

"Am I Jesus Christ?" I demand.

"Yes," they reply. *"Yes. Yes. Yes."*

"No!" I cry, losing my breath. I feel dizzy. If what I am receiving is correct (and it has to be because I firmly believe the voices don't lie) then I *am* the Messiah. The voices then become invisible entities. Not only from within, and around me, but above me. I feel like a pet in a tank watched by the Gods, Gods greater than *me*, Jesus, if such a thing is possible. They aren't just distant Gods, they are friends, and they are family.

"All right, let's just say I'm Jesus," I say, trying to negotiate. "What about this 'dead in two days' stuff? Is that true? I mean, isn't there *something* I can do?"

"No."

"No? Aw c'mon! Don't tell me that! And what about the 'cure for AIDS'?" Just then, above all the voices familiar and unknown, come the soft tones of my former girlfriend, Scarlett.

"Channeling's the cure. We all developed our skills, reaching into one another's minds, discovering alternative stimuli. Nowadays, we don't fuck genitally. We fuck mentally. It's much more satisfying. It's been going on for some time."

I am flabbergasted and also a little peeved. "You mean you've been fucking anybody and everybody you've wanted to? Just as simple as thinking about it?"

"Yes. But don't be jealous, it's beneath you. Listen, you've got very little time and so much to accomplish. We're all behind you, though. We love you very much." Then Scarlett says with respect, *"I'm really glad I got to know you."*

Scarlett's voice crackles and fades as if there is static interference. I lose her frequency, her channel overridden by a stronger signal.

"Hello, Iss," greets a deep male voice that I recognize immediately. My eyes bulge in disbelief. I acquire crystal-clear contact with my dead father, making me feel like Hamlet.

Staring into the shadowy hallway I see an ethereal, shrouded Jamil Ibrahim as I'd seen him last—frail, with most of his lower jaw removed after preventive surgery. He looks sad, but not because he was operated on and lost his good looks and his mellifluous singing voice, or that he'd been stricken with cancer, or that he is dead. His sadness is for me.

"Dad? Is that you?" My father doesn't say but two words to me, his voice choked with pain.

"I'm sorry."

"Aw shit!" I cry and run from my art studio/kitchenette, running from the many unseen eyes, the expectant and hopeful voices. "I can't do this!" I run into my rear bedroom, but the beings, their presence, is here too. Suddenly, running around my upstairs apartment, I feel like a lab rat in a maze viewed by a superior intelligence. I have an audience but my frightened scampering does not amuse them.

"Calm down!" Scarlett returns. *"Yeah, this is a shock but deal with it! It's all very complex, Jesus, but you were one of us."*

"What? A deity?"

"For lack of a better word, yes. But you were altered, interfered with, poisoned. That's why you're so confused now."

"But by who?" I ask, but I already know the answer. I just refuse to accept it as truth.

"She couldn't help it." Scarlett says.

"No! No! I don't want any of this. I can't go through with it. I don't wanna be Jesus. I can't do it," I protest to the empty room.

"Well, you don't want to get the wrong end of the reincarnation stick, do you? It can be arranged, you know. You always thought yourself a bit of a stud," she jeers. *"How'd you like to come back as a fucking horse?"*

Hearing these damning words I feel my posture stiffen as I involuntarily thrust my butt and chest up and out. My right leg kicks out in front of me, striking the floor in a counting gesture. Snorting, my head rearing up and around, completing the charade, I begin braying like a horse. I struggle to regain my composure and human characteristics.

"No! Please! Stop! I'll do it. I'll do whatever you want if I have no choice. I'll be Jesus. But I'm not going to kill anyone."

HOURS HAVE GONE BY without my realizing it and dawn is breaking. Gazing out my bedroom window, I feel that I am a marked man. I duck down out of sight, imagining unmarked government cars driving up to assassinate me.

"This is my destiny. This is my destiny," I whisper to myself, as I crawl along the floor trying not to be spotted and shot.

Mom has been implicated in the devilish plot to keep me from coming back to deliver my people to salvation. I do not want to believe it. Now that I face assassination, Mom is the only one I want to be with. Still on my belly, I slide down the stairs, desperate not to be seen. I am certain there are evil people who were tuned into the Channeling and know I've woken up but figure they aren't sure who Jesus is or where he lives. I have to protect my anonymity.

Once downstairs, stripped of everything but my tights and black Chuck Taylor high-tops, I seek out Mom. She is already up and ready for work. I meet her in the living room.

"Look Ma, Jesus in sneakers!"

"Hmm. Sounded like you had company up there," she says.

I dismiss her subspeak and ask, "Am I Jesus, Mom? Tell me, am I Jesus?"

Mom looks into my eyes, waits a thoughtful moment, then says, "Yes, son."

"Wow," I exclaim. Stunned by her affirmation, breathless with shock, I feel important, majestic, and powerful. "Thanks, Ma," I say, kissing her on the head. "Well, I'd better get going, there's a lot I've got to do, even though I don't quite know what I'm doing."

"I know, son."

This remark strikes me as strange. Doing a double take, I glance back at her. She is dressed and made up, but sloppily, like a homeless harridan. Mom used to be beautiful, yet this morning her caked black eye liner, spidery mascara, and crude red eye shadow make her look crazier than I feel. I try to be cool but I am panicking inside. It must be true what "they" said about her. She knows that I know who I am now and I'm seeing her now for what she really is—a possessed witch.

My fear goes up a thousandfold when I suddenly hear the sound of gigantic, pavement-shattering hooves, galloping down the street. I look out onto Linden Boulevard from the picture window in the living room and see nothing but an occasional early morning driver. I know these thunderous hooves do not belong to any vehicle, or the ghosts of Indians on spectral horses, but the devil himself, looking to kick ass. Looking for me!

59

A CAR PULLS UP AND SPITS OUT a fresh copy of the day's *New York Times* before driving off. I fear that car is one in the fleet of unmarked government assassin vehicles. I step outside nearly nude to retrieve the paper. I don't need to peel back the blue plastic sheath and read because I am certain I'll see my picture, or references to my Second Coming, touted throughout the paper like a beloved heavyweight fighter's return to the ring. I'm sure I make it above the fold.

I feel duty bound and sanctified while lurching, peeking, ducking, and weaving about my own house. I dare not look too long out my windows. I fear every car that passes contains at least one possessed soul looking to take me out. This is evidenced by the demonic red glow of each auto's taillight. I hide from the world in my rear bedroom and smoke the confusion away.

MY ATTENTION FALLS TO THE TELEVISION, which has been watching me all afternoon. I see a bunch of little brown men bouncing a little brown ball back and forth on a court surrounded by spectators. But this is not just any televised basketball game. This is a means of communication, a Channeling tool.

"SCORE *for Magic Johnson!*" The announcer shouts. I take their commentary personally. They are talking about me as if I were one of the players. *"Magic Johnson is on fire tonight!"* the announcer affirms within his play by play. Since Dad's birth name was John Johnson, and I am the magic man of the moment, it makes perfect sense that this game is about me and for me. I begin to focus harder. As I do, the announcer reports a sudden upswing in the game, a marked effort by my team to score points and take the lead. The crowd cheers behind this discovery. The roar of the crowd intensifies with my eagerness to succeed and "score."

I know my role in the game. I know whom to root for and channel my energy toward. But whom am I opposing? This isn't a game pitting good against evil. Not yet, anyway. This is a friendly game, a tutorial. Just as I think this, the crowd of spectators cheers loudly again. I search my mind for friends I'd cut off in the last eight months, someone who would enjoy engaging me in an aggressive game of psychic pro b-ball. Kubir was a devout hoops lover. The crowd goes wild once I think this. The announcer shouts, *"That's another score for the home team!"*

"Koob!" I exclaim. The cheering continues. Perhaps he wants to apologize for all his mischief that I'd endured during his crack addiction. A psychic nod and wink is all I get in acknowledgment. He wants to congratulate me on graduating from failed prodigy and full-time nebbish to *Jesus Fucking Christ.*

Watching the game with a glued gaze, I briefly consider phoning Kubir, to reestablish our friendship. I realize how important his role is in my becoming the Messiah. From my first high to the Independence Day awakening last summer to this very moment, he proved to be one of many catalysts. Being like family, Kubir already knows he's got a place set for him at the Divinity Dinner when all of this is behind us. He is merely sending his regards and offering himself as a capable guide down tonight's long, hard road. As his signal fades then dies I feel that, in a roundabout way, he's done enough.

The broadcast continues but the Channeling does not. I am concerned because even though I decline Kubir's offer to be my flashlight tonight, I still need one. Without a guide I could wander the Channeling labyrinth until Armageddon. Thinking that a blast of marijuana will improve my Channeling abilities, I light up my pipe, breathing in the intoxicating smoke. Now I am ready. Feeling pangs of desperation, but not knowing what else to do, I get up and change the channel.

Staring into the television, a huge, abstracted, unblinking eye stares back at me while a deep commanding voice proclaims, "This is See B.S." I stumble onto the premier station for Channeling, subspeak, and mind reading. The big-brother-inspired, all-seeing-eye logo and fatherly voice should sway the uninitiated and naysayers into the camp of the converted. On this channel, with concentration, you can *See the B.S.* Programming continues as always, but the frequency allows the good, the righteous, and the saved to channel in and "understand," receiving bulletins about the sudden demonic coup, the imminent apocalypse, and, best of all, my status as deliverer.

Every show on See B.S. is about me and my evolution. When the program ridicules the star for comic relief, I feel low, spoofed, Jesus struggling with the simplest of subspeak. It becomes clear to me that I have within the duration of each program to summon all of my strengths and spirituality and come into Christhood. I'd pissed away most of the 6 to 7 PM hour discovering how this thing worked. I make an effort not to let subsequent programming hours escape me. During the closing credits I hear Scarlett's voice in my head.

"I see you're having problems." I am embarrassed and confess my fears.

"I need help. I don't have it all figured out yet. I'm scared."

"Don't be," Scarlett soothes. *"Just relax. Let it flow. You're really close. All you need is a little more concentration . . ."*

What I had barely touched on earlier with Kubir is even clearer with Scarlett. Previously I got feelings and vibes. I am now communicating free and strong with my former love. After surfing smoothly on a strong wave I panic when I begin to lose her signal.

Running into the front bedroom, I rummage through several dresser drawers for specific items. I find only one photograph of Scarlett—it's overexposed but I can make out her beautiful face, smiling comically close. With this I can formulate a better connection with her and she can see me. I also have a sample of her handwriting in the form of a birthday card she'd written to me in happier times. To top it off, I have two of her extracted bloodstained wisdom teeth that I placed in the colorful maw of a conch shell she'd bought for me when we vacationed in Florida. As crude and unnatural Mom's bedroom altar appeared to be, mine is absolutely awful. It reeks of bargain basement voodoo.

I skitter back and forth, busily gathering every conceivable item that bears Scarlett's mark. Hairpins, LPs we'd listened to, everything and anything that has some connection to Scarlett. Her voice in my head eggs me on to find more and more.

Seated on the floor before my sacred altar, Scarlett's voice rings clear in my head and in certain phrases within the televised dialogue. Then I begin to smell something, faint at first, musky but not unpleasant and very familiar. Something is missing. The odor needed a woman. Not just any woman . . . Scarlett.

The odor is insistent, replaying many ecstatic episodes. Looking around for the odor's origin I discover it emanating from the conch shell. Yes, the conch shell with the extracted teeth within, providing that extra-special personal touch, allowing Scarlett to send her feminine scent to me, and with it she also sends a message: *"Let's make love."*

I do not hesitate. I strip off my Adidas tights, rubbing my now erect and wanting cock against the conch shell's seductive pink opening, breathing deeply Scarlett's vaginal vapors. In wild abandon, rubbing becomes thrusts, thrusts become hard pumping, sweating in the heat of passion. The Channeling cannot get better than this.

It's 10 PM. I am on my knees in my littered bedroom, kneeling in reverence to Scarlett's pussy, the television, and the Celestials. They are in attendance thanks to the large mirror I'd sat upright next to the TV. Better to see my delusional decline into decadence and depravity.

"How was that?"

"Amazing!"

"Welcome to Channeling, Jesus."

Listening to Scarlett's pleasant voice whisper pillow talk, while still drained from our celestial sex, I contemplate her role in my life as Christ, equating her to a new age Mary Magdalene. And what must my mother's role be in this sci-fi take on the Second Coming? Virgin Mother? Judas? I dare not think too long on it for fear of discovering the truth.

I need to be with Mom. I rise and wrap my nude body in a large white blanket that covered the bed. This makes a fitting holy garb. Looking and feeling pious, I walk with regal pride downstairs. Mom is on the living room sofa stroking Budwiser.

"Hello, son."

I cannot speak; instead I laugh like a maniac. My mouth is dry after all the pot smoking. I step into the kitchen, unsure what to drink but I know better than to open the faucet at the sink. The evildoers would just love to do away with me via a jolt of toxic-demonic tap water. I settle for orange juice. On the container is a cartoon drawing of a smiling sun. It must be a hint for *this* son, as in Son of God, that the beverage is safe for Messiahs-in-training.

Mom is smoking a joint, watching the ten o'clock news on TV. Not on See B.S. but an affiliate of evil. All the stories are intricately connected to my awakening; however, the reportage is dark and sarcastic. Giggling, I decode the unraveling plots, schemes, and counterstrikes. The war is already in effect. My people are doing their best to keep the menace from discovering their weakened leader. With such devotees, how can I let them down? I am committed to Christhood.

I can tell my mad laughter is making Mom uncomfortable but she says nothing. Perhaps she thinks I am just a little too high. Maybe she has grown accustomed to her children having a few bad trips.

Back in my room, See B.S. television dispatches more Christ-watch bulletins. Scarlett's presence returns, crying out from the distance like a carnival barker, *"This ain't no free ride."* I hear familiar voices from the TV speaker. Though the faces on the screen are of famous people, they speak in the voices of women I've known. Women I've bedded. One by one, and then in conversational groups, these women give testimony to my shallow lifestyle as a noncommittal playboy. From Queenie's daughter Jewel to all the hit and runs I've had in my carnal career. The gang's all here. Their voices surround me much like I was surrounded this morning by the Celestials, only I am not coddled and informed of my imminent greatness. Now, I am slammed hard with anecdotes and sound bites conjuring all the wrong I've done in the ways of love.

Scarlett leads the march down misery lane, twirling the barbed baton in my walk of shame. Though all of the women come and go like ethereal wisps of smoke, Scarlett's presence lingers. Swept up in reliving my past and fearing the future, I drop to my knees and beg forgiveness, blubbering to all of my exes, "I'm sorry. I'm so, so sorry."

I believe these women are paraded through my consciousness one last time to give Jesus a sense of humility. Perspective of where I've been compared to where I'm going, which is still unclear but I know I'll appreciate it more than the vacuous, empty life I am leaving behind. The embarrassing past-partners party is a rude but necessary awakening to what I was and promise of what I am to be, a shot in the arm for my failing faith in the metamorphosis.

It is now 11 PM. The awakening blossoms into a star-studded party of the mind. Everyone whom I ever wanted to know, all of my idols, past and present, make an appearance as if stepping from behind a velvet curtain. Scarlett remains as hostess, introducing each celestial celebrity guest with the playfully cliché yet appropriate question, *"Do you recognize* this *voice?"* Most of the guests Scarlett escorts out of the ether are long-dead painters and an incongruous assortment of film greats and recording artists, people whose work I've respected most.

It is like a ceremonious send off reserved for retiring presidents. All of my heroes are saying good-bye to the last vestiges of Issa Ibrahim, greeting the new Messiah. With all of these once-worshipped mortals turning out for my coming of age celebration, I picture them all smiling and saying proudly, *"To think, we knew him when . . ."*

As awed as I was by the flood of voices this morning, I am floored recognizing a familiar Liverpudlian Scouse accent coo, "'*Ello, luv.*"

My eyes dart to my framed copy of the December 9, 1980, edition of the *Daily News* with the sad headline "John Lennon Slain Here." Underneath the front page is the man's autograph, absconded from a former girlfriend, who left it behind after spending six months living here with me without my parent's consent. As evidenced with Scarlett earlier, I realize that if a personal sample of someone's life, such as his or her handwriting, were in your possession the Channeling will be much clearer.

"John?" I inquire, teary eyed.

"Good luck, son."

Lennon's greeting exhilarates me. I stand, but just barely, exhorting "Whoa!" loud and breathless, shaking my head in disbelief. Scarlett laughs at my reaction to her bringing out the big guns.

"I thought you'd enjoy that. There's someone else who'd like to meet you," Scarlett says, disappearing momentarily, returning with the presence of another. My head swivels to face the large framed poster of Beach Boys founder Brian Wilson, autographed and personalized.

"Did you get your shot?" Wilson asks.

I am warmed by Brian's presence, as if reconvening with an old, dear friend. I've long admired his musical acumen and grew up feeling tremendous pity for his psychological ills. After *my* breakdown I now empathize. I believe Wilson is referring to the tremendous opportunity offered to amend the underachievement that plagued my life. I can now do something wonderful and important. As the man who would be king I accept the challenge.

All of the beings from the awakening—family, friends, and the gaggle of stars and admired performers—flit, drift, and settle about my room and mind like motes of pollen in a spring breeze. But the back-slapping and accolades are fleeting. My attention is drawn back to the television. The late evening newscast is in progress. I've come to fear the news more than any other program. While the other shows dramatize my past, present, and possible future, and commercials encapsulate my plight or majesty in tight, tuneful thirty-second spots, the news pretty much cuts to the chase. I can depend on the See B.S. talking heads to dispatch the sorry state of affairs in their typical deadpan style. After all, this is no laughing matter. This is the end of the world.

I am especially curious about a proposed space shuttle launch that is slated for 1 AM. "That's an odd time to launch a shuttle," I muse. But it is not a regular shuttle at all. This will be their instrument of destruction. The Celestials all chime in their agreement and cheer that I quickly see through the B.S.

"Shhhhhh!" I warn. The voices obey. Computer animation of the plotted course of the shuttle indicates a launch in Florida, soaring over the eastern seaboard. In its flight, the great white craft will dust all of the states in its trajectory with a toxin that limits Channeling and will kill all the "good" people, *my* people! I feel frightened and sick. Surely there isn't anything I can do now. Here I am, deemed the Savior, delivering a planet full of followers, while earlier I had difficulty deciding what to drink from my mother's fridge. The guests at my inaugural bash disappear from my internal awareness. I've never before felt so alone.

60

See B.S. News Special Report goes to a remote broadcast from Florida, televising the lift-off of the deadly shuttle. The fucking gall. Ripping the drape from the nearest window, revealing a steady snowfall, I scream into the blue-black winter sky, "No! No! No!" On television the rockets ignite. My head whips from the sky to the tube.

"It's really happening," I whisper in disbelief. "They're really gonna do it."

I grab the nearest heavy object, my father's electric bass guitar that I rescued from the back of Mom's closet downstairs. I want to shatter the screen, but manage only to switch the power button off. I swing again, turning the TV back on. Aping Pete Townshend on the Smothers Brothers Show, Jimi Hendrix at Monterey, and Paul Simonon from the Clash's iconic LP *London Calling*, I swing the mighty axe, anticipating damage and release. All I get is more See B.S. News and the dreaded shuttle, now zooming up into the sky.

"No! No! No!" I scream, striking anything and everything in the room with the instrument. The huge mirror placed beside the TV mocks me in my rampage. Staring into the mirror, I no longer see myself as I remembered me, or the sentient Celestials, but rather an evil presence, a possessed soul, and finally Satan himself.

Crying aloud in anger and fear, kicking the mirror onto my bed, I chop at the looking glass with the bass guitar, creating countless jagged fragments of reflected insanity. Breathing wildly like a crazed bull, swinging the bass again, hoping to shatter the damned television, results only in shutting the power off one last time. I raise the instrument over my shoulder, determined to give the blackened screen one sure, final blow.

Mom enters the room.

"What's the matter, son?"

61

THE CASE HAS BEGUN. My Mental Hygiene Legal Service attorney is eating, sleeping, and breathing it. Balding and small, with the frame and moxie of a boxer, Barry Newfeld is pure Brooklyn mensch. For the entirety of my time in Creedmoor he has given me a spiel with a schmear he says he gives all his clients. It's more of a mantra. "Stay on your meds, stay out of trouble, and be patient because it's all good time."

MHLS is an outside state agency embedded within the grounds of Creedmoor. The attorneys see the doctors and administrators, their supposed adversaries, every day, at lunch or in the elevator, exchanging pleasantries: "How's the kids? How's the wife? Did you finish that deck yet?"

With those subtleties at play one can't expect the attorney to then turn around and tear the doctor a new asshole, like we patients expect—it might be necessary. I believe Barry walked that fine edge and after thirty years fell on the side of acquiescence. He always took my calls and listened to my complaints. But, as this was my first experience in the system, I didn't know what to do to seek justice when I felt I was being wronged, and I believe he just let it ride. It was only when I'd had enough and started strategizing, "Let's get a doctor. Then let's get *another* doctor," that Barry realized, this kid's thinking, and started to move his ass. It being his last case before retirement I figure Barry dusted off his VHS copy of *To Kill a Mockingbird*, shed a tear, and said to himself, "Hey, wait a minute . . . I'm a lawyer. Let me help this guy out." I take Barry's advice to remain "cautiously optimistic," vacillating between taking it to the wall and taking the first good offer that's thrown at me.

But I find out via Dr. Maggoty's testimony on the stand that Albany has turned me down. Again. No Level 4. Nothing. This latest denial is the result of Maggoty's legacy of damning reports on me. I am feeling edgy and depressed but show no emotion in the small courtroom. So I guess I play for all the marbles now. "Shoot for the moon," Barry quietly says.

Barry promises to guide me in making the right decision, understanding that I really just want to get the hell out of here. I stand outside every day waiting for the Creedmoor Circle Line Bus that transports the patients to their various programs on the campus and quietly survey the other insanity plea patients, some who've had Level 4 privileges for decades. I don't want to be another one of them, a Creedmoor zombie, beaten down by the system, haunting these grounds till I'm toothless and frail, no longer seen as a threat.

I feel as if I finally see the truth over the course of my hearing.

"I never gave Mr. Ibrahim individual psychotherapy," Dr. Maggoty declares, lying brazenly in her Irish brogue. So what the hell was that? All ten months of it? Is this what she does at all of her appearances? Does she always sink so low just to win a case? Apparently so, according to Barry's investigations. She glares at Barry as he successfully introduces into the record her various episodes of psychiatric and legal impropriety in several landmark mental health cases in which she gave erroneous "expert witness" testimony. Barry's research also uncovered a patented "sociopathic predator" profile that she cultivated, branding virtually every offender with it, almost as her insurance of justice.

Even worse than dubious Maggoty's performance on the stand is the congratulatory ringside cut man antics offered up from her toady, Patricia Crapella. Sitting directly behind me I hear her whisper "Job well done" as the doctor leaves the stand in a crane-like stride. This conspirator's comment hammers the last nail in the coffin of my respectful admiration begun when Crapella was an ambitious, whip smart psychology extern on 6-B but which corroded and died as she became an employee and finally Maggoty's pet, good cop to the forensic director's sick cop. Funny, but through the years I also watched the glimmer of youthful happiness flicker and die in her eyes. Maybe she saw the same in mine.

I also see my Living Museum program director Dr. Marton subpoenaed and deliver glowing testimony on my behalf. My hired doctor Allen Richman and independent court appointed forensic psychiatrist Lawrence Seagull also do a marvelous job impressing upon the court why I should be released.

Judge Freed has been very kind and welcoming to me, complimenting me on my attire, my "dignified presence," and finally equating my plight to that of an iconic political freedom fighter. "I get good vibes from you, Mr. Ibrahim," Judge Freed says. "Like Nelson Mandela being released from Robben Island, you seem to have come out of this long experience with grace, without bitterness and resentment." This totally embarrasses me but if it helps I'll wear that hat. This flattery is all well and good but will you cut me loose, Judge? *That* is the $64,000 question.

Barry's retiring as soon as he can get his closing arguments wrapped up. The drag is the court may ask for briefs from both sides—homework, as it were. Judge Freed wants examples of past insanity plea cases similar to mine in which the patient petitioned for and gained release without going through the furloughs, in addition to examples of various orders of conditions that allow for autonomy but also with some necessary restrictions. It looks like I may be a first.

"In my opinion this patient requires a safe transition," Maggoty says on the stand. "This is essential for him, and the community." My being released without Level 4, unescorted off-grounds furloughs, would forego that period of the "safe transition." Judge Freed sees that I am a very good candidate for early release (early, after nineteen years?) but he is also reluctant to make such a powerful decision. He has numerous sidebars during which I hear him bully the assistant attorney general to pressure his people up in Albany to "get a furlough down here!" So far OMH has stood firm and I pray they remain arrogant. With all the positive testimony and "good vibes" I am at Judge Freed's mercy. I hope he can find some for me.

62

"**W**HAT'S THE MATTER, SON?" Mom asks again and again, but it is too late for the word-and-mind games now.

I am standing in my bedroom, littered with shrine items and damaged furniture. Mom is wearing a long nightshirt with Chester Gould's *Dick Tracy* emblazoned on the front. His grim but determined scowl and steely eyes beneath the yellow fedora watch me as my body becomes taut and defensive.

"Tell me, Iss. What's wrong?"

Mom is asking me this question with all the snide sarcasm that could exist in the world, which is just about over. I see Mom as an integral part of the evil scheme to hold me back and as a result have untold millions suffer and die. I have to act.

I lunge at my mother. Mom anticipates this and turns to run. She makes it just out the door, but I tackle her and we spill into the dark hallway. She tries to wriggle free, but I grapple with her. Satan, or some dark, terrible, malevolent force, is in the closed, empty bedroom up the hallway that my nephew, her grandson, used to reside in before I banished him just before Christmas. I try to keep Mom and myself from this drafty doorway, which cracks open repeatedly, slamming as if something within were trying to get out. As if this fear weren't bad enough, the voices return and begin screaming damnations upon my Mom.

"You're not the son of God, you're the son of the Devil!"

"She's possessed!"

"She's possessing YOU!"

Mom begins to scream. She struggles up and crawls quickly away from my ripping hands. I get a handful of her nightshirt as she clambers up and away from me. I jump up and tackle my Mom again. Her screaming becomes desperate. We land on a long strip of carpeting in the kitchenette. Whatever I have to do to save her might be interfered with in some way by the fabric or pattern of the rug, so I drag my Mom onto the cold, hard linoleum floor.

I argue with the voices while still fighting to hold Mom down. "You said it yourselves, she's possessed. Well, I'm Jesus, right? And I can help her, can't I? I have to save her!"

The voices flood my head with their litany of admonishments against Mom, using her present behavior as proof that she is more evil than even I can handle. She writhes and bucks as if possessed by some powerful, evil spirit, but I am determined to rescue my Mom from the throes of hellish agony and demonic bondage.

"Get off of me, damn it! Let me loose! Damn it, Issa, let go of me!" I am amazed by Mom's tremendous strength as I hold her, cradle her, protecting her from evil, trying to will the demon out of her and into me.

I become frightened staring into her face and into her eyes, which look cloudy, filmed over. On her forehead I see beads of sweat form but they are shiny, metallic, and black, like ball bearings popping up from her pores. I start to panic. I see the demon deep within her, corrupting her, rotting her from the inside out.

"Leave her alone!" I scream.

I see such pain and rage in Mom's face that I almost jump up off her, knowing, as her son, that when she grows *this* angry there will be hell to pay. But I cannot abandon her and my mission. "No!" I yell at the hell inside her, "This woman *will be saved!*"

But it only gets worse. Mom's face shimmers, like a paved horizon in the summer sun. It is as if the demon living within her is going to show itself. But I am cheated out of seeing its true face. What remains is Mom's confused visage, to play on my sympathies. When convinced I have Mom in the sufficient crucifix position, ideal for exorcism, or so I believe, her hands twist and wring underneath mine, which are clamped down at her wrists.

"Watch it! The demon is using puppetry," the voices warn and sure enough, it looks as if she is controlling a marionette. With each of her struggling hand gestures, twists, and pulls, my body twists and turns with them. It hurts, my body torn between heaven and hell. I shake off the control and, with determination, set about completing this exorcism. I need rites and invocations but I don't know what adequate words to say to save Mom's tortured soul. And of course, when I need them most, to tell me how to finalize this exorcism, the voices are silent.

"I don't know what to say," I scream. "Tell me what to say!"

The believed evil within Mom takes advantage of my momentary lapse and gasps hoarse and breathless, "Let's go downstairs and have some coffee. Come on, son. Let's go downstairs and have some coffee." I take this to be a demonic ruse.

I am at a loss. What can I do next? I am not capable of seeing this through but *something* needs to be done . . . to help her, to *save* her. I need to buy some time, more time to think of where to take this. Wishing only to catch my breath, clear my head, and keep her body stable beneath me, I kneel on Mom's chest . . . and hear the breaking of bones.

63

FROM OUTSIDE I HEAR A CAR DOOR OPEN and slam shut. A motor starts and then drives off. This is a sure sign that whatever demon had inhabited Mom's body is now taking its leave. This same demon (could it have been Satan himself?) will undoubtedly set its evil plans into motion at breakneck speed. Why? Because the motherfucker had a hand in the death of *my* mother, that's why! How long does it think I'll wait to exact revenge? If this devil wasn't hip to my Jesus objective before, I'll surely carve it into its backside after this!

I contemplate ways of bringing Mom back to life. Maybe, with my powers as Christ, and a little luck, I can save Mom's recently departed soul. Before I set about righting the tremendous wrong I'd just committed, I consider phoning 911 for an ambulance, the police, *anybody*, but think again knowing that my thoughts will broadcast worldwide, alerting the evil ones to where I am. This will bring a deluge of demonic creepy-crawlers shambling down Linden Boulevard looking to tear me to shreds, as well as jeopardizing many benevolent freedom fighters that believe in Issa the Messiah. So for now, Mom's death will go unreported.

A strange feeling comes over me, like I am a fish in a huge bowl. But I do not make a very good fish for I feel as if I am suffocating, standing on tiptoe, reaching, grabbing for a light at the surface of the murky waters I believe myself to be drowning in. I realize that there is a ceiling, a sheet of glass keeping me from surfacing. Like someone trapped beneath the ice of a frozen pond, I imagine vague, divine images on the other side. The Celestials are watching me but saying and doing nothing. These indiscernible images will not help me break through. I have to will myself through. This is something that I cannot do.

I drift back down to the dark depths of my fate, my life. I cannot

escape what I have done, no matter how hard I try. I attempt to res-
urrect Mom. If I cannot raise her then I will try to deliver her soul to
Heaven. I start this process by inhaling great gusts of air. My secret?
Not to exhale.

Step two of the resurrection ritual is to audibly recite the alphabet,
only I must say it backward—while still inhaling. I begin with Z and
get only up to V before needing to stop and think what comes next,
and finally exhale. I inhale and start again, get to a certain point, P,
and again have to stop, think it through forward to the end, reverse it
audibly, and then am forced to exhale. Each time I stop I have to start
the process all over again.

Implementing step three, I walk counterclockwise around Mom's
body. I begin slowly by inhaling through clenched teeth while intoning
"Z, Y, X, W . . ." then step carefully. The act is nullified by my lack of
breath and remembrance of what letter comes before which.

I stop and start and stop and start and stop and start again. Finally,
at 3:30 AM, one half hour after Mom's death, I stop the ritual for the
final time. I have failed. Mom cannot be saved. I stand and stare for a
long while at my mother.

"Why? Why, Mom? Why did this happen? How can God allow this
to happen? Why?" She does not answer.

I CANNOT LOOK AT MOM'S BODY ANY LONGER. I stumble into my rear
bedroom. It is an unadulterated mess, but I am far from caring. I have
to do something to amend this atrocity I've committed. I tried to
bring Mom back but if I cannot then maybe I can sacrifice myself.
That will bring us closer together. I feel low. I want to die.

I lie on my bed strewn with broken mirror glass. I continue to
inhale without exhaling. Extending my arms, as if crucified, I writhe
and roll my body against the glass. I hope to die the miserable death
that I deserve, rocking back and forth on the broken glass and praying
for death. Be it quick as Mom's, perhaps with a long sharp shard into
a major artery, or slow by means of bleeding out from countless small
lacerations, I pray for death.

64

S NAPSHOTS. My brain only processes blurred Polaroid snapshots at first. Brief, muddy glimpses of long, marble-floored corridors with many closed doors on either side. Bright, irritating fluorescence lighting walls painted in thick layers, muted colors. Beige is the reigning hue coupled with subdued greens and yellows and blues. Everything speaks of sedation. The smell of fresh paint sneaks out of the stairwells, with cigarette smoke and stale urine cresting above the latex.

I am escorted into this room or another by a resigned black orderly. He appears to be in some pseudo-officious position, "in charge" of me but very little else. Handed my snakeskin cowboy boots and black jeans and asked to dress. I didn't realize I was undressed, and I shrug off the flimsy blue-and-white gown open at the back from my shoulders. A few steps are all it takes. In the mirror I see my face. I do not look well. I am in shock. My love for myself is all gone.

I am surrounded by the dead. Hollow-eyed haunted souls in ill-fitting clothes shuffling about like recently raised zombies. I too walk with the slow, persistent, shell-shocked slip, slip, slip of barely lifted, dragging feet, constant movement with no important destination. There is a TV bolted to the ceiling of a large room dispensing indiscriminate dialogue. The voices are feeding post-apocalyptic commentary. Perhaps this is the place where souls arrive once passing through that gelatinous bubble separating the earth from the netherworld, the triage area for those lost in the war over Heaven.

My earth parents are here—Dad after cancer, Mom after the possession, in addition to various past life acquaintances who made a difference. They look so different now, altered a bit. I can tell who's who by a passing resemblance, despite the trickery and visual deception. It becomes apparent now that we've been dying slowly on earth. Poisoned, contaminated by Satan's hatred. I see it now in the baleful, faraway eyes and tight, twisted mouths of the people here I used to love. I can't muster the love I used to have for them because they look different from what I remember—distorted, and strange. Though the shrunken black man and bruised light-skinned woman could be my parents I just can't be sure. I want to rush to them, and others who are doppelgängers for former friends and family, but my uncertainty keeps me away. I shuffle alongside them, stare into their hopelessly lost eyes, hoping they will approach first.

Settling finally in the large common room, a woman introduces herself. "Hi, I'm Sharon." She slips me a Snickers bar and then sits close by. She mumbled "Sharon," but in subspeak Sharing is intended. This close-cropped, hammy, caramel-skinned female must be someone I used to love in the old world. With her thick body type and light brown skin she resembles Scarlett, my former flame. She acts as a guide, a crossing guard over the river Styx, perhaps. The aides introduce me to the others as "Isaac Abraham." Sharing is intrigued. The name she gives me, "Saki," is apparently a new corruption of my already mangled moniker, but in the backward tongue of this awful place. It's not much different from the old world.

She gives so much of herself. Is she something I didn't learn before? The care she takes comforts me, like a wet kitten brought into the warmth of her home and nourished by her kindness. Sharing is Scarlett because Scarlett was sharing . . . way back when, before I had even a clue to who I was. Scarlett shared her heart, her hopes for a long life of loving me, of all people. Back when I was Fuck-up Number One. But I am transformed. Now I am Number One who has fucked up. Sharing invites me to her table when it is mealtime. She is usually watchful and silent except when lovingly instructing me on how to hold my plastic dinnerware or wiping my face when I dribble my milk. I have regressed so much and appreciate her help and patience even though I never voice this. I assume she knows.

Disembodied female voices wake me every morning from a fitful slumber, announcing the date, the time, and the temperature, but I forget what is said in the haze. "Medication!" is screamed out and for the second or third consecutive day I am asked to swallow a thick, clear, bitter liquid. Is this for my good or detriment? All who accept their Thiquid or capsules shuffle anticipatorily down the long, dirty hallway and into a small room to collect and inhale stale cigarettes. I join them and become dizzy, feeling my thoughts getting loose. The others can hear me clearly, this thought sent and disseminated among the sickly smokers.

There is no grand plot, plan, or scheme that needs hiding from these readers. They can bask in the majesty of my presence but will never have access to my great design for liberation, largely because I seem to have hidden the blueprints from myself. This must be an internal safety mechanism that was installed for occasions such as this. I am captured and precious information must not fall into the wrong hands. That is why even Sharing is suspect. As Scarlett on old earth I loved her like no other, but here, in this strange and disturbing environment, I can't be so sure. Though many of the white-smocked aides speak softly, smile kindly, and attend to our needs there is an underlying despair here. It is not a good place . . . so ultimately it must be evil.

They may be tempting me. That Thiquid I drink may be the water of old earth, ripe with pollutants. It has a sludge-like consistency. Do they want to see if I will change, if I *can* be changed? Corrupted? My eyes avert to the scraped and clotted neck of a sullen white female. The dried and congealed red looks jarring against the pale of her throat. I make a wan attempt to elicit her attention. I want her to allow me to touch her bloodied neck, to heal her. She resists, first with moans of opposition and finally with a sharp scream, swatting my hand away from her shoulder. Sharing becomes incensed, throwing a chair at the suicidal woman, both requiring sequestering and sedation.

I haven't bathed for a while, since long before the terrible offense last evening (or was it last week? Last month? Last year?). An aide asks if I want to take a midday shower. I comply, eager to be cleansed and feel the warm water that will make this strange place somewhat tolerable. Sharing, recently freed from the locked dungeon with the Plexiglas window called the Quiet Room, follows me into the shower. After seeing her nude body I am positive she is indeed my former love, Scarlett Simpson, unadorned by any altering atmosphere. Misshapen and bruised, she looks to have been beaten. I immediately think of Mom back home and quickly blot that thought, that horrible visual, out of my mind. Did it truly happen? I welcome Sharing's flesh. A staff member enters to watch us in the steam. Not amused, not disturbed, he just sits, smokes, and watches our primitive sex. It must be planned. They want me corrupted and, validating the black man's lustful sexual stereotype, I succumb.

65

NOTICE THE DAILY REGIMEN OF "MEDICATION" starting to take effect. My thoughts clear and my memories slowly return. What happened back home ceases to be an elusive haunted dream and more of a reality. A reality that I believe I must voice, however gruesome the truth and impactful the consequences may be.

Escorted into a small room, I am met by a slender, brown-skinned, wise-eyed old woman who resembles the paternal grandmother I had on earth. Is this really Granny Naomi? Am I seeing her too for the first time without the altered air? So persuasive are her eyes and kind ways that I release the stranglehold I have had on myself since crashing Kal's car and getting picked up by the fire department and EMS and sent here. I speak, telling of things not asked and things I'm sure she won't want to know. I confess my transgressions, starting with the immediate one against Mom. I tell of where I came and how I got where I am now, once they let me know exactly where this is. I am a patient at Rockland Psychiatric Center in the township of Orangeburg, New York. This grandmotherly woman is the ward social worker.

I recount the fateful evening, only days ago but seemingly of another lifetime. I recall the marijuana addiction, the hallucinations, the possession, the exorcism attempt, and finally her accidental death. When I say, "and I knelt on her chest and it collapsed," the social worker gasps. I recall the sound of Mom's cracking ribs, a sound that reverberates often in my sleep and waking hours, the inescapable, irrevocable sound of her cause of death. Her sternum and ribcage breaks daily in my memory, in my ears, in my mind. This health care professional is shocked and mortified by the act, *my* act, sending a shudder across the distance between us, up my body and deep within my bones, allowing me to own my culpability in Mom's death.

She sits with her back straight up and the air lingers in a desperate silence once I confess what I have done. I feel temporarily cleansed until a glance into this woman's face reveals the disgust she is trying unsuccessfully to hide. This is a look I will have to get used to. I know why she feels this way and I feel it too. For myself, for what I have done . . . God, what have I done?

THE AIDES COME IN THE DEAD OF NIGHT, rousing me from a chemical slumber. Peeking up from beneath the blanket of sleep, I am not sure if this is all a dream, but reality asserts itself as I am escorted through long hallways and several stairways into a small, windowless office. Once seated I am greeted by two well-fed white men, dressed in cheap polyester slacks, conservative sport jackets, and ugly ties. These men are officious, hardened man-hunters. Homicide detectives. You can spot them. It's in their eyes. They've seen all manner of horror, including the one I left in Queens. Here I will again make a confession, only this time it will stick. They say they're investigating "The Incident." They speak of it in a way that intimates my having prior awareness. I know what I have to do.

"I think I killed my mother," I mumble, wiping the sleep from my eyes.

AFTER SEVERAL DAYS my thinking becomes even clearer and the same detectives return. The main one, a barrel-chested expressionless gentleman who does all the talking, eyes unblinking, asks if I know why he's here.

"I think so. It's about my Mom, right?"

"Yes, Issa. You're under arrest now. Do you understand? We're going to take you back to Queens and book you. OK?"

My time at this rest stop called Rockland Psychiatric Center must be complete. I know the answers to all their questions, officially gaining entrance to hell. My journey has just begun. In a way I was waiting for them to return. I expect bravado, high-fives, Mountie posturing—they've got their man. But they remain calm and businesslike, even nice.

"Do you have to put on the handcuffs?"

"Yes, I do. But I won't put them on too tight, OK?"

The staff brings out a plastic shopping bag, in it a mound of shredded leather that was once my motorcycle jacket. I am made to sign my name on a property slip. Just as I begin to write "Jesus Christ" the impatient attendant screams, "Nah, man, your *real* name!" Shocked solidly into reality I write the name "Issa Ibrahim" and it is unfamiliar, like I never have seen or written it before, yet I believe I will have to become accustomed to it, answer to it, own it and all that this person has done . . . good and bad.

The long ride back is thick with cologne and silence. There are four stone-faced detectives to escort me from this foreign place upstate. Their big pink hands are slung over the front seat, close enough to subdue me in case I start to fight. But I go quietly, peacefully. After a long ride downstate I see New York City as we approach the Triborough Bridge going into Queens. Looking out the auto's window, the stone and metal spires capture my imagination as they did in my youth. The towering labyrinths are still somewhat impressive. This will be the last time for a long time that I will see them. The dramatic Manhattan skyline is preserved in my memory, like a photograph.

66

"**L**OOK AT THAT SMILE!" Barry Newfeld says, beaming proudly. I meet with Barry one last time at the MHLS offices on campus. We embrace and he looks tearful. He *should* be proud, not only of me but of his victory in such a difficult, seemingly unwinnable case.

"You did great, Barry. Thanks so much."

"*We* did great! Yeah, this is some swan song, huh?" We both are overcome with emotion. It's been a long road and I suddenly realize Barry's always been there, if only as a voice on the phone, familiar with my pain, comforting me, consoling me, urging me not to give up even during the many long stretches when there was no movement, no hope. He gave me hope. "You've got the rest of your life ahead of you, Issa. I always said you'd do great things and now it's your time. It's your time."

"It's been a long time, and you've carried me through most of it. Thanks for believing in me, Barry."

I hand Barry a painting, one that I like and am reluctant to part with, but he deserves it. He got me sprung. "Let me give some background on the painting. It's the first semi-abstract in oil I ever attempted, painted in Gaia's office in 1995."

"Ah, yeah, Gaia Sapros. I hope you learned from *that* episode." If he only knew.

"This was shown at my first one-man show, after I got the grant. It's called *Icarus Reflects*, with the artist, me, looking back on my life of poor choices, flying too high, crashing down to earth a wounded bird. You have given me new wings, Barry. Thank you."

CREEDMOOR HAS NEVER BEEN UP FRONT WITH ME, and usually under-handed, so I am prepared for any last minute digs as I go through the process of discharge planning. Dr. Marton is just as wary of the administration as I am, maybe more so because as an employee he *really* knows how they operate. He's mentioned recent instances of the administration punishing him for his testimony but I can tell by his vagaries and reluctance to offer details that he doesn't want me to feel obligated or burdened by this. Smiling with benevolence he simply says, "We showed them, eh? Now just keep your nose clean . . . as if."

IT'S BEEN MANY YEARS SINCE MOM'S DEATH. Now, on Mother's Day, almost a year after my discharge, Gaia and I reconnect and take a long drive as we used to, before things got complicated. We relate as mature people who share a history, crossed boundaries, yet still remain close.

"I'm glad that you haven't had any disturbing anniversary reactions," she says.

"Well, I still get very sad in the wintertime, in February. That's when it happened."

"I know, Issa, I know. And I've seen you down. I remember you staring off into space. But you've remained stable. Healthy."

"I don't have any choice."

"Sure you do. You can bug out. React like a patient. Give in. Give up. But I appreciate your resilience and desire to hang in there."

I don't respond. I just look away, out the passenger side window of Gaia's car as we drive far into Long Island. I generally appreciate her support, but today she is taking me to the last place I want to be. And the only place I will find peace, and closure.

We arrive at Calvary Veteran's Cemetery. At the reception office I give my father's name. As a veteran of the Korean conflict he is buried here. Near his grave is a plot for my Mom.

During the long walk through the grounds toward their resting place, I link arms with Gaia. She's offering comforting advice on what to say when I get there and how to feel. It seems strange yet I need her prompts. My heart has been frozen up since the incident, the arrest, the various dark, dirty places I had to stay, to be evaluated, deemed fit to be judged, and then finally determined to be defective, diseased. Having to process this was hard enough. There seemed little room for reflection, contrition, healing. I had to keep moving to survive. If I slowed for just a moment I felt I would be taken over and destroyed—by the system, its denizens, and ultimately myself.

Gaia slips her arm from mine and steps back. I stand above Mom's headstone, alone. This is my first time seeing it. I feel my heart start to tremble. I feel, and it frightens me. Reading her name on the bronze plaque, her date of birth and date of death, assaults me, thrusting responsibility and ownership into my hands and deep within my soul. I accept it, as hard and immovable as the stone and metal that sits above her deceased body. Encased in wood, covered in dirt, and eulogized by the offending party, me, her youngest son. In accepting this tragedy as my own I feel my offering today, and evermore, will never be enough. But I also come to the sober realization that I have a life to make up for, to honor, and now a purpose.

As I cry, I place a bouquet of roses by the side of the plaque, and a small painting, done in watercolor, of a mother, my mother, cradling her child.

"I'm sorry, Mom. I love you. Please forgive me. I didn't mean it. I'm sorry. I'm sorry."

67

I AM A FREE MAN. I am always free when I create. And I've always felt this way, especially when I was locked up—institutionalized in a state mental hospital, just four miles from my old family home and yet a world away.

Now here, in my small but cozy studio apartment in Richmond Hill, the first place I could ever call my own, I am also free to keep the light on and paint or bang out songs on my guitar and record all night long to my heart's content, and not worry about rousing and/ or angering a twenty-year parade of broken souls. These haunted men never had the same enthusiasm for my art, all just literally sick and tired, grateful to have a bed to lie in, greeting the evening's sleep as a just and appreciated respite and reward for surviving another day. A day not only of the cold and sometimes cruel "care and treatment" of Creedmoor, but also another day of the interior passion play in which their fragile minds and wounded hearts ricochet within their hollow bodies, careening and colliding, fighting, crying, trying to comprehend the whys and why-not-just-end-it-alls.

Though I did spend a good chunk of that time in my own room, where I created unbridled, uncontrolled, I still think of those many men whom I roomed with—the maniacal midnight laughter, ominous silences, habitual masturbation, noxious gases, raging sweet teeth, cloak-and-dagger stogies, and stolen money. I think of all those guys and reflect on whether my late night painting sessions had as much of an effect on their lives as those men have had on mine. I also reflect on the Mahatas, unit chiefs, and forensic directors.

And I think about Mom.

ONE DAY BEFORE MY FINAL COURT APPEARANCE, I am scheduled for my last treatment team meeting as an inpatient. Similar to my first team meeting at Kings County Hospital nineteen years earlier, when I entered a room with almost twenty professionals all looking at me as if I were a swab of gunk on a slide to be magnified to the nth degree, reenacting the crime for an audience, hopefully to be found competent to stand trial, this will be my last meeting to go over my treatment plan for discharge. Gathered around an impossibly long boardroom table is a different set of at least twenty mental health workers, all with eyes on me. Here is the old team, the new team, and peripheral professionals who have been or will be involved in my case. Dr. Maggoty presides over the whole affair and is just as combative till the very end.

I hear from Leslie Boobala, who was in the mass meeting of professionals before she was exposed as my attorney and then extricated until I arrived, that the preamble of the meeting was the doctor's assassination of my character. Leslie says, "Like an ugly drunk on payday giving a nasty toast to her boss in a noisy bar, Maggoty let everyone know of her opposition to your discharge, and even stated that she pleaded with the attorney general to appeal it." Sadly for her, and lucky for me, she was overruled.

My final court date is just a formality and goes very quickly and smoothly. Judge Freed signs the release order, wags his finger, and I am cut loose after a resounding, "This case is closed." Though cautious and sorrowful throughout, I knew after a while that I'd atoned, healed, and done my time. And I always believed if a competent and honest judge heard my case he would do what was right. People are a little too used to the system chewing people up and spitting them out. I'm glad that in this one case I fought back, by getting my head right, selling my artwork, mounting a case, doing whatever I could to escape from OMH and the system. I just have to fight back the occasional feeling of it all being a hollow victory, for though I am free, in the eyes of some I will always be a "murderer" and my Mom is no longer living.

My first full day of freedom is my birthday: my *re*-birthday. I wake up in Stepping Stones Transitional Residence, a halfway house on the campus grounds, sleeping in a different bed, in a room with windows that open, smelling the morning rain . . . things I hadn't done for almost twenty years. I start to cry.

I have been granted my conditional release but it is not a discharge. It is as it states, a release on conditions. Though I was acquitted and have no criminal record, I am still and will remain on Criminal Procedure Law status for five years, living under conditions that Maggoty drew up and Judge Freed found satisfactory and signed. I must remain drug and alcohol free and undergo random mandatory urinalysis to support this. After five years I can petition to be fully discharged from this status. Perhaps the most depressing stipulation in my order of conditions is that I can't leave New York State within this time. There's nothing I'd love to do more than travel after being locked up for half my life. But there are always postcards, travelogues, and the Internet, which has a way of bringing people closer and showing you the world.

My computer allows me to log on to the Citi Field site, break through the cyber-throng, and purchase tickets to see Paul McCartney on tour the summer I get out. Being a lifelong Beatle-freak and having been denied the opportunity several years earlier, I am overjoyed and enjoy the show. As Sir Paul once sung to me when he was just a Scouser and I was a cherub, "It's getting better all the time."

PLENTY DON'T UNDERSTAND OR ACCEPT marijuana's negative impact in my case. I get the same surprised reactions, nervous laughter, and ignorant resistance: "Are you sure it wasn't laced? Pot doesn't make you kill people."

Rather than chafe the very vocal stoner culture by casting aspersions on the reefer decriminalization juggernaut, and wishing not to solely blame pot for my illness and Mom's death, I prefer to attribute the tragedy to a cluster fuck of coincidences. It would seem my hard knock lifeboat capsized under a perfect storm of young adult angst, familial grief, racial tension, social anxiety, marijuana abuse, and falling within the age of onset for developing mental illness.

Like Dad's endorsement when I was young, I do acknowledge that cannabis does indeed have medicinal properties, helping glaucoma and cancer sufferers, among others, deal with their symptoms and pain. However, in my case no pain was evident, except that of a broken heart. All I know is marijuana does me no good.

Whenever I smoke I get symptomatic, with irrational paranoia, delusions, ideas of reference, and bizarre behavior. I have teased it out enough times to know this. Like a tragicomic action serial, the insanity picks up right after the last cliffhanger as if no time had passed, or all that "normal" time was part of a secondary storyline. Sort of like *The Domestic Life of Clark Kent*, complete with many seasons of all the mundane things a nerd would do, pretty much forgetting he's the Man of Steel. But when I smoke again . . . up, up, and away!

I only hope to add my own personal caveat to the marijuana glamorization and minimization of its dangers, and catch other young dreamers, possessed with talent and promise or just the good fortune of youth, from flying too high then falling so far. Making the same mistakes I made, having to travel the same dark road.

ONCE I GOT RELEASED the sex between Lily and I started to wane. Was it the sudden lack of danger, the absence of the possibility of our getting caught that tempered both our libidos? Or did we just run our course and were now going through the motions, united in hardship and strife but rudderless and apathetic when faced with normalcy? It doesn't help when I admit to Lily that I have been unfaithful, giving my juices to other women these last few years while still seeing her.

I used to tell Lily that I am married to the state, tied to the hospital, and she had to understand that she would always be the mistress in this affair. "OK, but now that you're out are we going to make good on all those faraway promises of moving in together?" she asks. "Are we going to get married?"

It breaks my heart to tell her, "I can't marry you or anybody right now. I have to find myself and my place in this world after being locked up for half my life."

After fifteen years in this stunted relationship, and with my getting released, Lily feels me slipping away. "OK, I understand," she says. "But I also feel rejected . . . and betrayed." I should have let her go to find that husband and house full of children, cats, and rabbits. After coming clean about my other girlfriends and years of multiple infidelities, like my Dad purging his guilt to Mom many years before, Lily cries. "The only reason I stayed was because I thought you were faithful."

We both cultivated and nurtured love lies to each other and ourselves. She loving the perfect man in a box, unable to move and thus a captive audience and eager receptor for her attentions. And me loving the only woman in town, desperate to believe that our union was more than just convenience.

In truth, Lily will stay close because we get along so well and I'm the only man for which she's ever had any feelings of real love. And I love her. She's my best friend, kind of like a sexy army buddy, both of us having an unbreakable bond, a psych hospital symbiosis. But I find it strangely ironic to have cultivated a serious long-term relationship with an angry, implosive woman who says she would willfully do to her mother what I did accidentally to mine.

AFTER NOT HEARING FROM GAIA for a long while, our mutual friend Sherri Ferrone calls with dread in her voice. "Gaia's had a stroke," she says.

"It happened in the middle of the night. No one knows how long she was lying there. John woke up and saw her there unresponsive and called the EMS. She's in Flushing Hospital now, hooked up to all sorts of tubes. She can't breathe on her own so she's had a tracheotomy. She can barely talk. God, I don't know if she'll pull through but pray for her, Issa. Pray for her. She's in a bad way. You wouldn't recognize her, Issa, and I wouldn't want you to see her as she is now. She's eighty-five and quadriplegic and I've made peace with how I knew her, how alive she was and how good she was, to me, to you, to everybody she met. It breaks my heart seeing her like this. I don't think I'll be visiting her much anymore. It's tough for me, working as I do, only to run after work all the way to Flushing Hospital and have her crippled daughter, alcoholic son, and emotionally unavailable husband sit at her bedside like ghouls, all waiting for her to get better, get up outta that bed and go back home to cook and clean up after them like she did all her life. The fuckin' bastards. If the stroke doesn't kill her they will. I whispered to her that I loved her and she mumbled back to me 'Will I ever get out of this place?' I heard her say that and I knew it was time to go and turn the page. She's a good woman and God will take care of her more than I or those crazies she left at home ever could. She was so good to you too, Issa. She loved you. Take those memories; cherish those times you spent with her and pray for her, Issa. Pray for her."

Gaia Sapros was the mother of all mother figures. She took great care of me, seeing that I was lonely, needing affection, human contact, someone to smile at me and look me in the eye—the things that made me a human being. With both Gaia and Bella happily offering up fine Mediterranean and Spanish cuisine, as an alternative to the nauseating mess the hospital usually served up, I don't see my accepting these and other amenities as manipulation, as Maggoty opined. It was survival. I knew I was doing a potential life sentence. I was cold, scared, hungry, and angry that I couldn't express myself without repercussions, where everything I said, did, and felt was held against me. Gaia and Bella soothed that uneasiness for a little while, even as I knew they were authority figures breaking the law.

I do cherish those times. I remember most the sessions spent in Gaia's office, not engaged in therapeutic heavy lifting or even having hot sex, but with me painting at an easel set up in the corner while she busied herself with her progress notes, looking up occasionally to survey the emerging work and calling out quiet encouragement. Just like Mom.

THE DA'S OFFICE HAS FOR YEARS been in touch with my family. My sister Carol is the loudest voice in the family choir to keep me locked up.

However, for reasons unknown to me, my release has gone unnoticed by my family. This is a good thing, as for years I have worried about finally being freed and one or more members of my family angrily trumping up some false claims, getting me sent back to the hospital. I understand their resentment and pain. Not only have they lost their mother but they've also lost a brother.

I may never be on civil ground with them ever again. After more than twenty years without their concern or positive involvement I think of them and I miss them but believe it may be best to let them be. I only hope they feel the same. I pray for my family, especially my sister Carol, the nurse, who did not offer help when I ran to her in Oakland. And I cry for Mom, who tried to help but didn't know any better than to rub healing oil on my head.

I AM NO LONGER SYMPTOMATIC but I do occasionally hear a voice, Mom's voice, offering artistic advice and personal encouragement. She guides me through difficult stages, aiding me in making wise choices. Like supernatural pep talks, she is my spirit guide, holding my hand through moments of doubt. Mom's voice reaffirms what she knew from my birth and reinforced all my life: "You are a great artist, son." I honor her by living up to this dream. My art keeps me in touch with Mom and keeps me sane. I am finally whole, at peace, and resolute in honoring my greatest influences, the artists who taught me the most, my Dad and Mom.

As dawn approaches and I move freely about my space, from the mixing palette to unfinished canvas, ready to fill in the blanks with color and wit and bite, I think of Mom. And I feel her. Here with me now, as always, full of love and radiating warmth, never wanting me to suffer. Dancing to *my* music, calling out, "That's great!"

Standing in my periphery, just out of sight, Mom surveys my work, as I finish this piece. Coming around the clubhouse turn, I can hear her say, "That's it, son. That's it. Perfect."

I smile, pleased and proud, and say, "Thanks, Ma."

Acknowledgments

AUDREY JACOBS-IBRAHIM, Jamil Ibrahim, Susan Spangenberg, Herman Worthy, Patricia Worthy, Dr. Janos Marton, Geo Geller, Lawrence Newman, Esq., Consuelo Alsapiedi, Teri Farrell, Tim Noe, Jamie Hoover, Steve Stoeckel, Tucker Mitchell, Monica Tarver, Jessica Yu, Kit Shapiro, Claudia McDaniel-Khan, Dr. Elisabeth Berger, *DSM5*, Laura Starecheski, Sean Sorensen, Adam Chromy, my editor Yuval Taylor, the man upstairs, my friends at the Living Museum, and all the patients, peer counselors, advocates, and freedom fighters on the front lines.